CONTENTS

Introduction xvii

Policy Guidelines xix

**Chapter I. General Responsibilities
and Information** I–1

Individual Team Member Checklist I–2
    Personal Items: I–2
    Optional Items (brought at your own risk): I–3
    Personal Health Items and Medical Tips: I–3
    OFDA-Provided Items: I–3
    Information To Be Left with OFDA: I–4

Team Support Checklist I–4

Documentation I–5
A. General I–5
B. Types of Documentation I–5

Accountability and Liability I–6

Administration I–7
A. Time Records I–7
B. Per Diem and Vouchers I–8
C. Procurement and Contracting I–9

DART Setup and Closeout Guidelines I–9
A. General I–9
B. Setup I–10
    1. Files and Record Keeping I–10
    2. Diskettes I–10
    3. Contact List I–11
    4. Program Management I–11
    5. Packaging I–12
C. Closeout I–13
    1. The Date I–13
    2. Administration I–13
    3. Personnel I–13
    4. Moving and Transferring Files I–14
    5. Program Management I–14
    6. Public Relations I–16
    7. Petty Cash Funds I–16

    8. Transfer of Property I–16
    9. Communications I–16
    10. Memorandum of Agreement (MOA) I–17

Safety and Security I–17
    Safety and Security Checklist I–18

Personal Health and Critical-Incident Stress I–19
    A. Briefings I–20
    B. Managing Culture Shock I–20
    C. Critical-Incident Stress I–21
    D. How Team Members May Be Affected by
       Stress During Disaster Operations I–21
    E. How To Minimize Stress During a Disaster
       Operation I–22

Medical Emergencies and First Aid I–23
    The Initial ABCs of Medical Emergencies/First Aid I–23
    Choking I–26
    Other Emergency Situations I–26
       Shock I–27
       Bleeding I–27
       Burns.................................... I–28
       Fractures (broken bones) I–29
       Frostbite I–30
       Heat Exhaustion I–30
       Heat Stroke............................... I–30
       Hypothermia I–30

Working with the Media........................ I–31
    A. General I–31
    B. Rules for Dealing with Reporters................ I–31

OFDA Guidelines for Drug Donations I–33

Chapter II. Assessments II–1

Introduction II–2

Purpose of an Initial Assessment II–2

Types of Assessments II–4
    A. Situation (Disaster) Assessment II–4
    B. Needs Assessment II–5

Assessment Team Composition II–5

Elements of an Assessment II–6
A. Preparedness Planning II–6
B. Survey and Data Collection II–6
C. Interpretation II–7
D. Forecasting II–7
E. Reporting II–7
F. Monitoring II–7

Data Collection Methods II–8

Keys To a Successful Assessment II–10

Assessment Process Main Points II–12
A. General II–12
B. Assessment Recommendations and Their
   Impact on Recovery II–13

OFDA Assessment Cable Reporting Formats II–14
A. Slow Onset Disaster Cable Format II–14
   1. Subject II–14
   2. References . . . . .
   3. Summary . . . .
   4. General Situation
   5. Food and Logistics
   6. Health . . . .
   7. Water and Sanitation
   8. Shelter . . . .
   9. Capability and Capacity II–17
   10. Coordination II–17
   11. Recommendations II–18
   12. Who Should Get the Cable? II–18
B. Fast Onset Disaster Cable Format II–19
   1. Subject II–19
   2. References II–19
   3. Summary II–19
   4. General Situation II–19
   5. Health/Nutrition (Situation) II–20
   6. Shelter II–21
   7. Water/Sanitation II–21
   8. Infrastructure/Logistics II–21
   9. Coordination II–22
   10. Capability and Capacity II–22
   11. Recommendations II–22
   12. Who Should Get the Cable? II–22

D0126232

W9-BVO-841

Assessment Checklists II–23
A. Introduction II–23
B. Victims/Displaced Population Profile II–24
   1. General Characteristics II–24
   2. Priority Health Status Conditions II–24
   3. Capacities and Assets II–25
      Capacities II–25
      Physical Assets II–25
C. Health and Nutrition II–26
   1. Health II–26
   2. Nutrition II–28
D. Water II–29
   1. Displaced Population Situation II–29
   2. Functioning Water System Disruption II–29
E. Food and Agriculture II–30
   1. Food II–30
      Baseline Data II–30
      Effect of the Event on Food II–30
      Food Availability II–31
      Distribution Systems II–31
      Social and Market Impact of Food Aid .. II–32
      Other II–32
   2. Agriculture II–32
      Baseline Data II–32
      Effect of the Event on Agriculture II–33
      Agricultural Production Capabilities ... II–34
      Other II–34
F. Shelter II–35
   1. Affected Population Profile II–35
   2. Materials II–35
   3. Distribution II–36
G. Search and Rescue (SAR) II–37
H. Sanitation II–38
   1. Displaced Population Situation II–38
   2. Nondisplaced Population Situation II–38
I. Logistics II–39
   1. Airports II–39
   2. Civil Aviation II–40
   3. Alternative Aircraft II–40
   4. Seaports II–41
   5. Transfer Points II–42
   6. Trucking II–42
   7. Railroads II–43
   8. Warehousing II–43

J. Coordination Capacity II–45
K. Infrastructure II–45
   1. Communications II–45
   2. Electric Power II–47
   3. Water/Sewage II–48
   4. Hydro Facilities (Hydroelectric, Irrigation) II–48
   5. Roads and Bridges II–50

Chapter III. Information on Populations at Risk III–1

Introduction III–2

Immediate Response III–2
A. Protection of Displaced Persons (DPs) III–2
B. Organizational Considerations III–3
C. Material Assistance III–4

Water III–5
A. General III–5
B. Assessment and Organization III–6
   1. Assessment III–6
   2. Organization III–7
C. Needs III–8
   1. Quantity III–8
   2. Quality III–10
D. Immediate Response III–11
E. Water Source III–12
   1. Surface Water III–12
   2. Ground Water III–13
   3. Rainwater III–15
   4. Seawater III–16
   5. Water Source Considerations III–16
F. Storage III–16
G. Distribution III–17
H. Treatment III–18
   1. Storage III–19
   2. Sand Filtration III–20
   3. Coagulation and Flocculation III–21
   4. Chemical Disinfection III–21
   5. Boiling III–21

Food and Nutrition III–22
A. General III–22
  1. Food Security III–22
    a. Food Availability III–22
    b. Food Access III–22
    c. Food Utilization III–22
  2. Assessing Needs III–23
B. Nutritional Assessment and Surveillance III–24
  1. Systematic Random Sampling III–24
  2. Cluster Sampling III–25
  3. Assessing Malnutrition III–26
    a. Weight-for-Height (Weight-for-Length) III–26
    b. Mid-Upper-Arm Circumference (MUAC) III–31
C. General Feeding Program III–32
  1. Types of Food Distribution III–36
    a. Dry Ration Distribution (Take Home) III–36
    b. Wet Ration Distribution III–38
D. Selective Feeding Programs III–38
  1. Supplementary Feeding Programs III–39
    a. Blanket SFP III–40
    b. Targeted SFPs III–40
  2. Exit Criteria III–41
  3. Supplementary Food Quantities III–41
  4. Organization and Management of an SFP III–42
E. Therapeutic Feeding Programs III–43
  1. Phase One (24-Hour Care) III–44
  2. Phase Two (Day Care) III–45
F. Infant Feeding and Milk Products III–45
G. Basic Facts about Food and Nutrition III–46
  1. Nutrients III–46
  2. Energy and Protein Intakes III–49
  3. Food and Diets III–49

Health III–49
A. General III–49
B. Initial Health Assessment, Mortality Rates,
   and Morbidity Rate III–50
  1. Health Assessment III–50
  2. Mortality Rate III–51
  3. Morbidity Rate III–52
C. Epidemiology and Disease III–52
  1. Epidemiology Concepts III–53
    a. The Epidemiologic Triangle III–53
    b. Epidemiologic Definitions III–53

   2. Definitions of Environmental Characteristics III–56
   3. Disease Cycle Intervention III–58
D. Disease Control III–59
   1. Immunization III–59
   2. Common Diseases III–60
       Protozoa III–60
       Bacteria III–60
       Virus. III–61
       Acute Respiratory Infections III–61
       Cholera III–61
       Dengue Fever (Breakbone Fever) III–62
       Diarrheal Diseases III–63
       Diphtheria, Tetanus, Pertussis III–64
          Diphtheria. III–64
          Tetanus III–64
          Whooping Cough (Pertussis) III–64
       Intestinal Parasites III–65
       Lassa Fever. III–65
       Leprosy III–65
       Malaria. III–66
       Measles III–66
       Meningitis III–69
       Meningococcal Disease III–69
       Nutritional Diseases III–69
          Protein-Energy Malnutrition III–69
             Nutritional Marasmus III–70
             Kwashiorkor III–70
             Marasmic Kwashiorkor. III–71
          Micronutrient Deficiency Disease III–71
             Vitamin A Deficiency III–71
             Vitamin C Deficiency (Scurvy) III–71
             Niacin Deficiency (Pellagra) III–71
             Anemia III–72
             Thiamine Deficiency (Beriberi) III–72
       Polio III–72
       Shigellosis (Bacillary Dysentery) III–73
       Skin Infections. III–74
       Tuberculosis (TB) III–74
       Typhoid III–75
       Typhus Fever III–75
       Yellow Fever. III–76

  D. Displaced Person Health Care III–76
     1. The Provision of Health Care III–77
     2. Medical Supplies III–79
        a. WHO Emergency Health Kit III–79
        b. Vaccines III–80
        c. Donations of Unsolicited Drugs III–81
     3. Health Education III–81

**Displaced Person Camps: Site Selection,
Planning, and Shelter** III–81
A. General III–81
B. Criteria for Site Selection III–82
     1. Social Needs III–82
     2. Water III–82
     3. Open Space III–83
     4. Accessibility III–83
     5. Environmental Considerations III–83
     6. Soil and Ground Cover III–83
     7. Land Rights III–84
C. Site Planning III–84
D. Specific Infrastructure Design Considerations III–85
     1. Latrines III–85
     2. Water Distribution III–85
     3. Roads and Pathways III–85
     4. Firebreaks III–85
     5. Administrative and Community Services III–85
     6. Physical Layout III–86
E. Shelter III–87

Sanitation and Environmental Service III–89
A. General III–89
B. Importance of Organization, Integration, and
   Selection III–89
C. Disposal of Excreta III–90
     1. Selection of a System—Immediate
        Considerations III–91
     2. Immediate Action III–93
     3. Long-Term Options III–93
     4. Latrine Styles and Considerations III–94
        a. Number and Siting of Latrines III–94
        b. Population Density III–95
        c. Soil III–95
        d. Available Water III–96
        e. Drainage III–96
        f. Construction Materials III–96

D. Wastewater, Garbage, and Dust III–97
   1. Wastewater III–97
   2. Garbage III–97
      a. Storage III–97
      b. Collection III–97
      c. Disposal III–98
   3. Dust III–98
E. Insect and Rodent Control III–98
F. Fires III–100
   1. Prevention III–100
   2. Control III–100
G. Disposal of the Dead III–101

Figures
Figure III–1. Methods of Well Construction III–15

Tables
Table III–1. Water Needs for Displaced People III–9
Table III–2. Characteristics of Different Types of
   Well Constructions III–14
Table III–3. Weight-for-Length Expressed as a
   Percentage of Median Weight III–27
Table III–4. Weight-for-Height Expressed as a
   Percentage of Median Weight III–28
Table III–5. Weight-for-Length and Associated
   Z-Scores III–29
Table III–6. Weight-for-Height and Associated
   Z-Scores III–30
Table III–7. Examples of Survival Food Rations for
   Populations in Protracted Crisis Situations III–34
Table III–8. Example of Planning Figures to
   Determine Food Needs for Survival Food
   Rations for Populations in Protracted Crisis
   Situations III–35
Table III–9. Approximate Nutritional Values of
   Commodities III–47

**Chapter IV. Disaster Assistance
Response Team** IV–1

Overview IV–3
A. Purpose IV–3
B. Structure IV–4
C. DART Activation and Deployment IV–5

General Checklist for All DART Members IV–6
    Predeparture: IV–6
    In Travel: IV–7
    In-Country: IV–7
        Immediate Actions: IV–7
        Ongoing Actions: IV–8
    Demobilization: IV–9

Team Leader IV–9
    Predeparture: IV–10
    In-Country: IV–11
        Immediate Actions: IV–11
        Ongoing Actions: IV–12
    Demobilization: IV–13
A. Press Officer IV–14
    Predeparture: IV–14
    In-Country: IV–14
        Immediate Actions: IV–14
        Ongoing Actions: IV–15
    Demobilization: IV–16
B. Safety Officer IV–16
    Predeparture: IV–16
    In-Country: IV–16
        Immediate Actions: IV–16
        Ongoing Actions: IV–17
    Demobilization: IV–17
C. Liaison Officer IV–17
    Predeparture: IV–17
    In-Country: IV–18
        Immediate Actions: IV–18
        Ongoing Actions: IV–18
    Demobilization: IV–18

Logistics Coordinator IV–19
    Predeparture: IV–19
    In-Country: IV–19
        Immediate Actions: IV–19
        Ongoing Actions: IV–21
    Demobilization: IV–21
A. Supply Officer IV–21
    Predeparture: IV–21
    In-Country: IV–21
        Immediate Actions: IV–21
        Ongoing Actions: IV–22
    Demobilization: IV–23

B. Transportation Officer IV–23
    Predeparture: IV–23
    In-Country: IV–24
        Immediate Actions: IV–24
        Ongoing Actions: IV–25
    Demobilization: IV–25
C. Aviation Officer IV–25
    Predeparture: IV–25
    In-Country: IV–26
        Immediate Actions: IV–26
        Ongoing Actions: IV–27
    Demobilization: IV–28

Communications Officer IV–29
    Predeparture: IV–29
    In-Country: IV–30
        Immediate Actions: IV–30
        Ongoing Actions: IV–30
    Demobilization: IV–31

Operations Coordinator IV–31
    Predeparture: IV–31
    In-Country: IV–32
        Immediate Actions: IV–32
        Ongoing Actions: IV–32
    Demobilization: IV–33
A. Medical Officer IV–33
    Predeparture: IV–33
    In-Country: IV–33
        Immediate Actions: IV–33
        Ongoing Actions: IV–34
    Demobilization: IV–34
B. Search and Rescue Task Force Leader IV–34
    Predeparture: IV–34
    In-Country: IV–35
        Immediate Actions: IV–35
        Ongoing Actions: IV–35
    Demobilization: IV–35
C. Technical/Scientific Operations Specialists IV–35
    Predeparture: IV–36
    In-Country: IV–36
        Immediate Actions: IV–36
        Ongoing Actions: IV–37
    Demobilization: IV–37

Planning Coordinator IV–38
   Predeparture: IV–38
   In-Country: IV–39
      Immediate Actions: IV–39
      Ongoing Actions: IV–40
   Demobilization: IV–41
A. Information Officer IV–41
   Predeparture: IV–42
   In-Country: IV–42
      Immediate Actions: IV–42
      Ongoing Actions: IV–43
   Demobilization: IV–43
B. Field Officer IV–44
   Predeparture: IV–44
   In-Country: IV–44
      Immediate Actions: IV–44
      Ongoing Actions: IV–45
   Demobilization: IV–45
C. Program Officer IV–45
   Predeparture: IV–45
   In-Country: IV–46
      Immediate Actions: IV–46
      Ongoing Actions: IV–46
   Demobilization: IV–46
D. Technical/Scientific Specialists IV–46
   Predeparture: IV–47
   In-Country: IV–47
      Immediate Actions: IV–47
      Ongoing Actions: IV–48
   Demobilization: IV–48
   Types of Technical/Scientific Specialists: IV–48
   1. Water and Sanitation Specialists IV–48
      In-Country: IV–48
   2. Health Specialists IV–49
      In-Country: IV–49
   3. Food Specialists IV–50
      In-Country: IV–50

Administrative Officer IV–50
   Predeparture: IV–51
   In-Country: IV–52
      Immediate Actions: IV–52
      Ongoing Actions: IV–52
   Demobilization: IV–53

A. Procurement Specialist IV–53
   Predeparture: IV–54
   In-Country: IV–54
      Immediate Actions: IV–54
      Ongoing Actions: IV–55
   Demobilization: IV–57
B. Administrative Support Specialist IV–57
   In-Country: IV–58
      Immediate Actions (upon being hired): IV–58
      Ongoing Actions (performed for various
       functions): IV–58
   Demobilization: IV–58

Contracts Officer IV–59
   Predeparture: IV–59
   In-Country: IV–60
      Immediate Actions: IV–60
      Ongoing Actions: IV–61
   Demobilization: IV–61

Figures
Figure IV–1. DART Organization IV–2

Chapter V. Forms and Instructions V–1

Transportation Tracking Form V–2
Transportation Manifest Form V–5
Resource Request Form V–8
Commodity Issue Form V–11
T-Card V–14
Field Situation Reporting Format (SITREP) V–16
Unit Log V–18
Communications Log V–20

Chapter VI. Reference Information VI–1

DART Communications VI–2
A. Requirements VI–2
B. Systems VI–2
  1. General VI–2
  2. The Local Phone System (PSTN) VI–3
  3. Satellite Terminal Systems VI–3
  4. HF/VHF/UHF Radio Networks and Systems VI–4
C. Policy on the Use of Frequencies VI–6

D. Radio Identification and Communications
   Procedures VI–7
   1. Radio Identification VI–7
   2. Communications Procedures VI–7
   3. Phonetic Alphabet VI–7

Maps and Mapping VI–7
A. Predeparture VI–8
   1. Obtaining Maps for Field Use VI–8
   2. Predeparture Arrangements for Field Data
      Collection and Map Production VI–9
B. Mapping in the Field VI–9
   1. Field Applications VI–9
   2. Terms and Concepts VI–10
   3. Options for Thematic Map Production VI–11
   4. Procedures VI–12

Aircraft Information VI–12
A. General VI–12
B. Points to Consider when Dealing with Aircraft VI–13
C. Aircraft Loading and Offloading Methods VI–14
D. Points to Consider when Planning To Receive
   Aircraft Cargo VI–16

**OFDA Stockpile Commodities and DART
Support Equipment** VI–21
A. OFDA Office Supply Kit VI–22
B. OFDA Individual Support Kit VI–25
C. Tents VI–25
D. Blankets VI–25
   1. Wool Blankets VI–25
   2. Polyester Blankets VI–25
E. Chainsaw Kits VI–27
F. Water Container, 5-Gallon Collapsible VI–27
G. Water Tank, 3,000-Gallon (10,000-Liter)
   Collapsible—UNICEF Type VI–27
H. Water Tank, 3,000-Gallon Collapsible—
   U.S. Military Type VI–27
I. Plastic Sheeting VI–27
   1. General VI–27
   2. Distribution VI–29
   3. How to Use Plastic Sheeting VI–29
      a. Hot-Weather Conditions VI–30
      b. Cold-Weather Conditions VI–30
      c. Useful Construction Techniques VI–30

J. Other Supplies VI–32
   1. Hard Hats VI–32
   2. Face Masks VI–32
   3. Gloves VI–32

Working with the Military in the Field VI–33
A. Military Operations Involving Coordination With
   OFDA Disaster Response Activities VI–33
   1. Point-to-Point Logistical Support VI–33
   2. Peace Operations VI–34
   3. Disaster Relief VI–34
B. Characteristics of Military Culture VI–35
   1. Organizational Culture VI–35
   2. Meetings VI–36
   3. Coordination VI–36
   4. Operational View of the Mission VI–36
   5. Deployment VI–37
C. Military Structure During Operations VI–37
   1. Chain of Command VI–37
   2. CINC Authorities During Critical
      Humanitarian Relief Situations VI–38
   3. Humanitarian Assistance Survey Team VI–39
   4. Joint Task Force VI–39
   5. Civil Military Operations Center VI–40
   6. Civil Affairs VI–42
   7. Psychological Operations VI–42
D. Your Deployment with the Military VI–43
   1. Before Departing VI–43
   2. Arrival. VI–43
   3. Getting Visibility. VI–43
   4. Your Mission VI–45
   5. Meetings and Briefings in the JTF VI–45
   6. Contact and Visibility with the Affected
      Country, UN/PVO/NGO/IOs, and Donor
      Governments VI–46
   7. Staffing VI–46
   8. Reporting. VI–47
   9. Support VI–47
  10. When Are You Done? VI–48
  11. Closeout VI–48
  12. Other Assignments VI–48
E. More Information VI–49

Figures
Figure VI–1. Plastic Sheeting VI–28

Tables

Table VI–1. Characteristics of Radio and Satellite
   Communications VI–5
Table VI–2. Types of Aircraft That May Be Used by
   OFDA During Disaster Operations VI–17
Table VI–3. Types of Helicopters That Might Be
   Used by OFDA During Disaster Operations VI–20
Table VI–4. Overland Transport Capacities VI–21
Table VI–5. Contents of OFDA Office Supply Kit VI–23
Table VI–6. OFDA Individual Support Kit VI–26
Table VI–7. Title, Insignia, and Rank of U.S.
   Military Commissioned Officers VI–44

Chapter VII. Commonly Used Acronyms and Terminology VII–1

OFDA Acronyms and Terms VII–2

Department of Defense Acronyms and Terms VII–19

INTRODUCTION

This *Field Operations Guide for Disaster Assessment and Response* (FOG) was developed by the U.S. Agency for International Development/Bureau for Humanitarian Response/ Office of Foreign Disaster Assistance (OFDA) as a reference tool for individuals sent to disaster sites to perform initial assessments or to participate as members of an OFDA Disaster Assistance Response Team (DART).

The FOG contains information on general responsibilities for disaster responders, formats and reference material for assessing and reporting on populations at risk, DART position descriptions and duty checklists, sample tracking and accounting forms, descriptions of OFDA stockpile commodities, general information related to disaster activities, information on working with the military in the field, and a glossary of acronyms and terms used by OFDA and other organizations with which OFDA works.

In the development of the FOG, OFDA has drawn on several sources for information, including: the United Nations High Commissioner for Refugees *Handbook for Emergencies*; the United Nations Office for the Coordination of Humanitarian Affairs *United Nations Disaster Assessment and Coordination Field Handbook*; the World Health Organization booklet *New Emergency Health Kit*; the United Nations Children's Fund handbook entitled *Assisting in Emergencies*; the U.S. State Department's Bureau for Population, Refugees, and Migration *Assessment Manual for Refugee Emergencies*; the U.S. Public Health Service *Handbook of Environmental Health*; reference materials from the Centers for Disease Control and Prevention, the University of Wisconsin's Disaster Management Center, and InterWorks; USAID policies and directives; information from the Office of Food for Peace; and OFDA procedures, files, and staff expertise.

The FOG's size and format is modeled on the National Wildfire Coordinating Group's *Fireline Handbook,* which is used by wildland firefighters throughout the United States.

The search and rescue (SAR) component of a DART is more fully described in a separate operations guide developed by the Federal Emergency Management Agency, which specifically addresses SAR activities.

It is hoped a variety of field operations will find the FOG to be a useful source of information, in a compact, usable format. In the interest of conserving space and keeping the FOG to a manageable size, there is no index at the end of this guide. However an extensive Table of Contents is included at the beginning of the FOG to assist in locating information quickly by specific subject. Comments for revision should be directed to:

> USAID
> BHR/OFDA
> Operations Support Division
> Washington, D.C. 20523

The FOG is also posted on the World Wide Web at:

http://www.info.usaid.gov/ofda/

It is planned that this publication will be made available through the U.S. Government Printing Office (GPO) in the future.

This version of the FOG represents a second revision of the original *Guide to Field Operations for Disaster Response*, produced in 1992, and initially revised as the FOG in 1994. The FOG was developed for OFDA by the U.S. Department of Agriculture/Forest Service under its International Programs Office. That office's Disaster Assistance Support Program (DASP) is managed jointly by the Forest Service and USDA's Foreign Agricultural Service/International Cooperation and Development, with funds and direction provided by the U.S. Agency for International Development/Bureau for Humanitarian Response/OFDA under USDA Resources Support Services Agreement: AOT-R-00-96-90149.

OFDA
August 1998

POLICY GUIDELINES

The U.S. Agency for International Development/Bureau for Humanitarian Response/Office of Foreign Disaster Assistance (OFDA) has the responsibility to provide foreign disaster assistance and to coordinate the U.S. Government's (USG) response to disasters abroad. The authority to provide and coordinate USG foreign disaster assistance comes from the Foreign Assistance Act of 1961, as amended. **OFDA's mandate is to save lives, alleviate suffering, and reduce the economic impact of disasters**. OFDA does so by:

- Providing rapid, appropriate response to requests for assistance.

- Providing sufficient warning of natural events that cause disasters.

- Fostering self-sufficiency among disaster-prone nations by helping them achieve some measure of preparedness.

- Enhancing recovery from disasters through rehabilitation programs.

OFDA carries out these responsibilities in coordination with the government of the affected country, other donor governments, international organizations, UN relief agencies, and private voluntary and nongovernmental organizations. The primary responsibility for disaster relief rests with the government of the affected country. OFDA responds only when the U.S. Chief of Mission in an affected country has declared a disaster based on the following criteria:

- The magnitude of the disaster exceeds the affected country's capacity to respond.

- The affected country has requested or will accept USG assistance.

- It is in the interest of the USG to provide assistance.

OFDA's assistance is intended to supplement and support, not replace, the efforts of the government of the affected country. It is the responsibility of the U.S. Chief of Mission to make certain that USG assistance is appropriate and based on priority humanitarian needs. To ensure that the response is appropriate, timely, and cost effective, OFDA provides technical assistance through damage and needs assessments. That initial technical assistance may come in the form of an OFDA **Assessment Team** whose objectives are to:

- **Assess** the scope of the disaster's damage.

- **Assess** the initial needs of victims.

- **Report** to the Chief of Mission and OFDA headquarters in Washington (OFDA/W) on the situation and needs.

- **Recommend** follow-up USG relief actions, if any.

Assessment Team findings and recommendations must be clear, concise, timely, practical, and operational. They become the blueprints for USG decisionmaking and planning for disaster response activities.

Disaster relief that OFDA furnishes may take the form of OFDA relief commodities, services, transportation support, or grants to relief organizations.

If a more rapid or continuous response is necessary, OFDA will deploy a **Disaster Assistance Response Team (DART)**, which provides specialists trained in a variety of disaster relief skills **to assist the U.S. Chief of Mission and the USAID Mission (if present) with the management of the USG response to a disaster**. As with an Assessment Team, DARTs continue to assess and report on the disaster situation and recommend follow-up actions. But DARTs also:

- **Provide** an operational presence on the ground capable of carrying out sustained response activities.

- **Develop and, upon approval, implement** OFDA's field response strategy based on the DART mission objectives.

- **Coordinate** the movement and consignment of USG relief commodities.

- **Coordinate** USG relief efforts with the affected country, other donor countries, relief organizations and, when present, military organizations.

- **Fund** relief organizations (when delegated the funding authority).

- **Monitor and evaluate** USG-funded relief activities.

The Team Leader of a DART reports to the Chief of Mission as the lead USG person in the affected country to ensure that USG disaster relief efforts are coordinated and to OFDA/W to ensure that OFDA's mandate and mission are being carried out.

OFDA views disaster relief provided to victims in the immediate aftermath of a disaster within the context of long-term recovery and development activities. Disasters can provide the opportunity to reduce the vulnerability of the affected country to future disasters. Rehabilitation and reconstruction, properly formulated, can do much to introduce mitigation techniques to protect against the effects of future disasters.

OFDA stands ready to continue the American tradition of providing humanitarian relief for disaster victims worldwide.

Chapter I

General Responsibilities and Information

GENERAL RESPONSIBILITIES AND INFORMATION

This chapter provides information on general responsibilities for individuals sent to disaster sites to perform assessments or to participate as members of a Disaster Assistance Response Team (DART). Lists of needed equipment and supplies are also included.

Individual Team Member Checklist

The following pages contain five types of supply checklists for team members:
- Personal items.
- Optional items.
- Personal health items and medical tips.
- OFDA-provided items.
- Information to be left with OFDA.

Team members should be as individually mobile as possible. Unless you are deploying as a member of a long-term DART, try to limit your personal belongings to what you can carry.

Personal Items:
[ ] Valid passport. Copy the picture page and keep separate.
[ ] Immunization record (Yellow Book).
[ ] Personal health items (see below).
[ ] Adequate amount of U.S. currency/traveler's checks (check to see if you will be able to cash them) for length of assignment.
[ ] Personal checks and major credit cards.
[ ] Food for 36 hours (high energy, low weight).
[ ] Drinking water for 36 hours (2–3 liters).
[ ] Four changes of clothing appropriate for the location, elevation, time of year, and kind of assignment.
[ ] Toilet articles.
[ ] Six extra passport photos.
[ ] Flashlight with spare batteries.
[ ] Alarm clock.
[ ] Pocketknife.
[ ] Earplugs.
[ ] Business cards.

Optional Items (brought at your own risk):

[ ] Camera with film, batteries.
[ ] Pocket-size binoculars.
[ ] Electrical adapters for appliances.
[ ] Pocket calculator.
[ ] Swapping items (pins, buttons, pencils, stickers, etc.)

Personal Health Items and Medical Tips:

[ ] Prescription medicine for expected length of stay.
[ ] Medication for colds, allergies, diarrhea, athlete's foot, menstrual cramps, hemorrhoids, constipation, and headaches.
[ ] Sunscreen (SPF-15 or higher).
[ ] Insect repellent.
[ ] Antiseptic ointment.
[ ] Lip salve.
[ ] Vitamins.
[ ] Small scissors.
[ ] Tweezers.
[ ] Soap.
[ ] Small bottle or individual swabs of isopropyl alcohol.
[ ] Water-purification tablets or system.
[ ] One packet of oral rehydration salts.
[ ] Baseball cap or hat for sun and rain.
[ ] Flipflops.
[ ] Extra pair of glasses or contacts (record your prescription in the back of your Yellow Book).
[ ] If you wear contacts, be aware of dusty conditions at disaster sites.
[ ] Write down your blood type in your Yellow Book.
[ ] Don't take any of these first aid kit items in glass bottles.
[ ] Make a copy of your Yellow Book and keep the copy separate, in case you lose the original.

OFDA-Provided Items:

[ ] *Field Operations Guide for Disaster Assessment and Response* (FOG).
[ ] Individual's office supplies (see OFDA Office Supply Kit list in Chapter VI, "Reference Information").
[ ] Position description and checklist pertaining to your assignment.
[ ] Country clearances for affected country and visa if required.
[ ] Personal health kit, if needed; see U.S. Public Health Service officers in OFDA.

[ ] Short-term immunizations, boosters, and malaria pills needed at time of departure (contractors check when negotiating contract).
[ ] Travel authorization (TA) (make extra copy), travel advance, and airline tickets if travel is under OFDA. Make sure TA covers your potential needs such as car rental, local ticket purchase, excess baggage, and double per diem.
[ ] OFDA Individual Support Kit (if needed). DART members will usually be issued an OFDA Individual Support Kit by the OFDA Logistics Officer, if requested. The contents of the kit are listed in Chapter VI, "Reference Information."
[ ] Overseas workmen's compensation and medical evacuation insurance (contractors only).

Information To Be Left with OFDA:
[ ] Personal information sheet for personal and family emergencies.
[ ] Copy of passport picture page and immunization record.

Team Support Checklist

This checklist addresses overall team needs and complements the Individual Team Member Checklist contained in the first section of this chapter and the position checklists contained in Chapter IV, "Disaster Assistance Response Team." The Team Leader ensures that the following team support items are acquired prior to deployment:

[ ] Contact list for USAID/Embassy, private volunteer organizations, nongovernmental organizations, international organizations, United Nations agencies, donor and assisting countries, and appropriate affected country officials.
[ ] FOG.
[ ] USAID decals.
[ ] Camera and film/VCR tapes (35-mm and television camcorder) for documenting events and DART response (optional).
[ ] Telecommunications equipment commensurate with the assignment.
[ ] Copies of reference documents pertaining to affected country (If available):
    [ ] OFDA's Country Profile (if updated).
    [ ] State Department background notes.
    [ ] Mission Disaster Relief Plan (if available).
    [ ] Lessons-learned file.

- [ ] Maps covering the affected and surrounding areas.
- [ ] OFDA's Disaster History and Commodity Services Report.
- [ ] Travel advisory alerts.
- [ ] Public health bulletins.
- [ ] List of do's and don'ts.
- [ ] Assessment guides.
- [ ] Copy of all cable traffic pertaining to the disaster.
- [ ] Copy of all directives and team support documents:
  - [ ] OFDA's team support funding documents.
  - [ ] Overseas workmen's compensation and medical evacuation insurance for contractors.
  - [ ] Travel authorizations and itineraries.
  - [ ] Special authorizations and instructions from OFDA Director.
  - [ ] Photocopy of passports, visa, and personal information sheet.
- [ ] OFDA Office Supply Kit (see Chapter VI, "Reference Information," for contents).

Documentation

A. General

Team Leaders may make team members responsible for maintaining a daily log of activities with which they are involved. This log should include a chronology of significant events (departures, arrivals, meetings attended, individuals contacted, work accomplished, etc.). The log should be turned in to supervisors on request. The log is then turned in to the Plans function, where it becomes a part of the disaster response documentation and may also be used in the development of situation reports.

B. Types of Documentation

Each DART function receives and develops information that becomes a part of the disaster response documentation. The following is a list of the types of documentation generated by each function:

- **Management**—Delegation of authority, disaster relief objectives, press releases, safety plans, liaison plans.

- **Plans**—Situation reports, disaster chronology (developed from individual logs and information gathered by plans), maps, assessments, daily plans, personnel tracking, grant status (submitted, approved, funded, or being implemented).

- **Logistics**—Equipment and commodities tracking, accountability documents, equipment use information.

- **Operations**—Work assignments, work accomplishments, assessments, maps.

- **Administration**—Fiscal accounting, rental and procurement agreements, receipts, personnel records, petty cash.

Accountability and Liability

General—Team members are responsible for three types of equipment and supplies at a disaster: expendable, nonexpendable, and personal.

Expendable—Those items that are issued for use at a disaster site and are either used up, consumed, or possibly left at the disaster site for use by victims or by local individuals involved in continuing disaster relief efforts. Expendable items would include office supplies, gloves, small water containers, plastic sheeting, blankets, tents, hardhats, and hand tools. When issuing expendable items to local relief workers, be sure that the items are needed for the immediate relief effort. Some expendable items have proven to be personally attractive and particularly susceptible to being used for purposes other than relief activity.

Nonexpendable—Those items that are issued for use at a disaster and can be returned and refurbished for use on future assignments. Nonexpendable items would include radios, generators, specialized tools, and computers.

Personal—Those items such as clothing, toiletries, extra glasses, and medications that an individual takes to a disaster to attend to his or her personal needs. Cameras, binoculars, radios, and such items are considered personal items unless specifically required by OFDA.

Accountability—If OFDA deploys a DART or an Assessment Team to assist the USAID Mission or Embassy in the affected country, OFDA will become accountable at the field level for the distribution of all funds, supplies, equipment, and com-modities used in disaster relief operations. Team members have the responsibility to account for all items they consume, use, damage, destroy, or lose. This accounting must be done through a documentation system that tracks items from receipt through use or subsequent issuing to the ultimate users or disaster victims. Team members should always receive and keep an inventory of items for which they are responsible. Supervisors are responsible for identifying the method and level of tracking necessary for each disaster, based on direc-tion from the Team Leader. Lost or damaged items must be accounted for with a written statement explaining the circum-stances. When a question arises over whether an item is expendable, the Team Leader is responsible for making the decision. Certain disaster situations may call for issuing nonexpendable items to local agencies for use beyond the deployment of the team. Such issues should be documented through a hand receipt, with accompanying written justification becoming part of the team documentation. The Team Leader has the final team authority to decide what will or will not be left.

If OFDA does not deploy a DART or Assessment Team, then the accountability for funds or relief supplies, materials, and equipment provided by OFDA rests primarily with the recipient USAID Mission in the affected country.

Liability—Team members are liable for items lost or destroyed through poor accounting or performance. Problems arising from poor accounting or performance will be resolved with the appropriate representatives of the member's parent agency. Applicable USAID regulations will be used during the resolution.

Administration

A. Time Records

Depending on the relationship with OFDA, team members may or may not need to keep track of hours worked during a de-ployment to a disaster. OFDA will determine what method of timekeeping is necessary. If there will be reimbursement for all or a portion of a person's time, the team member must make sure that he or she and his or her agency are clear on what method of reimbursement will be used by OFDA. Types of agreements under which team members may be serving OFDA are:

- **USAID-Direct Hire**—See USAID Directives and discuss with your supervisor.

- **Personal Services Contractor**—Reimbursement and reporting documentation determined by contract. Check with OFDA at time of contract issuance.

- **Resources Support Services Agreement**—Includes individuals whose salaries are reimbursed through a resources support services agreement (RSSA). Some agencies donate employee salaries up to 6 weeks. The method of reimbursement for overtime worked must be agreed to beforehand by OFDA. If overtime will be approved, claims for reimbursement must be accompanied by a time record signed by the senior OFDA person on the team. Compensation time for overtime worked is an issue that must be determined by the individual's parent agency.

- **Individual Working for an Institutional Contractor, Grantee, or an Organization with a Memorandum of Understanding (MOU) with OFDA (may include volunteers)**—Reimbursement and reporting documentation are determined by the contract, grant, or MOU. Parent agencies must determine the required documentation.

B. Per Diem and Vouchers

Current General Services Administration (GSA) per diem rates and normal per diem rules will be used by all team members to determine amounts to be reimbursed for expenses incurred during a team deployment, unless otherwise specified in a contract, grant, or MOU.

Team members will fill out travel vouchers with the agency that prepares their travel authorization. Depending on the urgency of the team mobilization, a team member may travel on one or more travel authorizations, such as one for airline tickets, another for food and lodging, and possibly a third for a travel advance. Make sure the agency issuing a travel authorization has a mechanism and authorization procedure in place for reimbursement from OFDA.

Team members must keep lodging receipts for which they have paid. If a team member will be reimbursed based on actual expenses, he or she must obtain receipts for all expenses. Team members should keep a daily log of activities as well as expenses. The log is very helpful when filling out travel vouchers. Remember, only those expenses authorized on a travel authorization can be reimbursed.

C. Procurement and Contracting

The hiring or contracting of goods and services for team requirements at a disaster is the responsibility of the Team Leader. The Team Leader may delegate this responsibility to an authorized person on the team, depending on the size and complexity of the disaster. Unless authorized, team members cannot purchase, hire, or contract for goods and services, or make informal commitments to do so. If team members have any questions as to the limits of their procurement or contract authority, they should contact their team supervisor.

DART Setup and Closeout Guidelines

A. General

These guidelines propose some systems and suggestions to be used during DART setup that will increase the efficiency of DART operations and ease the closeout or transition of the DART to the USAID Mission (USAID), U.S. Embassy (Embassy), or OFDA Washington (OFDA/W). The Mission and Embassy are often referred to together as USAID/Embassy because both (if there is a Mission in the country) will normally be involved with DART operations.

The goal of a DART closeout should be to effect a seamless transition to the USAID/Embassy or OFDA/W. This transition will assist them in continuing support for the situation in terms of reporting, program management, and situation analysis.

The philosophy of setup and closeout should be one of cooperation and collaboration with the USAID/Embassy and, therefore, thinking ahead to the needs of the USAID/Embassy is critical. This cooperation and collaboration must also include agency partners who may be establishing a presence as the DART withdraws. Initiating planning for the transition when the DART is first set up will facilitate the eventual transfer to the USAID/Embassy and the closing out of the DART.

Many of the tasks identified in this section fall within the area of responsibility of the DART's Administrative function, but it is the responsibility of all team members to assist in the setup and closeout of a DART by setting up and maintaining proper files within their functional area.

B. Setup

1. Files and Record Keeping

Set up a simple, clearly documented filing system for cables, correspondence, and e-mail, commencing on Day One of the operation. Files should be set up by *Subject* and *Organization*.

Establish a financial tracking system that includes obligating documents, records, and receipts.

Establish grant files for each grant as funding is put in place. One side of the file folder should contain the grant document and the other side the related correspondence and memoranda.

Establish filing for rejected proposals.

Make and maintain a master filing list. Files can then be more quickly reviewed and separated or thrown out as needed.

Set up In/Out boxes.

In addition to the grant files, it has been found useful to maintain a desktop binder that contains copies of the final grant documents, by UN/PVO/NGO/IOs and grant number. This enables DART members to rapidly find documents when having discussions with grantees and to have a handy reference when working on Sitreps, replying to e-mails from Washington, etc.

Set up ingoing and outgoing binders for e-mail. E-mail messages that are relevant to a program or subject should be copied and filed appropriately. Save only 10 days of hard copies of e-mail. The historical file of e-mail should be put on diskettes. See *Diskettes* below.

2. Diskettes

Set up master diskettes. Use separate diskettes to store e-mail, memos and strategy pieces, Sitreps, and UN/PVO/NGO/IO grant documents. Mark the diskettes clearly. Team members can have their individual diskettes but final documents should go on the master diskettes that are placed in a separate disk storage box.

The Information Officer is normally responsible for the Sitrep diskettes and the Program Officer for the grant diskettes. Another diskette should hold copies of strategy documents, analyses, etc. Working diskettes for Sitreps and proposal reviews should also be set up to allow the team flexibility in daily movements and to make it easier to pass information on to others.

3. Contact List

Develop and maintain a contact list. This list should be sorted by organization, name, and function. Noting the date of initial contact may also be useful, especially for long-term DARTs. Periodic review and update of the list is often useful. Obtaining contact information that provides both temporary (field) and permanent (headquarters) contact information can be very helpful. For extensive or long-duration events, it may be advisable to use spreadsheet or contact manager software to facilitate updating, sorting, and displaying the information.

4. Program Management

DARTs are deployed with an initial strategy that is updated periodically by the Team Leader and OFDA/W with input from the USAID/Embassy. The strategy identifies the priority areas for OFDA support for relief activities. The strategy enables team members to work with UN/PVO/NGO/IOs in a focused and professional manner. The strategy should be shared with the relief community. Involvement in the development of the strategy will also allow the USAID/Embassy to see the evolution of the program over time prior to their inheritance of the operation.

As proposals are reviewed, written comments by team members should be recorded on a diskette. Such a system enables team members to provide input when they have time. It provides an archive of the discussions that took place regarding each proposal before reaching the final funding stage. It is also useful if there is a split DART with contracting occurring away from the center point of the team; a consolidated comment paper from the team can be forwarded to the Contracts Office for inclusion into the final file and discussion with

UN/PVO/NGO/IOs. This will also ensure that when the DART leaves there are complete historical records of grant actions to pass on to the USAID/Embassy (or back to OFDA/W, as the case may be).

Any adjustments to grantee programs, even if amendments are not called for, should be recorded in writing and put in the appropriate grant files.

All DART members should be familiar with the whole program, even if they have a specialty area that they focus on. This is important to ensure backup systems throughout the deployment. A map showing the area of all DART-funded programs will help in this regard.

If funding is taking place in the field, start a computer spreadsheet describing the proposals under review, their status, the name and number of the grant, the amount, etc. It should be updated regularly, especially during a funding cycle. The printout should be available to all team members and to OFDA/W if they request it. DARTs, which do not have funding authority, should expect a similar spreadsheet from Washington.

Build into the team some continuity into the future by using Foreign Service Nationals (FSNs) or locally hired personnel in some way. Discuss with them how OFDA works, the special authorities, etc., so that when the actions transfer completely to the USAID/ Embassy, any remaining staff funded by OFDA are well briefed. A time for overlap with incoming staff must be planned.

To facilitate closeout, petty cash funds should be reconciled every 30 to 60 days.

A daily schedule of programmatic review meetings should be posted.

5. Packaging

Save any reuseable packaging for equipment or supplies that will be returned during closeout.

C. Closeout

1. The Date

Difficult as it might be to project, the DART should determine a target closeout date as far in advance as possible. The message must go out early to all concerned groups, organizations, and offices that the DART is leaving.

Once a date is roughly determined, OFDA/W, working with the DART, must define the scope (operationally and programmatically) of the activities that will remain and begin to prepare the USAID/Embassy or OFDA/W for the takeover of the program. This entails discussions on staffing, levels of funding available, disposition of equipment and supplies, etc.

2. Administration

The Team Leader with the Administrative Officer should prepare a checklist for all actions that need to be taken to close the DART. Assign a lead person for each action. Distribute a checklist to each team member and monitor progress toward completion of actions. A master list should be maintained by the DART Team Leader or Administrative Officer, who will note when actions are completed. Distribution of a task list allows team members to work their part of the closeout into their ongoing DART schedule.

3. Personnel

The DART should discuss with OFDA/W the possibility of funding one (or more) DART members to stay on with the USAID/Embassy to provide program and historical continuity.

The DART Team Leader should plan for overlap with the USAID/Embassy and appropriate staff. Sufficient time should be scheduled to allow for "stress-free" relaying of important information. Also, if possible, a return visit shortly after transition by the Team Leader is useful. This allows for the new staff to draw up a list of questions that arise during the first days of posttransition. This is especially important if no DART members are staying on.

It is critical to ensure that the USAID/Embassy understands and agrees with the plans for the transfer or separation of FSNs and locally hired staff.

4. Moving and Transferring Files

A DART transition may require a physical relocation of files and documents to the USAID/Embassy. Before moving:

- Provide a copy of the file list to OFDA/W. In the event that some files are needed back in OFDA/W, they should be drawn out of the files and put aside for sending. If the USAID/Embassy desires the same files, copies need to be made.

- Plan for a "moving" day if you need one.

- Visit the new location and identify the new space for DART files. If an Executive Officer has already been assigned, work with him or her on these details.

- Decide what needs to be moved and what you need to move it. Make sure appropriate DART members are available that day.

If organizational systems were put in place early, the actual transfer becomes easy. The files are catalogued by subject and grant, and a list can be handed off to the mission. Diskettes are organized by topic as noted above and can easily be copied by the USAID/Embassy for their records. Originals can be returned to OFDA/W if required.

The Sitrep diskettes are passed to the USAID/Embassy, giving them a format on which to base any continued reporting that may be required. (The USAID/Embassy should restart the numbering of Sitreps to clarify that the transition has taken place.)

Ingoing and outgoing e-mail binders may not be desired by the mission. However, if you have filed important e-mails in the subject and grant files, you will have ensured that the USAID/Embassy has all the information necessary on various issues to provide a complete history. E-mail diskettes may also replace the need for paper copies.

5. Program Management

The most challenging part of the transition is ensuring that all matters regarding programs and grants are "complete" from the DART field perspective. Following is a list of actions that need to be taken:

- Grantees must be notified as early as possible that a transition is imminent. DART must explain how the transition will affect their programs. Individual meetings with grantees are recommended.

- A general letter to all grantees explaining the transition should be sent to all grantee headquarters and field offices at least 2 weeks before the DART's final day of operation. The letter can be drafted in the field but should be cleared with OFDA/W and by them with the USAID/W Contracts Office. Besides noting the administrative changes generally, the letter should also thank the grantees for their collaboration with the DART.

- If a DART is shifting from field contracting to USAID/W contracting, each grantee, for each grant, must receive an Amendment Letter noting the change in the Action Officer and any other blanket changes that are being caused by the DART's move.

- Depending where the grant funding has been executed, it will be important for the DART to work out arrangements with the USAID/Embassy or REDSO involved as to the handling of DART grants. Options presented below have been tried recently:

  - Transfer of all grant actions back to Washington, including those grants executed by DART in the field. This requires changing all grant numbers to conform to USAID/W numbers, returning funds to Washington, and amending all grants to indicate the change. All grant files must be shipped back to Washington immediately to permit the Action Officer to continue the program without a break.
  - Maintain all DART-executed grants in the field until their expiration dates with only nonfunded amendments authorized. REDSO takes charge of these simple amendment actions upon cable request from the Mission. (If the DART is already in a Mission that has contracting authority, this is very simple). All new funding is taken on by OFDA/W, including ongoing grantee programs requiring new funds. The latter must be resubmitted as new activities. Complete grant files then remain in the field until they expire and are shipped back to OFDA/W at that time.

6. Public Relations

Send letters to key colleagues (for example, the Special Representative of the U.N. Secretary General, Force Commander, ICRC, local officials), explaining the DART closeout and transition and expressing DART's appreciation for their collaboration.

As appropriate for the DART, send a cable announcing the DART transition and thanking missions and embassies in the region for their support.

7. Petty Cash Funds

Vendors should be encouraged to submit final vouchers before the DART closeout. Keep some funds in the field to clear DART accounts that may come due after the team's departure. If a DART member stays on, it is possible to transfer administrative approval for the bills to that individual; otherwise the USAID/Executive Officer can assist. After a certain period (1–3 months) when the accounts are clear, remaining funds should be returned to the cashier who set up the petty cash fund. Remember that each person granted petty cash authority must close out his or her own petty cash drawer prior to leaving.

To clear the fund, gather all receipts together. A ledger should have been maintained showing the drawdown of the funds. This information should be returned to the point where the funds were issued. Any residual funds will be returned by the controlling mission to OFDA/W.

8. Transfer of Property

The disposition of any DART property to be left must be completed during the closeout. The disposition should include an agreement on whether the property will be transferred, left in place for use for a set time, or left as pre-positioned equipment. This agreement should state whether OFDA will be expected to provide support for the equipment and, if so, how and to what degree.

9. Communications

Find out early what sort of pouch services might be available for returning heavy equipment to the States or if channel flights or other military assets might be available. Pick a deadline date when the DART will disconnect its satellite and make sure OFDA/W knows that the DART will no longer have independent communications. Inform the Embassy Communications Officer. He or she may be able to assist with any technical aspects of the disassembly of the communications equipment. If you have an especially complex setup you may require special OFDA technical assistance.

Identify packing materials early on. Have one person in charge of supervising the packing of the materials, checking each item off on the inventory as it is packed away. Label all boxes, address them correctly, and number them along with a notation of their contents. Notify OFDA/W when the pack-out is complete and provide the approximate date items were put into the pouch.

10. Memorandum of Agreement (MOA)

The DART Leader, during the final closeout with the USAID/Embassy, may want to develop a MOA (Memorandum of Agreement) that defines all follow-on relationships between the DART and the USAID/Embassy. Here is where issues such as outstanding petty cash, transfer of property, and disposition of FSNs or locally hired staff can be addressed. The Team Leader should confer closely with OFDA/W in preparing the MOA because the task of following up on the MOA will likely fall to OFDA/W.

Safety and Security

Being aware of personal and team safety and security is a part of every team member's job, regardless of his or her task at the disaster. The goal is to prevent accidents and protect the safety, health, and security of all team members on and off the job.

Assessment Teams and DARTs are sent to a disaster because of an emergency situation. The tasks they perform are ones for which they are trained. An emergency occurs for a team member and the team when a member becomes sick or injured and must be cared for or evacuated, diminishing the ability of the team to deliver the maximum assistance possible to the victims. The safety, security, and well-being of all members is an asset to the team and the victims. **THINK SAFETY AND SECURITY AT ALL TIMES!!!**

The following checklists for safety and security cover some of the general issues you as a team member should think about and become knowledgeable of, both before you depart and throughout your deployment. If there is a written generic safety and security plan available, take one with you.

Safety and Security Checklist

- WEAR YOUR SEAT BELT ALWAYS!!

- Slow down in vehicles; if you have drivers, insist that they maintain safe speeds.

- Be aware of potential hazards at a disaster site, such as working in or near damaged buildings, aircraft operations, vehicle operations, and unsanitary living and eating conditions.

- Report hazardous conditions and other safety concerns to your supervisor and also to the safety function, if there is one on the team.

- Familiarize yourself with the medical emergency plan and medical evacuation plan, if they have been done.

- In lodgings, find out about fire detection and protection procedures; check for exits and smoke detectors.

- Team Leaders should be aware of potential health issues of team members.

- Familiarize yourself with the security plan for the team.

- Get a briefing on who will be the security focal point on the team.

- Be aware of personal security issues:
  - Signs of danger (culturally, politically).
  - Areas of danger (crowds, mined areas, factional borders).
  - Physical danger (increase in criminal activity, increase in factional fighting, shelling, shooting).
  - Location of secure areas or locations for team members.
  - List of personal items to take or leave in an emergency and location of those items (use Individual Team Member Checklist as a reminder list).
  - Need for protective clothing.

- Establish a communications plan:
  - Frequencies in use by team and others (UN/PVO/NGO/IOs or donors).
  - Contact system between team members and among groups above.
  - Secondary backup systems.
  - Radio procedures.
  - Copies of frequencies, procedures, etc., available in the office and vehicles.
  - Reporting or call-in procedures.

- Establish a travel plan:
  - Get a briefing on road and security conditions.
  - Routes to be driven.
  - Planned stops.
  - Points of contact at stops.
  - Timeframe for trip.
  - List items taken for safety or security reasons (personal gear, extra food or water, vehicle equipment spares, security items, etc.)
  - At the conclusion of the travel, debrief on the road and security conditions.

- Establish an emergency evacuation plan:
  - Coordination with Embassy/Mission.
  - Shutdown procedures (collection or destruction of sensitive materials and equipment).
  - Assembly points (stay-or-go procedures).
  - Survival equipment and supplies (amount, location, access).
  - Transportation methods for evacuation (road, air, water).
  - Evacuation points and routes (airport, border, specific road) marked on maps.
  - Vehicles equipped and prepared for evacuation.
  - Plan rehearsed or discussed.

- Share this plan with appropriate cooperators and seek to obtain their plans.

- Maintain a points-of-contact list (internal and external).

Personal Health and Critical-Incident Stress

This section provides a guide to recognizing and meeting common physical and emotional problems encountered during disaster relief activities. Experience has shown that promoting and maintaining good health, especially by coping with the stresses encountered overseas, are the keys to successful performance.

A. Briefings

The most important key to personal health and safety is to follow briefings given by OFDA, the State Department, the DART Team Leader, the USAID Mission in-country, the U.S. Embassy or Consulate in-country, and affected country contacts. They can provide up-to-date details on disease, sanitation, food and water safety, personal and property security, and other information to keep team members healthy and safe during the assignment.

Team members should never knowingly put their lives in jeopardy. "Stay alert, keep calm, think clearly, and act decisively" should be their motto. Tasks should be accomplished by putting safety first.

B. Managing Culture Shock

Team members may experience two different but interrelated types of stress. The first is culture shock, which comes from suddenly being placed in a strange foreign environment. The second is the emotional and physical impact that often comes from being immersed in a disaster.

Between arriving in-country and reaching the disaster site, team members may experience classic culture shock. The team member is a foreigner and may be frustrated because of an inability to communicate with the local population; anxiety and frustration may erode his or her customary level of self-confidence.

The team member should expect to be disoriented and confused and realize that this is natural and often happens to others in similar situations. Patience, realistic expectations of an ability to make a difference, and a sense of humor are good coping strategies in these circumstances. The team member should not expect the affected country and the victims to change their ways of doing things to accommodate to relief workers.

C. Critical-Incident Stress

No one who sees a major disaster remains emotionally untouched by it. Typical reactions are feelings of frustration, hopelessness, and that there is simply too much suffering and relatively little impact one person can have.

The combined effects of cultural and job stress make team members vulnerable to physical and emotional exhaustion. Some people refer to this as "burnout." It can happen to anyone.

The disaster-related stress caused by these factors is often referred to as critical-incident stress, or CIS. A critical incident is any incident so unusually stressful to an individual as to cause an immediate or delayed emotional reaction that surpasses available coping mechanisms. Critical incidents take many forms, including all emergencies that cause personnel to experience unusually strong reactions.

The effects of critical incidents can include profound behavioral changes that may occur immediately or may be delayed for months or years.

D. How Team Members May Be Affected by Stress During Disaster Operations

Following are some ways team members may be affected by stress during disaster operations

- They may experience physical symptoms associated with stress, such as headaches, upset stomach, diarrhea, poor concentration, and feelings of irritability and restlessness.

- They may become tired of the disaster and prefer not to talk about it, think about it, or even associate with coworkers during time off. They may become tired of continual interaction with victims and may want to isolate themselves during time off.

- They may have feelings of frustration or guilt because they miss their families and are unavailable to their families both physically and emotionally due to their psychological involvement in the disaster, fatigue, and so forth.

- They may feel frustrated with family and friends when they are able to contact them because the relief workers feel that families and friends simply cannot understand the disaster experience. If family and friends become irritated, it can compound the problem, and temporary isolation and estrangement may occur.

E. How To Minimize Stress During a Disaster Operation

Following are some ways to minimize stress during a disaster operation:

- As much as possible, living accommodations should be personal and comfortable. Mementos from home may help disaster workers to keep in touch psychologically.

- Regular exercise consistent with present physical condition and relaxation with some activity away from the disaster scene may help.

- Getting enough sleep and trying to eat regular meals even if the workers are not hungry will help. Workers should avoid foods high in sugar, fat, and sodium, such as donuts and fast foods. Taking vitamin and mineral supplements may help the body to continue to get the nutrients it needs.

- Excessive use of alcohol and coffee should be avoided. Caffeine is a stimulant and should be used in moderation as it affects the nervous system, making relief workers nervous and edgy.

- Although relief workers need time alone on long disaster operations, they should also spend time with coworkers. Both experienced and new relief workers should spend rest time away from the disaster scene. Talking about normal things (home, friends, family, hobbies, etc.) other than the disaster is a healthy change of pace.

- Humor helps ease the tension. However, use it carefully as victims or coworkers can take things personally, resulting in hurt feelings if they are the brunt of "disaster humor."

- When on the job, it is important for relief workers to take breaks during the day, especially if they find themselves making mistakes or unable to concentrate.

- Team members should try to stay in touch with family back home if they can. Communication helps prevent the sense of being strangers when they return after the disaster.

Team Leaders can take specific, practical action to prevent and reduce the effects of CIS, consequently avoiding the personal and organizational costs associated with them. Steps include:

- Learning to identify and respond to CIS in personnel.

- Educating team members in advance about the potential harmful effects of critical incidents.

It's normal to experience stress during a disaster operation, but remember...stress can be identified and managed.

Medical Emergencies and First Aid

This section contains very basic information on medical emergencies and first aid. More complete information can be found in the booklet in the OFDA personal health kit.

Most field medical situations you encounter are not immediately life threatening. The few that are can generally be addressed by anyone with basic first aid skills and a rational approach. Maintain a calm, thoughtful manner. Panic will cause or contribute to a "shock" response in the victim and may cause others to act irrationally as well.

When confronted by a medical emergency, your first step is to determine whether or not you can safely and effectively render assistance. Do not move the victim unless you have to for your safety or his or hers. Once you have determined that you are not endangering yourself and that the victim is in a relatively safe position, get help if you are able to do so.

WARNING—There is a definite risk to the first aid responder from the bodily fluids of the patient. These include blood, mucus, urine, and other secretions. You should take the steps necessary to protect yourself before attempting to treat the patient. Use surgical gloves if you have them (they are provided in the OFDA medical kit). Also, it is strongly advised that you use a cardiopulmonary resuscitation (CPR) barrier device if giving mouth to mouth. A facemask will also reduce the potential for rescuer infection.

The Initial ABCs of Medical Emergencies/First Aid

The basic steps in assessing your victim and initiating treatment are as follows:

- **Airway**—Open and maintain an adequate airway.

- **Breathing**—Check for breathing by listening at the mouth and watching the rise of the chest.

- **Circulation**—Check for circulation by feeling for a pulse at the wrist, ankle, or throat.

In a fully unconscious person you can clear the airway by using a "finger sweep"—reaching into the back of the throat to remove a visible object but being careful not to push the object in further. Place them on their back, look inside the mouth, and do a finger sweep. If the victim is not unconscious, be careful not to get bitten. Falling unconscious and relaxing may loosen the object from the throat. If it does not, kneel astride the person and place your hands at the base of the rib cage. The heel of one hand should be down, the fingers of the upper hand between those of the lower, grasping the palm. Deliver five quick upward thrusts to the abdomen.

If you are able to clear the blockage but the patient has not resumed breathing, perform mouth-to-mouth resuscitation, part of cardiopulmonary resuscitation (CPR).

1. **Position the Victim.** Lay the victim on their back. Kneel and position yourself at a right angle to the victim's body, with your knees perpendicular to the victim's neck and shoulders.

2. **Head Tilt/Chin Lift.** Position your palm on the person's forehead and gently push backward, placing the second and third fingers of your other hand along the side of the victim's jaw, tilting the head and lifting the chin forward to open the airway.

3. **Modified Jaw Thrust.** If you suspect a neck injury, a modified jaw thrust (without the head tilt) may be used. This is done by placing your hands on each side of the victim's face, your thumbs on the cheekbones but not pushing, and pulling the jaw forward with your index fingers. Again examine the mouth for foreign objects. If you find any, use the finger sweep to clear them.

4. **Check for Breathing again.** Put your ear directly over the victim's mouth to listen and feel for air being exhaled. Look at the victim's chest to see if it is rising or falling.

5. **Mouth-to-Mouth Resuscitation.** Position yourself at a right angle to the victim's shoulder. Use the head tilt/chin lift maneuver and pinch the victim's nose closed, using your thumb and forefinger. Open your mouth wide, and place it tightly over the victim's mouth. Exhale into the victim just enough to see the chest rise. Take another breath and repeat. Check to see if the victim's chest is rising when you exhale. If the stomach bulges the air is going into the stomach and not the lungs. The airway may be blocked still. Check the airway again.

6. **Check for a Pulse.** After you have delivered your two breaths into the victim, check for a pulse using two fingers just to the side of the Adam's apple. If the victim has a pulse but is not breathing, continue mouth-to-mouth resuscitation, using the same technique of big breaths every 5 seconds (12 times/minute). Remove your mouth between breaths. Continue to check for signs of breathing and watch for chest movement. If the victim's breathing is weak, you may have to continue mouth-to-mouth, following the victim's breathing pattern, ensuring a breath at least every every 5 seconds.

7. **Restore Circulation**. If you are unable to find a pulse in the victim, you must begin heart compressions to restore circulation. The compressions must be coordinated with the mouth-to-mouth resuscitation. Kneel and position yourself at a right angle to the victim's chest. Find the base of the breastbone at the center of the chest where the ribs form a V. Position the heel of one hand on the chest immediately above the V; with the other hand, grasp the first hand from above, intertwining the fingers. Shift your weight forward and upward so that your shoulders are over your hands; straighten your arms and lock your elbows. Shift your weight onto your hands to depress the victim's chest (1½ to 2 inches in an adult). Count aloud as you do it, five times in an even rhythm, slightly faster than 1 compression/second (80–100 beats/minute). Repeat the pattern for a total of 15 chest compressions.

8. **Continue Breathing for the Victim.** You must continue to give the victim oxygen through mouth-to-mouth resuscitation. Give two breaths. Repeat.

9. **Alternate Pumping and Breathing.** Pump the victim's chest 15 times, then breathe for him or her twice. Establish

a regular rhythm, counting aloud. Check the pulse and breathing after four cycles. Continue until help arrives, if possible.

10. **Performing CPR on a Child.** The procedure is essentially the same, but you use only one hand for chest compressions and pump the child's chest five times. You then breathe for the child once, more gently than you breathe for an adult.

11. **Two-Person CPR.** One person provides breathing assistance while the other pumps the heart. Pump the heart at a rate of 80 to 100 beats per minute. After each five compressions, a pause in pumping is allowed for a breath to be given by the other person.

Choking

The victim will be unable to speak or breathe effectively if their airway is obstructed. If they are coughing or gasping strongly for air, leave them alone. If they are unable to speak, trying to clear their throat, or coughing weakly, stay with them and carefully monitor their breathing. If the victim is unable to speak and puts their hands around their throat, act promptly; this is the universal sign for choking. Clearing the airway is easiest if the patient is standing. Step behind them, make a fist with one hand and place it over the abdomen, thumb side towards the patient, between their navel and the bottom of their rib cage. With your other hand, grasp your wrist. With a sharp inward and upward thrust, compress the abdomen. Repeat until the airway is clear. If the person has passed out, is too big for you to reach around, or cannot be stood up, lay them flat on their back, turn their head to one side, and use an abdominal thrust with both hands similar to a CPR chest compression. Continue to monitor the ABCs and treat for shock, if indicated.

Other Emergency Situations

Once you know that your patient's ABCs are OK, you can move on to determining what other problems they may have. If you saw the injury occur and the patient is conscious and able to communicate effectively with you, this step is fairly simple. If a language barrier exists or the patient is not conscious, it becomes more difficult. Be sensitive to cultural barriers or obstacles, especially when your patient is of another culture.

Shock

The most commonly encountered form of shock in the field is traumatic shock, induced by injury. *If left untreated, it may result in death.* Always monitor for signs of shock and routinely treat for it in cases of severe injury. The patient may be cold and clammy, have pale skin, a rapid, weak pulse, rapid, shallow breathing, or a combination of these symptoms. Except in cases of head injury, have the patient lie flat on their back and elevate their legs. Cover them with a blanket or other thermal cover and monitor the ABCs.

Bleeding

There are several ways to control the bleeding. These should be attempted, in the following order:

- Using a sterile gauze square, apply pressure directly over the wound. When it stops bleeding, tape or otherwise secure the gauze in place. Immediately removing the gauze may cause the bleeding to restart.

- If you have knowledge of the arterial pressure points, apply pressure, using one or both thumbs over the artery. Once this has controlled the bleeding, apply pressure bandages to the wound site.

- If you are unable to control the bleeding in any other way, and professional help is many hours away, apply a tourniquet to the affected extremity. There is a high risk of losing the extremity, particularly if professional attention is not immediately available. This is a last resort.

- Bleeding from the torso does not lend itself to control by any method other than direct pressure. Elevation may help, and if ice is available in sufficient quantity, it will also help.

- Bleeding from the head can usually be controlled by direct pressure, elevation, icing, or a combination of all three. Do not apply a tourniquet.

Burns

Burns may be three basic types: chemical, electrical, and thermal. The treatment for each is different, but in every case, treatment for traumatic shock should be part of your approach.

Chemical burns—These may arise from inadvertent spills when handling chemicals, coming in contact with improperly disposed chemicals and chemical waste, or chemical warfare acts. Take precautions to ensure that you are not contaminated or exposed to the chemicals before attempting treatment. If you can determine the nature of the chemical that caused the burn, it will be helpful in determining the followup treatment.

- Remove all contaminated clothing.

- Thoroughly rinse with copious amounts of clean, lukewarm water. Rinse for at least 20 to 30 minutes or longer if possible.

- Seek professional medical attention as soon as possible, regardless of the apparent severity of the burn.

Electrical burns—These usually stem from electrical shock. Before approaching the patient, be certain that no further risk of injury is present. If you know the patient is still in contact with the electrical source and you know it is low voltage, you can move the wire or the patient to a safe position with a dry pole or rope. If the wire is of unknown or high voltage, get professional help to shut off the current or move the wire. Attempting to do so yourself will likely result in an increase in the body count for this incident. Don't do it.

- As soon as it is safe to do so, check the ABCs and continue to monitor them. Patients with electrical burns often suffer cardiac or respiratory arrest.

- If there are evident burns, cover them loosely with sterile dressings.

- Seek professional help in treating the burns. Do NOT apply burn creams or ointments.

Thermal burns—These range from mild sunburn to the severe burns associated with open flames and heated metal. Thermal burns are categorized by degree. Appropriate treatment is keyed to the severity of the burn.

- **First-degree burns**—Symptoms are minor swelling and redness of the affected area.
  - Apply cool running water or wet compresses as soon as possible, continuing until the pain subsides.
  - Leave the burned area exposed. Do NOT apply ointments or salves. If pain recurs, reapply cold water.

- **Second-degree burns**—Symptoms are definite redness of the affected area, swelling, and blistering.
  - Treat as above for first degree burns for 15 to 30 minutes, preferably using sterile water.
  - Cover with a dry, sterile bandage.
  - Elevate the burned area, and treat the patient for traumatic shock.
  - Seek professional help.

- **Third-degree burns**—Typically, these are areas of deeper burning, surrounded by areas that display first and second degree burn characteristics. Charring or a leathery appearance are also common.
  - Check the ABCs and continue to monitor them.
  - Treat for traumatic shock.
  - Cover the burned area with a sterile, nonadhesive dressing.
  - Elevate the burned area.
  - Immediately seek professional help.

Fractures (broken bones)

Usually, the patient will know if they have broken a bone. The symptoms are bruising around the fracture site, localized pain, deformity, and swelling. In treating a fracture, the objective is immobilization of the ends of the broken bone. Immobilize any fracture before moving the patient. This is especially important in the case of known or suspected spinal injury. When splinting a fracture, immobilize the adjacent joints as well as the fracture site. After splinting is completed and on a continuing basis until professionally treated, check circulation in the affected extremities. In the case of an open fracture, you will most likely need to control the bleeding using pressure points instead of direct pressure. Monitor the patient for the onset of traumatic shock symptoms. Treat for shock routinely in fractures of major bones and open fractures (when the bone breaks the surface of the skin). Get medical attention for open fractures.

Frostbite

Frostbitten tissue will feel cold to your touch, and either numb or painful to the patient. In extreme cases, the tissue will turn white and harden. Do not attempt to thaw frozen tissue until you can ensure it will not be immediately refrozen. It is better to delay treatment a few hours than to refreeze previously frozen tissue. To treat, gently warm the affected areas in a heated space, using lukewarm water where it is possible to immerse the affected area. Give the patient warm fluids and be alert to signs of shock. Rewarming that is too rapid will cause circulatory problems and possibly worsen the tissue damage. If the tissue blisters, avoid breaking the blisters and cover the affected area with a dry gauze bandage. Prevent injured fingers, toes, etc., from rubbing against each other by place gauze pads between them. Seek medical attention for all but mild cases, as there is risk of septicemia and gangrene in more severe cases.

Heat Exhaustion

The patient usually sweats profusely, feels clammy to the touch, may complain of a headache or nausea, and may be disoriented and feel weak. If you suspect heat exhaustion but the patient is not sweating, see *Heat Stroke*, below. Get the patient out of the direct sun and cool them down by applying cold compresses and fanning. If they are conscious, give ORS and water, or plain water. If recovery isn't fairly immediate upon treatment, seek medical attention.

Heat Stroke

The patient will have hot, dry skin and a temperature well above normal. *This situation is life threatening and must be treated immediately and aggressively.* In more advanced cases, the patient will lose consciousness and may convulse. Get the patient out of the sun and into a cool space. Remove their clothing and immerse them in cold (NOT icy) water until the onset of shivering. Seek medical attention. *You must immediately lower the body temperature or it is quite likely that the patient will die.*

Hypothermia

The patient will shiver in the early stages of hypothermia, but once the body's core temperature goes below about 92 degrees, they may not. They will be uncoordinated and may demonstrate mental confusion, slurred speech, and irrational behavior. Merely bringing the patient into a warm space will not reverse severe cases. Remove any wet or constricting clothing, place the patient in a prewarmed bed or sleeping bag, and add water bottles of warm (NOT hot) water around the torso. If warm water is not available, use one or more warm, dry rescuers in the sleeping bag or bed to provide heat. If the patient is sufficiently conscious to protect their airway, give them warm (100–115°F) fluids such as lemonade or Tang. This provides readily absorbed fuel (sugar) and a means to provide heat to the body core. Do NOT give coffee, tea, other stimulants, or any form of alcohol. The patient has lost the ability to produce sufficient heat and heat must be provided externally. While this is a "cold" injury, it is most common at temperatures above freezing and in wet, windy conditions.

Working with the Media

A. General

The Team Leader sets the guidelines for relations with the media covering the disaster. If a Press Officer is a member of the DART, he or she is the contact point with the media. If not, the Team Leader takes on the direct media relations function. The following rules are mainly for Press Officers. However, these rules are helpful to any member of the team who may become involved with answering media needs.

B. Rules for Dealing with Reporters

- Never pick a fight with the news media:
    - They air or print every day and you don't.

- There are no secrets:
    - Assume what you say and do will get on the air or the printed page.
    - While you can say things "off the record," that doesn't mean the media won't print it and give you attribution.

- Don't assume anything:
    - Reporters may not be well informed or technically proficient about your profession.
    - Explain terms to ensure they are understood.

- Keep it simple:
  - Simplify and summarize your major points.
  - Write facts and data down to hand out.
  - Use English. Talk in a relaxed style that is aimed at laypersons, not subject experts. Avoid acronyms.
  - Remember that the audience is the general public.

- Give reporters a good story to write...or they may find one you don't like and write it:
  - Listen for trends in the questions. Is the reporter asking leading questions? Are there obvious misconceptions? Offer to clarify or redirect.

- Treat reporters professionally:
  - Treat them with respect.
  - Initiate background conversations.
  - Always answer their calls immediately.
  - Leave word in your office where you will be so you can answer calls immediately.

- Don't lie:
  - Make sure your information is accurate.
  - It doesn't have to be all-encompassing. You don't have to tell a reporter your views on everything.

- Before you do an interview, decide what you can discuss and what you can't—and stick to it.

- Use humor to defuse confrontational situations.

- Choose your words carefully and well:
  - They will likely be reported as you say them.

- If a critical or controversial story is going to be written anyway, your point of view should be in the story:
  - Silence is not always golden.

- Repetition is the essence of retention:
  - The public will remember what they see, hear, and read repeatedly in the media.

- Once a story is out that you don't like, it is usually too late and fruitless to try to correct it:

- Use objective and authoritative sources of information to back up your statements to reporters, if you can:
  - Don't make charges you can't back up or make stick.

- Try to anticipate questions. If you can't or you don't know the answer, get back to the reporter after you are asked such questions so you can give a considered response.

OFDA Guidelines for Drug Donations

OFDA/W, Assessment Teams, and DARTs may receive offers of drug donations from a variety of organizations. These organizations often also seek assistance in transporting the donated drugs. OFDA/W will normally work with the organizations on the transport issues, but Assessment Teams and DARTs will often be requested by OFDA/W to validate the field requirement for the drugs and to ensure the capability of the identified consignee to receive, transport, store, distribute, and monitor the use of the drugs. Clearance for medical and pharmaceutical products is granted if the goods are determined to be appropriate, based upon adaptations relevant to OFDA's disaster-related activities, and in the WHO Guidelines for Drug Donations. The following OFDA adaptations serve as a tool to assist Assessment Teams and DARTs to be objective and consistent in providing field input on whether to accept or reject donated drugs. The major principles to remember are as follows:

- Donations must be based on an analysis of needs.

- Product selection and distribution must conform to existing policies and capabilities (adherence to any existing national policies, the WHO Essential Drug List, etc.).

- Products must be easily identified through labels and written materials.

- The shelf life must allow time for transportation and distribution (expiration dating >9 months in emergency situations).

- Unsolicited and unnecessary donations are wasteful and should not be encouraged.

Chapter II

Assessments

ASSESSMENTS

Introduction

The purpose of this chapter is to provide Office of Foreign Disaster Assistance (OFDA) staff and others who participate on OFDA Assessment Teams with a guide to conducting an initial assessment for sudden or slow onset disasters. It includes information on the purpose, types, and elements of an assessment; collecting and analyzing data; preparing recommendations for U.S. Government (USG) response; and submitting assessment reports to OFDA Washington (OFDA/W). It also provides assessment checklists and reference information by sector and reference annexes for displaced populations at risk.

In addition to providing a guide to conducting an initial assessment, this chapter contains information on assessing specific sectional needs. However, it is not intended as a complete reference for comprehensive assessments conducted by sectorial experts. When sectorial experts such as epidemiologists and sanitarians are members of the Assessment Team, they will provide more specific materials related to conducting their portion of the assessment. This information will help when team members assist in conducting comprehensive assessments.

Purpose of an Initial Assessment

The overall purpose of an initial assessment is to provide OFDA/W with information and recommendations to make timely decisions on the USG disaster response. Initial assessments:

- Identify the impact a disaster has had on a society, and the ability of that society to cope.

- Identify the most vulnerable populations, especially women and children, that need to be targeted for assistance.

- Identify the most urgent food and nonfood requirements and potential methods of providing them in the most effective manner.

- Identify the level of response by the affected country and its internal capacities to cope with the situation, including those of the affected population.

- Identify the priorities of the affected population and their preferred strategies for meeting those priorities.

- Identify the level of response from other donor countries, UN relief organizations (UN), private voluntary organizations (PVOs), nongovernmental organizations (NGOs), and international organizations (IOs).

- Make recommendations to OFDA/W and to USAID/Embassy (if there) that define and prioritize the actions and resources needed for immediate response. Recommendations should include possibilities for facilitating and expediting recovery and development.

- Identify which types of in-depth assessments should be undertaken.

- Highlight special concerns that would not immediately be evident to OFDA/W or nonemergency persons.

Initial assessments should also provide baseline data as a reference for further monitoring. Monitoring systems should be identified so that relief officials will be able to determine whether a situation is improving or deteriorating. The systems must also be able to provide a means of measuring the effectiveness of relief activities. Each assessment or survey should be designed to build upon previous surveys and expand the data base.

Assessments should be conducted whenever there is uncertainty about the nature of an emergency response. If the disaster appears to require more than a $25,000 request, an assessment should be considered.

The Assessment Team must be sensitive to the situation of the affected country. The team needs to structure its assessment questions so that unreasonable expectations are not created. It should be clear to the affected country what the United States can/cannot and will/will not do. The Assessment Team must also be aware of the pressures it will feel from the affected country and others to "identify needs." A recommendation of "no additional assistance is required" may also be a valid response, given that the on-the-ground site visit yields a disaster that is not as severe as indicated in thirdhand reports and media coverage (focused on the most heart-wrenching cases) received in Washington prior to the Assessment Team's departure.

It is important to remember that the Assessment Team is supporting the U.S. Country Team, led by the Ambassador. The Country Team will have a strong desire to help. The Assessment Team must consider the Country Team's desire to help, but it also must be prepared to advise it on the limitations of OFDA, and that the United States cannot solve all the disaster problems alone.

OFDA Assessment Team findings and recommendations must be clear because they become the blueprints for USG decisionmaking and planning for the disaster response. Precise assessments are the foundation of what OFDA does.

Types of Assessments

Assessment Teams collect two types of information: what has happened as a result of the disaster and what is needed. The type of information that is usually available first to an Assessment Team concerns the effects of the disaster. Collecting this information is referred to as a situation or disaster assessment. It identifies the magnitude and extent of the disaster and its effects on the society. The other information gathered is a needs assessment. It defines the level and type of assistance required for the affected population. The gathering of information for the situation assessment and needs assessment can be done concurrently. The information collected in the initial assessment is the basis for determining the type and amount of relief needed during the immediate response phase of the disaster. It may also identify the need for continued monitoring and reassessing of the unfolding disaster.

A. Situation (Disaster) Assessment

This assessment gathers information on the magnitude of the disaster and the extent of its impact on both the population and the infrastructure of the society.

Areas assessed and reported on include:

- Area affected by the disaster (location and size)

- Number affected by the disaster.

- Mortality and morbidity rates.

- Types of injuries and illness.

- Characteristics and condition of the affected population.

- Emergency medical, health, nutritional, water, and sanitation situation.

- Level of continuing or emerging threats (natural/human-caused).

- Damage to infrastructure and critical facilities.

- Damage to homes and commercial buildings.

- Damage to agriculture and food supply system.

- Damage to economic resources, and social organization.

- Vulnerability of the population to continuing or expanding impacts of the disaster over the coming weeks and months.

- Level of response by the affected country and internal capacities to cope with the situation.

- Level of response from other donor countries and PVO/NGO/IOs.

B. Needs Assessment

The initial needs assessment identifies resources and services for immediate emergency measures to save and sustain the lives of the affected population. It is conducted at the site of a disaster or at the location of a displaced population. A quick response based on this information should help reduce excessive death rates, and stabilize the nutritional, health, and living conditions among the population at risk. A quick response to urgent needs must never be delayed because a comprehensive assessment has not yet been completed.

Assessment Team Composition

An ideal OFDA Assessment Team comprises of three to four people specializing in health, nutrition, water and sanitation, logistics, communications, disaster management, and OFDA policies and procedures. OFDA draws experts from within OFDA and USAID, other Federal agencies, contractors with disaster management experience, donor government aid agencies, and the UN/PVO/NGO/IO community.

The Assessment Team is lead by a Team Leader, who is usually selected from within OFDA or USAID. Team Leaders are familiar with OFDA's mandate and response capabilities. The scope of work for the Assessment Team is defined by OFDA management and the USAID/Embassy within the affected country.

Elements of an Assessment

The information that follows defines the elements of any assessment. Assessments are generally composed of six basic elements or activities:

A. Preparedness Planning

An accurate assessment depends on thorough planning, design, and preparation. Most information needs can be identified well in advance. The means of collecting the necessary data, and the selection of formats for collection and presentation of the information, should be established as part of an organization's predisaster planning. Seek advice widely from survey specialists, statisticians, and epidemiologists. By preparing to undertake assessments well in advance of an emergency: Both the data required and the process most appropriate for its accurate and speedy collection can be identified and refined prior to the emergency. Proper design of sampling and survey methods can increase substantially the accuracy and usefulness of assessment data. Standard survey techniques, questionnaires, checklists, and procedures should be prepared to ensure that all areas are examined and that the information is reported using standard terminology and classifications. Also, consideration of local factors, social organization and hierarchies of power at this stage can help greatly in formulating interview methods and identifying useful sources of information.

B. Survey and Data Collection

The gathering of the information must proceed rapidly and thoroughly. In an initial reconnaissance, surveyors should look for *patterns and indicators* of potential problems. Using the procedures developed earlier, key problem areas are thoroughly checked. Sources of all information should be identified. Examples include whether it was observed, reported by an informant in a discussion, collected through a survey of a randomly sampled population, heard by rumor, etc. The information will be more meaningful to those interpreting it—especially if there are conflicting reports, if a source is indicated.

C. Interpretation

Thorough analysis of the information gathered is critical. Those performing the analysis must be trained to detect and recognize trends and indicators of problems, to interpret the information, and to link the information to action programs.

D. Forecasting

Using the data that has been collected, the Assessment Team must construct estimates about how the situation might develop in the future so that contingency plans can be drawn up that will prepare for and mitigate negative impacts. Forecasting requires input from many specialists, especially persons who have had extensive experience in previous emergencies and who might be able to detect trends and provide insights as to what course an emergency might follow.

E. Reporting

When data analysis and forecasting are complete, it is necessary to report and disseminate the results in a format that enables managers to make decisions and formulate plans and projects. Essential information should be presented and structured so that the main patterns and trends are clear.

F. Monitoring

An assessment should not be seen as an end result in itself, but rather as one part of a continuing process of reevaluating the needs and the appropriateness of responses to the disaster situation. This is particularly true in long-term, complex disasters.

Data Collection Methods

It is useful to distinguish between the terms "data" and "information": data is simply a collection of words, numbers, and other characters with a structure. Information is "useful data." Data becomes information when it is useful, meaningful, relevant, and understandable to particular people at particular times and places, and for particular purposes. What is information to one person can simply be useless data to another. Three other considerations are important in assessment data collection:

- **The Need for Accuracy**—The information must agree with the reality it represents. The data on which it is based must be accurate.

- **The Need for Timeliness and Adequate Frequency**— Information must be produced as and when it is wanted. The frequency of data collection and reporting must match the rate of change in the situation being assessed.

- **The Question of Availability of and Access to Information**—Who should get what information? The way in which data is collected or the access to the data can affect the way it is routed, who it reaches, and where its flow may be blocked.

There is a range of data collection methods. The following list outlines some of the most common ways of collecting data in emergencies:

- **Automatic initial self-assessment and local assessment by key elements in the system,** for example, staff of "lifeline" systems. This can involve preplanned damage reporting by civil authorities and by military units.

- **Visual inspection and interviews by specialists.** Methods can include overflight, actions by special point-assessment teams (including preplanned visits), and sample surveys to achieve rapid appraisal of area damage.

- **Sample surveying of specific characteristics of affected populations by specialist teams.** Well conducted surveys have a number of advantages, not least of which is the relative confidence that may be attached to data collected using formal statistical sampling methods. There are several different types of sample surveys:

- **Simple random sampling:** every member of the target population is equally likely to be selected, and the selection of a particular member of the target population has no effect on the other selections.
- **Systematic random sampling:** every fifth, or tenth, member on a numbered list is chosen (may be wildly inaccurate if the lists are structured in certain ways).
- **Stratified random sampling:** the population is divided into categories (or strata); members from each category are then selected by simple or systematic random sampling; then combined to give an overall sample.
- **Cluster sampling:** the sample is restricted to a limited number of geographical areas, known as "clusters"; for each of the geographical areas chosen, a sample is selected by simple or random sampling. Subsamples are then combined to get an overall sample.

- **"Sentinel" surveillance.** This is a method used widely in emergency health monitoring, where professional staff establish a reporting system that detects early signs of particular problems at specific sites. The method can be applied to a variety of other problems where early warning is particularly important.

- **Detailed critical sector assessments by specialist.** This involves technical inspections and assessments by experts. It is required in sectors such as health and nutrition, food, water supply, electric power, and other infrastructure systems in particular. Critical sector assessments may be compiled from reports by specialist of these systems or by visits by specialist teams from outside.

- **Continuing surveillance by regular "polling" visits.** This again is a technique that is well developed in epidemiological surveillance of casualty care requirements and emergent health problems.

- **Continuing surveillance by routine reporting.** As the situation develops, it will be especially useful if routine reporting systems can be adapted and used to develop a comprehensive picture of events.

- **Interviews with key informants** in government and PVO/NGO/IOs and within particular groups of affected people, local officials, local community leaders, and (especially in food and displacement emergencies) with leaders of groups of displaced people.

Keys To a Successful Assessment

Several factors contribute to the design of a successful and accurate assessment:

- **Identify the Users**—Every element of an assessment should be designed to collect information for a specific user. The potential users should specify their data needs during the design phase. For example, health workers need certain types of information that will only be useful in certain formats, usually tables, while a procurement officer may need more quantitative or statistical data.

- **Identify the Information Needed To Plan Specific Programs**—Too often, assessments collect information that is incomplete or of little value for planning relief programs or specific interventions. In many cases, information is anecdotal rather than substantive; in others, valuable time is wasted collecting detailed information when representative data would be just as useful. Determine what information is vital, what method is best to obtain this information, and how much detail is necessary for the information to be useful. The type of assistance usually provided by an agency should be considered when listing the data to be collected. For example, an agency that provides food will need to know about availability of transport and fuel, road conditions, etc.

- **Consider the Format**—It is important to collect, organize, and present the data in a form useful to analysts and program planners. The results must be presented in a format that makes the implications very clear so that priorities can be set quickly. By applying baselines and standards to the presentation, key relationships can be quickly noted. For example, daily death rates in a displaced person (DP) camp should be calculated and compared to the international standard of 1.0 deaths per 10,000 per day.

- **Consider the Timing of the Assessment**—Timing may affect the accuracy of an assessment because situations and needs can change dramatically from day to day. Various types of assessments need to be timed to collect the necessary information when it is available and most useful. Relief needs are always relative but, as a general rule, initial surveys should be broad in scope and should determine overall patterns and trends. More detailed information can wait until emergency operations are well established.

- **Determine the Best Places to Obtain Accurate Information**—If the information must be obtained from sample surveys, it is important that the areas to be surveyed provide an accurate picture of needs and priorities. For example, carrying out a health survey in a medical center would yield a distorted view of the overall health situation, because only sick or severely malnourished people would be in the medical center.

- **Distinguish Between Emergency and Chronic Needs**— Virtually all developing countries have longstanding chronic needs in most, if not all, sectors. It is important to design an assessment that will distinguish between chronic and emergency needs. Attempt to acquire baseline data, reference data, and/or recognized and accepted standards in each sector. For example, if malnutrition is prevalent in a certain area of a country, a nutrition survey of incoming DP's will almost certainly reflect poor nutritional status. The surveyors must differentiate between what is normal for the location and what is occurring as a result of the disaster, so that emergency food aid and health care can be provided to those most in need. (It should be remembered that assessments may bring to light previously unrecognized or unacknowledged problems in a society. Thus, the data collection system should be careful to structure the information so that critical data such as health status, etc., can be used for long-term planning.)

- **Assess Needs and Vulnerabilities in Relation to Capacities**—Needs are immediate requirements for survival. Vulnerabilities are potential areas for harm and include factors that increase the risks to the affected population. Vulnerabilities create unequal levels of risk between groups. Needs are assessed after an emergency has occurred, whereas vulnerabilities can be assessed both before and during the emergency. Needs are expressed in terms of requirements (food, water, shelter, etc.); vulnerabilities are expressed in terms of their origins (physical/material, social/organizational, or motivational/attitudinal). The antidote to needs and vulnerabilities are capacities. Capacities are means and resources that can be mobilized by the affected population to meet their own needs and reduce vulnerability. Assessing vulnerabilities and capacities as well as needs provides a way of:

- Preventing a widening of the emergency in which today's vulnerabilities become tomorrow's needs.
- Targeting assistance to the most vulnerable groups.
- Effecting a sustainable recovery, based on local resources and institutions.

The last point is a particularly important contribution of capacity assessment, since externally provided assistance can actually slow recovery and impede a return to development if it is not given in a way that supports the efforts of the local populations to secure their own means of long-term survival. Capacity and vulnerability assessment requires direct engagement of members of the affected population in order to ensure that the required information is being shared.

- **Use Recognized Terminology, Standards, and Procedures**—Assessments will invariably be carried out by a variety of people operating independently. To provide a basis for evaluating the information, generally accepted terminology, ratings, and classifications should be used in classifying and reporting. The use of standard survey forms with clear guidelines for descriptive terms is usually the best way to ensure that all information is reported on a uniform basis.

Assessment Process Main Points

A. General

Following are the main points to consider regarding the assessment process:

- An assessment is only a "snapshot in time."

- Information changes over time.

- The significance of information changes over time.

- If a disaster manager can identify the unfolding scenarios, monitoring will ultimately be more important than assessment.

- What you can't see is often more important than what you can see.

- It is vital to use the first assessment to establish an ongoing data collection and analysis system.

- Most reports should be iterative, not detailed.

- The initial assessment should provide information that feeds directly into the program planning process.

- Timing of the report is vital. Without a point of reference, most assessment data is of little value.

B. Assessment Recommendations and Their Impact on Recovery

It is important that the recommendations made by the Assessment Team do not have a detrimental effect on the long-term recovery efforts of an affected country. Relief programs can set the stage for rapid recovery or prolong the length of the recovery period. Every action in an emergency response will have a direct effect on the manner and cost of reconstruction.

Many common relief programs can create dependencies and severely reduce the survivors' ability to cope with the next disaster. For example, food commodities brought into a disaster area without consideration for the local agricultural system can destroy the local market system and cause future food shortages where self-sufficiency had been the norm. Another example is when relief supplies, equipment, or technology are sent in that are not sustainable in the socioeconomic environment of the survivors. When this assistance wears out or is used up, the survivors may be left in the same condition as immediately following the disaster.

Sustainable recovery depends on restoring the affected populations' own capacity to meet their basic food, shelter, water, and sanitation needs. The victims have the most immediate and direct interest in recovering from a disaster, and most disaster survivors do so using their own resources. Consequently, they may place a high priority on restoring their means of livelihood. Understanding their priorities and providing assistance that supports the affected population's efforts to restore viable socioeconomic systems is critical to achieving a long-lasting, sustainable recovery.

Recommendations should be simple, support the use of local materials and systems, and be sustainable by the affected country. Don't discount alternative interventions that may be against "conventional wisdom," collide with bureaucratic obstacles, or need increased relief agency capacity. In the long run they may be more cost effective and sustainable.

OFDA Assessment Cable Reporting Formats

The following cable format outlines should be used by OFDA Assessment Teams when sending reporting cables to OFDA/W following a disaster assessment. A longer, more detailed assessment report may be prepared by the team to address the points outlined in the cable in more depth.

A. Slow Onset Disaster Cable Format

1. Subject

Country—type of disaster.

2. References

Cite any recent cables that are relevant to the report (REFTEL: cable # as appropriate). This is an action cable for OFDA (or other office); see paragraphs x, y, z. These paragraphs will most likely be at the end of the cable, although they can also be at the end of each technical section if the team prefers. A summary of the recommendations should be in the summary section of the cable.

3. Summary

This section of the cable can be more than one paragraph and should summarize the findings of the disaster assessment.

Describe the Disaster. How many people are affected? Where are they? For example, "a famine of horrifying proportions is developing in x as a result of civil unrest and drought. An estimated y people are affected and will require food for x months." Cite the sources for your statistics.

Summarize what is currently being done to handle the disaster on the local, national, and international level. (Mention the presence of relief agencies, both local and international; military participation; etc.)

What is the Mission/Embassy doing (briefly)? Has a disaster been declared? What are the team's summary recommendations?

4. General Situation

This introductory section should give the reader a more detailed overview of the disaster than the summary. Describe the OFDA Assessment Team. Who was on it? What was their expertise? Where did they go? How did they get there? How long did they stay? Who did they talk/meet with? Has the Embassy declared a disaster? When? Has the $25,000 been received? Expended? For whom/what?

Describe in more detail the disaster situation:

(a) What is the extent/enormity of the problem? When did the problem begin? What is the experience of the country in previous similar situations?

(b) Where is the disaster occurring? How many people are affected? How many have died/are injured/ homeless/ill/ displaced? If displaced, are they in camps? If yes, how many people are in them? What is the population profile (children/men/women/ages)? Are more on the move? Are they moving within the country or is there a potential refugee situation evolving?

(c) How are the affected country government, UN/PVO/ NGO/IOs, and donors responding?

(d) Are there particular political/social/economic/security factors that influence the event?

5. Food and Logistics

If it is a famine or food shortage, describe the magnitude of the food needs, numbers of people, tonnage required, and tonnage pledged to date. (For example, "The UN estimates that x metric tons of food are required in the next 6 months to avoid massive starvation. This comes to y metric tons per week.")

Describe the logistics of getting the food to the people, roads, water, air, relative costs, truck and worker availability, and any problems encountered (customs, contracts, etc.), including problems at ports and airports. In a conflict situation note in particular any security problems associated with food movement.

What is being done? Who is distributing? How? Where? What problems have been encountered? Is the food getting to vulnerable groups, especially women and children? Mention should be made of availability of food in markets, prices, and the potential for a market sales program or other ways of getting food to people, such as food for work.

What kind of rehabilitation programs, if any, are underway (for example, seeds and tools, fishing equipment)? Who is implementing the programs? Where?

Are there any security issues related to food distributions?

What more needs to be done? Further assessments? More pledges? Different foods? More funds?

6. Health

Describe nutritional conditions. What is the rate of malnutrition? Has it changed (improved/declined; in what areas/what groups). Be as specific as possible. Cite sources (for example, "MSF/F surveys conducted in (month) have determined that rates of malnutrition of the under-5 population in x are y. Similar surveys in other areas report the same/different information.").

Describe mortality. What is the death rate? Where?

Describe morbidity. What are the health effects of the disaster? Are there/have there been any epidemics?

Describe what is being done to handle the situation. Who is on the ground? Where? What are they doing (therapeutic feeding/ immunizations/health clinics/reproductive health)? With what staff (doctors/nurses, local, international)? How are they getting to the area (by road/air/ boat)? Are they staying overnight/traveling in by day only? Is there one organization taking the lead? What is the UN doing? What role is the host government playing (if relevant)?

Are there any security issues related to these programs?

7. Water and Sanitation

Describe where the population obtains water (wells/boreholes/ temporary facilities/piped city system). Are there water problems associated with the disaster? If in a camp, note the color of the water (clear/muddy/yellow/red/green on surface) and smell.

What is being done about the problem? Is the water being treated? How much water is available to people per day (liters/person/day)? Where are they getting it? Who is providing it? Is there a clean-water education campaign? Is there safe and easy access to water for women?

Describe sanitation problems. Is there overcrowding? If so, how is waste being handled? Are there separate washing/sanitation facilities for women? Is there damage to the sewer system as a result of the disaster?

Are there qualified people available to advise/assist? Is technical assistance needed?

8. Shelter

Shelter is not likely to be a major problem in a slow onset disaster unless there is a massive displacement of people, in which case the team should evaluate shelter needs at the camp or area where the displaced persons (DPs) have gathered.

Describe the need for shelter, clothing, and, eventually, cooking supplies and water jugs. Where are the DPs living? In abandoned buildings, under trees, in makeshift huts? Are there building materials nearby? Do the DPs have clothing? (In a civil war situation, very frequently DPs will arrive without clothing or household goods.)

Describe what is being done. Who is in charge? What is the role of local government, UN, and relief agencies?

What additional needs must be addressed?

9. Capability and Capacity

As best as possible, evaluate the overall response to the disaster; the capability of the NGOs; both national and international collaborative efforts between them and problems identified; and the capacity of the host government and its policies, biases, and interests in assisting or not.

10. Coordination

How is the relief effort being coordinated? Who is taking the lead? Are there donors' meetings or meetings with government officials? With NGOs? Where are they held and how frequently? Did the team attend any of them? What role has the Mission/ Embassy been playing?

What more needs to be done?

11. Recommendations

Outline immediate actions required (be sure to put paragraph numbers in paragraph 1 of the cable). If commodities are requested, specify the item, quantity needed, other specifications as appropriate; when it is needed; and how it will be received, transported, stored, and distributed. If by air, information should be provided about runway capability (dirt/paved, damaged/intact), air traffic control services, and possible security problems as appropriate. If additional expertise is needed, specify what type and when. Note any issues such as customs clearances, storage, special handling, and any holidays that may interrupt delivery. Recommendations in a slow onset disaster can also include making additional funds available to respond to project proposals, additional assessments by the U.S. Public Health Service, or mobilizing a Disaster Assistance Response Team (DART).

12. Who Should Get the Cable?

At a minimum, the reporting cable should be addressed as follows:

SECSTATE WASHDC (for BHR/OFDA, Regional Bureau, and BHR/FFP also for the State Desk and PRM); INFO AMEMBASSY BRUSSELS (for USEC); AMEMBASSY ROME (Rome pass FODAG); USMISSION GENEVA (for USAID and RMA); USMISSION USUN NEW YORK; AMEMBASSY SAN JOSE (for OFDA Regional Advisor—if in S/L.A.); AMEMBASSY MANILA (for OFDA Regional Advisor—if in Asia).

Additional INFO addressees will depend on the situation but could include:

(a) The neighboring country missions (for example, if it is Sudan, send also to Kenya, Addis Ababa, Cairo at a minimum).

(b) Other European capitals with particular interests in the country (for example, if it is in Iraq, send also to Paris, London, Bonn).

(c) SECDEF WASHDC.

(d) JOINT STAFF WASHDC.

(e) USCINCXXX—appropriate regional military addressee.

(f) Others as situation requires.

B. Fast Onset Disaster Cable Format

1. Subject

Country—type of disaster.

2. References

Cite any recent cables that are relevant to the report (REFTEL: cable # as appropriate). This is an action cable for OFDA (or other office); see paragraphs x, y, z. These paragraphs will most likely be at the end of the cable, although they can also be at the end of each technical section if the team prefers. A summary of the recommendations should be in the summary section of the cable.

3. Summary

This section of the cable can be more than one paragraph and should summarize the findings of the initial disaster assessment.

Describe the Disaster. When did it occur, where, and approximately how many people were affected? For example, "A typhoon of immense proportions hit the island of x, on y date. An estimated x people have been left homeless, agriculture destroyed, buildings damaged, ..." Cite the sources for your statistics.

Describe in summary form what is currently being done to handle the disaster on the local, national, and international level. (Mention the presence of local and international relief agencies, military participation, etc.)

What is the Mission/Embassy doing (briefly)? Has a disaster been declared? What are the team's summary recommendations?

4. General Situation

This introductory section should give the reader an overview of the disaster in more detail than the summary. Describe the OFDA Assessment Team. Who was on it? What was their expertise? Where did they go? How did they get there? How long did they stay? Who did they talk/meet with? Has the Embassy declared a disaster? When? Has the $25,000 been received? Expended? For whom/what?

Describe in more detail the disaster situation:

(a) What is the extent of the disaster? Where did it occur? How many people were affected (killed/injured/homeless)? Were buildings damaged? How badly (cite percentage if available)? Were public services disrupted (water/electricity/transportation)? What is the general mood (panic/under control)?

(b) Has there been a similar disaster in the country before or is this the first time?

(c) How are the affected country government, UN/PVO/NGO/IOs, and donors responding?

(d) Are there particular political/social/economic/security factors that influence the event?

5. Health/Nutrition (Situation)

This section should provide as much detail as possible on the health situation from as many sources as possible. Wherever possible, cite the source (for example, "According to a Red Cross worker at the site ...").

How many people have been killed, injured? Where are they? Are there potential disease risks? What are they? Who is affected (children/adults/the elderly)?

Describe what is being done in the health arena. What agencies (national and international) have been mobilized? Where? What are the constraints to doing a better job (for example, too many victims and not enough staff, not enough of the right kind of staff, shortage of medical supplies, problems of access)?

There are usually no immediate nutritional problems associated with a fast onset disaster. However, in certain cases, a food shortage could occur in the medium term if the disaster has destroyed or contaminated food supplies. What is the potential for a food crisis? What is being done about it? What are the constraints? Who is handling the issue?

6. Shelter

Describe damage to private and public buildings in the affected area. What type of housing has been damaged/destroyed? How many buildings (private and public) have been damaged or destroyed? Has a value been placed on the damage?

Estimate the population in need of shelter. Why is shelter important (weather, culture, etc.)?

What is being done to provide shelter? Are people at home? At campsites? Are there any local solutions? What is the host government planning? Are imported supplies required? How much? Are any agencies responding? What more is needed?

7. Water/Sanitation

Describe any water problems; for example, broken pipes, contamination, damaged pumping stations. Note color of water (clear/muddy/yellow/red/green on surface) and smell.

What is being done about the problem? Is the water being treated? How? Is there an education campaign? How much water is available to people per day (liters/person/day)? Where are they getting it? Who is providing it? Is there safe and easy access to water for women?

Describe sanitation problems. Is there overcrowding? If so, how is waste being handled? Are there separate washing/sanitation facilities for women? Is there damage to the sewer system as a result of the disaster?

Are there qualified people available to advise/assist? Is technical assistance needed? What was standard before the disaster?

Has the impacted population lost its supply of cooking, cleaning, and storage utensils? What is being done?

8. Infrastructure/Logistics

Describe damage to infrastructure. Is this posing problems of access to victims? What is being done? What logistics support, equipment, and facilities are available and undamaged (hospitals, airstrips, ports, aircraft, vehicles, etc.)?

9. Coordination

How is the relief effort being coordinated? Is the government in charge? Who is taking the lead? Are there donors' meetings and meetings with government officials? With NGOs? Where are they held and how frequently? Did the team attend any of them? What role has the Mission/Embassy been playing?

What more needs to be done?

10. Capability and Capacity

As best as possible, evaluate the overall response to the disaster; the capability of the NGOs; both national and international collaborative efforts between them and problems you identified; and the capacity of the host government and its policies, biases, and interests in assisting or not.

11. Recommendations

Outline immediate actions required (be sure to put paragraph numbers in paragraph 1 of the cable). If commodities are requested, specify the item, quantity needed, and other specifications as appropriate, as well as when it is needed and how it will be received, transported, stored, and distributed. If by air, information should be provided about runway capability (dirt/paved, damaged/intact), air traffic control services, or possible security problems as appropriate. Note any issues such as customs clearances, storage, special handling, and any holidays that may interrupt delivery. If additional expertise is needed, specify type and when.

If shelter is requested, discuss ability of local authorities to receive, store, and distribute equitably. What NGOs would be involved? Is there the expertise to demonstrate uses of shelter? Is technical assistance required?

12. Who Should Get the Cable?

At a minimum, the reporting cable should be addressed as follows:

SECSTATE WASHDC, IMMEDIATE (for BHR/OFDA, Regional Bureau, and BHR/FFP also for the State Desk and PRM); INFO AMEMBASSY BRUSSELS (for USEC); AMEMBASSY ROME (Rome pass FODAG); USMISSION GENEVA (for USAID and RMA); USMISSION USUN NEW YORK; AMEMBASSY SAN JOSE (for OFDA Regional Advisor—if in

S/L.A.); AMEMBASSY MANILA (for OFDA Regional Advisor—if in Asia).

Additional INFO addressees will depend on the situation but could include:

(a) The neighboring country missions (for example, if it is Sudan, send also to Kenya, Addis Ababa, Cairo, at a minimum).

(b) Other European capitals with particular interests in the country (for example, if it is in Iraq, send also to Paris, London, Bonn, among others).

(c) SECDEF WASHDC.

(d) JOINT STAFF WASHDC.

(e) USCINCXXX—appropriate regional military addressee.

(f) Others as situation requires.

Assessment Checklists

A. Introduction

The following assessment checklists are intended to assist the Assessment Team in planning, formatting, and conducting a complete initial assessment. The answers to the checklist questions will provide the information needed to complete the disaster cable formats outlined in the previous section on cable formats. These assessment checklists are divided into major sectorial areas. They are meant to be as inclusive as possible of the types of questions that need to be answered in initial assessments of various disasters. To be answered completely, some of the questions would require extensive survey work, which the team may or may not have the capacity to perform. However, the information may already exist, and the task of the team may be only to gather assessment information assembled by others and evaluate the information for accuracy, timeliness, and completeness. An Assessment Team may also find it necessary to develop new or expanded questions to gather the required information for specific disasters.

B. Victims/Displaced Population Profile

1. General Characteristics

- Determine the approximate number of displaced people.

- Determine their locations. Are they moving? To where? How many?

- Determine how many are arriving per week. How many more could come?

- Determine how they are arriving. Are they scattered individuals or families, or clans, tribal, ethnic, or village groups? By what means are they traveling? How did those already there arrive? What is the average family size?

- Determine the approximate numbers and ages of men, women, and children (ages 0–5, 6–14, 15 and over).

- Identify ethnic/geographic origin (urban or rural).
    - Sedentary or nomadic background?
    - What is the average family/household size?
    - How many households are headed by females?
    - What are their customary skills?
    - What is the language(s) used?
    - What is the customary basic diet?
    - What is the customary shelter?
    - What are the customary sanitation practices?
    - What is the general distribution of socioeconomic statuses—(poor, middle class, wealthy)—within the population?

2. Priority Health Status Conditions

- Determine how many deaths occurred in the past week.

- Determine how many children under 5 died in the same period, disaggregated by sex.

- Determine the main cause of death for each group.

- Determine the crude mortality rate.

- Determine whether measles vaccinations have been or will be provided. If provided, give dates of vaccinations.

- Determine the percentage of children vaccinated.

- Determine the incidence of diarrhea among adults and children.

- Determine the most common diseases among children and adults.

3. Capacities and Assets

Capacities

- What percentage of male and female population is literate?

- What emergency-related skills (for example, health workers, individuals with logistics/organizational relief skills) are represented within the population that could be drawn upon by relief organizations?

Physical Assets

- Determine what the displaced population has as personal property and what was lost as a result of the disaster.

- Estimate the number and types of blankets needed (according to climatic conditions).

- Identify what blankets are available within the country from personal, commercial, UN/PVO/NGO/IO, or government stocks.

- Determine what is needed from external sources for blankets.

- Describe the clothing traditionally worn, by season and area.

- If clothing is needed, estimate the amount by age group and sex. Determine if used clothing is acceptable, and if so, for which groups.

- Describe normal heating/cooking practices.

- Determine whether heating equipment and/or fuel is required.

- Estimate the types and quantities of heating equipment and fuel needed over a specific time period.

- Determine appropriate fuel storage and distribution mechanisms.

- Identify what fuel is available locally.

- Identify what is needed from external sources.

- Determine if other personal effects, such as cooking utensils, soap, and small storage containers, are needed.

- Determine if the DPs brought any financial assets. Would those assets be convertible to local currency?

- Determine if livestock was brought along.

- Determine if shelter materials were brought along.

- Determine if other possessions, such as cars, bicycles, or boats, were brought along.

C. Health and Nutrition

1. Health

- Ascertain demographic information:
  - Total number affected.
  - Age-sex breakdown (under 5, 5–14, 15 and over).
  - Identification of at-risk population (that is, children under 5 years of age, pregnant and lactating women, disabled and wounded persons, and unaccompanied minors).
  - Average family or household size, and number of female-headed households.
  - Rate of new arrivals and departures.

- Determine background health information:
  - Main health problems in home area.
  - Previous sources of health care (for example, traditional healers).
  - Important health beliefs and traditions (for example, food taboos during pregnancy).
  - Social structure (for example, whether the displaced are grouped in their traditional villages and what type of social or political organization exists).
  - Strength and coverage of public health programs in home area (immunization, reproductive health, etc.).

- Mortality rate:
  - Determine the crude mortality rates.

- Morbidity rate:
  - Determine the age- (under and over age 5) and sex-specific incidence rates of diseases that have public

health importance. Document the method of diagnosis (clinical judgment, laboratory test, or rumors).

- Immunization programs:
  - Determine the need for immunization programs or the effectiveness and coverage (percent of children under age 5 and between ages 5–14) of those in place, especially measles vaccinations.
  - Dates of vaccinations.
  - Determine the capability of relief officials to begin or sustain a program (for example, logistics, infrastructure, and cold chain availability).

- Determine or estimate the number of major injuries and the rate for each type of injury. Specify traumatic injuries requiring surgery or hospitalization (for example, fractures, head injuries, internal injuries).

- Determine the number and locations of health facilities that existed prior to the disaster.

- Determine the number of facilities that are still functioning and the total number of usable beds.

- Determine the number of indigenous health personnel who are available.

- Determine the amount and type of medical supplies and drugs that are available onsite or in-country.

- Determine additional amounts and types of medical supplies and drugs needed immediately from sources outside the stricken area.

- Determine what additional medical equipment is needed and can be readily obtained to deal with major injuries. Suggested data sources:
  - National/provincial health officers.
  - Hospitals.
  - Clinics.
  - Traditional healers.
  - Local leaders.
  - Fly-over.
  - Walk-through surveys.

- Environmental conditions:
  - Determine climatic conditions.
  - Identify geographic features and influences.

- Identify water sources.
- Ascertain the local disease epidemiology.
- Identify local disease vector.
- Assess local availability of materials for shelter and fuel.
- Assess existing shelters and sanitation arrangements.

- Determine if a health information system is in place to monitor the affected population and provide surveillance and intermittent population-based sample surveys that should:
  - Follow trends in the health status of the population and establish health care priorities.
  - Detect and respond to epidemics.
  - Evaluate program effectiveness and coverage.
  - Ensure that resources go to the areas of greatest need.
  - Evaluate the quality of care delivered.

- Determine if the affected country has in place or plans to begin programs in:
  - Health information systems.
  - Diarrhea disease control.
  - Expanded programs on immunization (EPIs).
  - Control of endemic diseases.
  - Reproductive health programs.
  - Nutrition programs.
  - Continuing education programs for health workers.
  - Vector control.

2. Nutrition

- Determine the prevalence of protein energy malnutrition (PEM) in population less than 5 years of age.

- Ascertain the prior nutritional status.

- Determine the prevalence of micronutrient deficiencies in the population less than 5 years of age (for example, scurvy, anemia, pellagra).

- Determine the percentage of children under 5 years of age with:
  - Either moderate or severe acute malnutrition.
  - Determine the average daily ration (food basket and calories/person/day) and method and intervals of distribution (for example, wet/dry on a daily/weekly/monthly basis).

- Determine the length of time the above ration level has been available.

- Determine the attendance and effectiveness of supplementary and therapeutic feeding programs.

- Determine the incidence of low birthweight.

- Determine rate of weight gain or loss of children registered in Mother-Child Health (MCH) clinics.

- Determine oral rehydration salt (ORS) needs and distribution system.

D. Water

1. Displaced Population Situation

- Determine the amount of water available per person per day.

- Determine the source and quality of the water.

- Determine how long the daily amount has been available.

- Determine the evidence of water-related diseases.

- Determine the length of time users wait for water.

- Determine whether there is safe access to water for vulnerable groups.

- Determine the types of wells, transportation, and/or storage systems used.

- Determine if there are problems with well repair/rehabilitation.

- Determine if there is equipment/expertise onsite, on order, or available if needed.

- Determine the availability of additional sources of safe water if required.

- Determine the need for water engineers to assist with evaluating requirements.

2. Functioning Water System Disruption

- Describe the types of systems and sources that existed prior to the disaster in the affected areas.

- Specify how many people have been deprived of a functional water supply.

- Determine who is in charge of the local water system(s) (community group, committee, national authority).

- Determine whether the system is still functional or what the requirements for repair are.

- Determine the need for an engineering specialist to assist with evaluating requirements.

E. Food and Agriculture

1. Food

Baseline Data

- Describe the normal consumption pattern (food basket) of the affected population, any taboos, and acceptable substitutes.

- Describe the normal food marketing system (including government involvement, imports, subsistence).

- Indicate what food aid programs, if any, exist and describe them.

- Outline the indigenous food processing capacity.

Effect of the Event on Food

- Ascertain the disaster's effect on actual foodstocks and standing crops (damaged/destroyed).

- Determine if access to food (for example, roads, milling facilities) has been disputed and, if so, how long it is likely to remain disrupted.

- Check market indicators of food shortages, such as:
  - Absence or shortage of staple grains and other foods on the market.
  - Price differential.
  - Change in supplies on the market (for example, an increase in meat supplies may indicate that people are selling animals to get money).
  - Change in wholesale grain availability.
  - Unusual public assembly at a warehouse or dockside when grain is being unloaded.
  - Changes in warehouse stocks.

- Black market price changes or increase in black market activities.
- Commercial import changes or proposed changes.
- Sale of land, tools, draft animals, etc.

- Check nutritional indicators of food shortages by sex, such as:
  - Signs of marasmus, kwashiorkor, or other signs of malnutrition.
  - Increased illness among children.
  - Change in diet (that is, quantity, quality, type).

- Check social indicators of food shortages, such as:
  - Increased begging/fighting/prostitution.
  - Migration from rural to urban areas.

Food Availability

- Determine how much food can be expected from future and/or specially planted, quick-maturing crops. Where in the production cycle was the affected area when the disaster struck?

- Estimate the local government stocks on hand and those scheduled to arrive. Is borrowing of stocks on hand a possibility?

- Estimate the local commercial stocks on hand and scheduled to arrive.

- Estimate the local PVO/NGO/IO stocks on hand and scheduled to arrive. Is borrowing a possibility?

- Estimate local personal stocks on hand and those scheduled to arrive.

- Determine regional availabilities.

- Canvass other donors to find out what they expect to contribute.

- Estimate how much food aid would be required during specific time periods.

Distribution Systems

- Describe existing food aid distribution systems (for example, government rationing, PVO/NGO/IOs).

- Describe the effectiveness of the distribution system.

- Describe the role of women in the distribution system.

- Describe government marketing mechanisms.

- Judge the capacity of the above to expand/begin emergency aid. What is their record of accountability?

- Describe potential alternatives.

- Explain the country's (agency's) previous experience with mass feeding.

- Determine the availability of facilities and materials, including fuel.

- Determine whether repackaging facilities exist.

Social and Market Impact of Food Aid

- Analyze the likely price impact on normal food suppliers. Describe the suppliers.

- Decide whether food aid would free cash and labor for other aspects of relief, or divert labor and create a dependent attitude.

Other

Research any legal impediments to importation of certain foods.

2. Agriculture

Baseline Data

- Describe crops grown in the affected area following the points listed below:
  - Crop name.
  - Average area planted (per data available).
  - Average production (per data available).
  - Planting season(s) (dates) and time to maturity.
  - Are crops climate-specific? If so, identify the climatic requirements.
  - Are hybrid seeds being used in the area? If so, identify them.
  - Are they cash or subsistence crops?

- Describe domestic animals present in each affected area following the points listed below:

- Approximate number of animals in the area.
- Value of individual animals.
- Use of animals for food.
- Use of animals for work.
- Use of animals for cash production.
- Are bred stocks used in the area?

- Describe the agricultural system, including the following:
  - Main agriculturist in family units (male/female).
  - Land-use systems.
  - Agricultural labor system/land tenure.
  - Crop preferences.
  - Inputs.
  - Seeds (reserved or purchases): Is treated seed used?
  - Fertilizer.
  - Machinery/tools.
  - Pesticides.
  - Storage (farm, government, private).
  - Agrobusiness facilities, processing of local or imported commodities.

- Describe the local fishing industry.

Effect of the Event on Agriculture

- Effect of the event on agriculture/livestock/fisheries.

- Ascertain the extent of damage to crop/livestock/fisheries by area, noting at what point in the production cycle the event occurred. State the source of the information.

- Estimate the loss in production (tonnage/head) by crop/livestock/fisheries and by zone within the affected area.

- Analyze whether losses will increase over time and state why.

- Describe the damage to agricultural machinery.

- Describe the damage to irrigation systems.

- Describe the damage to seed, fertilizer, and pesticide stocks.

- Describe the damage to fishing gear.

- For a drought, compare the current rainfall to the normal or recent past precipitation.

- Identify any unusual or untimely grazing changes.

- Describe any threats from insects or disease that might follow the disaster.

Agricultural Production Capabilities

- Availability of inputs by type (for example, seed, fertilizer, pesticides, tools, machinery, veterinary medicines, fishing boats, nets, breeding stock).

- Estimate the local government stocks on hand and when they are scheduled to arrive.

- Estimate the local commercial stocks on hand and when they are scheduled to arrive.

- Estimate the local personal stocks on hand and when they are scheduled to arrive.

- Ask the victims how they plan to cope with losses.

- Determine regional availabilities and elasticity of supplies.

- Ascertain what other donors plan to supply.

- Outline what further inputs would be required to restore minimum productivity.

- Find out if repackaging facilities for seed, fertilizer, and pesticides exist.

- Distribution systems/technical infrastructure.

- Outline host government (Ministry of Agriculture) operations in the affected area. Does it provide:
  - Extension service?
  - Crop storage/silos?
  - Veterinary services?
  - Irrigation services?
  - Research facilities?
  - Hybrid seed?
  - Fertilizer?
  - Other plants (fruit trees)?
  - Pesticides?

Other

- Describe any agricultural projects and inputs provided by foreign organizations/governments.

- Describe the operations of rural or agricultural credit organizations, cooperatives, or credit-sharing organizations that exist in the affected area.

- Judge the capacity of the above to incorporate rehabilitation disaster assistance.

F. Shelter

1. Affected Population Profile

- Determine the number of people requiring shelter and whether the need for shelter is temporary (a few weeks), or if it is a displaced population requiring shelter for an indeterminate time.

- Determine the average number of people in an individual dwelling.

- Identify obstacles that prevent victims from meeting their own needs, both for temporary and permanent shelter.

- Determine the area affected (for example, portion of city, several villages, large area of a country).

- Approximate the number of private dwellings (single-family, attached, low-rise and high-rise multiple family) and public buildings (schools, churches, hospitals) damaged or destroyed by city, village, or region.

- Determine the number of damaged dwellings that are habitable without immediate repair, that are habitable only after repair, and that are not habitable and must be destroyed.

- Inventory existing structures and public facilities that can be used as temporary shelters, giving careful consideration to access to sanitation and water.

2. Materials

- Identify the construction styles and materials normally used in the affected structures.

- Determine the availability and costs of indigenous materials to meet both cultural and disaster-resistance requirements.

- Identify any suitable material substitutes, locally or externally available, that would meet the cultural and disaster-resistance requirements.

- Identify the type and quantity of building materials that the victims can provide for themselves for temporary or permanent shelter.

- Identify the type and quantity of building materials that the affected government can provide for the victims for temporary or permanent shelter.

- Determine the type and quantity of materials needed from external sources for temporary or permanent shelter.

- Assess the suitability (that is, infrastructure support) of available sites for both temporary and permanent shelters, including, where necessary, mass sheltering.

- Determine if relocation is necessary due to the nature of the disaster. Identify the problems this may cause with the local population.

- Assess the potential hazard and security vulnerabilities of available sites for both temporary and permanent shelters.

- Assess the environmental conditions that would impose constraints on temporary shelters or camps, such as all-season accessibility, proximity to sources of essential supplies (shelter materials, cooking fuel, water, etc.), soil, topography, drainage, and vegetation.

- Identify any problems related to land use, such as grazing, cultivating, sanitation, and land tenure issues.

3. Distribution

- Determine the accessibility to the affected areas for both assessment and delivery.

- Determine the availability of a distribution mechanism (local, regional, national, international) to distribute shelter materials (temporary or permanent) to the victims.

- Identify committees, credit unions, government agencies, or co-ops that can mobilize forces to help implement a shelter program.

- Determine if an equitable means of allocation and an appropriate medium of exchange for the building materials can be implemented.

G. Search and Rescue (SAR)

- Determine how many collapsed structures in an urban area have been affected. What types?
  - Hospitals, multistory public housing units, schools.

- Buildings constructed of reinforced concrete or other materials that would leave voids where trapped victims could survive (not adobe or mud bricks):
  - Apartment buildings.
  - Industrial buildings.
  - Office buildings.
  - Hazardous installations creating secondary risks.

- Predominant building types and construction material:
  - Wattle and daub.
  - Masonry buildings (adobe, brick, concrete blocks, stone masonry).
  - Reinforced concrete structures (frames with brick infill, frames with load-bearing masonry walls, bearing walls, prefabricated structures).
  - Steel structures (multistory steel structures, steel frames in an enfilade arrangement with reinforced concrete).
  - Timber structures.
  - Other.
  - Type of roof (reinforced concrete, steel, wood, grass, etc.)

- Determine if the local authorities request search and rescue (SAR) assistance.

- Type of assistance needed:
  - Search with technical equipment and/or dogs.
  - Rescue with lifting, pulling, cutting, digging, and lighting equipment.

- Medical to oversee and aid in victim extraction.
- Special operations for removing hazardous materials, demolition, shoring of dangerous structures, or damage and emergency repair.

H. Sanitation

1. Displaced Population Situation

- Determine the placement, number, and cleanliness of latrines.

- Determine if the design and placement of latrines are affecting their use because of cultural taboos.

- Determine if there is a sanitation plan if the population increases.

- Determine if there is safe access to latrines for women and girls.

- Determine the evidence of water-related diseases.

- Determine the proximity of latrines and refuse areas to water sources, storage areas, and distribution points.

- Determine the placement and plan for the disposal of corpses.

- Determine if there is a plan for the collection and disposal of garbage.

- Determine if there is an insect- and rodent-control plan.

- Determine the need for a specialist to assist with evaluating requirements.

2. Nondisplaced Population Situation

- If the disaster occurs in a rural area, waste disposal is usually not a problem unless sewage "ponds" in a public area. Determine if this is occurring.

- If you are on an island affected by a hurricane or in an area affected by flooding, determine if the sewage drainage system is still open. (See also "Infrastructure.")

- Determine the adequacy of sewage disposal facilities in any public buildings or other areas being used to temporarily shelter homeless people.

I. Logistics

1. Airports

- Identify the airport being assessed by:
    - Name.
    - Designator.
    - Location.
    - Elevation.

- Describe the current condition of facilities.

- Ascertain whether the airport is fully operational. Daylight hours only?

- Furnish information on usable runway lengths and location(s).

- Determine whether taxiways, parking areas, and cargo handling areas are intact.

- Establish whether runway and approach lights are operating.

- Specify which navigational aids are operating.

- Describe available communications facilities.

- Determine whether the terminal building is operating.

- Check the availability and cost of aviation fuel.

- Find out if facilities exist for mandatory aircrew rest.

- Explore whether the cargo handling area can be lit for night cargo operations.

- Determine what cargo handling equipment is available, including fuel and operators:
    - Forklifts (number, capacity).
    - Scissors lift (capacity).
    - Cargo dollies (number).
    - Trucks with drivers and laborers for hand unloading

- Determine what start-up equipment is available, including fuel and operators.

- Describe maintenance operations (facilities, personnel, hours).

- Outline what storage is available:

- Covered?
- At the airport? Off airport? How far?
- Capacity and suitability for storage of foods or other perishables.

2. Civil Aviation

- Find out whether arrangements can be made for prompt overflight and landing clearances.

- Ascertain that the air controller service is functioning.

- Specify working hours for airport personnel.

- Explore having "no-objections" fees or "royalty" fees waived or paid locally.

- Find out if arrangements can be made to work around the clock, including customs.

- Identify personnel to tally and document cargo as it is received and transshipped.

- Ascertain that the host government will accept deliveries by means of military as well as civil aircraft.

- Describe security arrangements.

- Determine what repairs and/or auxiliary equipment would be needed to increase airport capacity. How soon an local authorities be expected to restore service?

- Determine if there are any local air carriers, their availability, and their rates.

3. Alternative Aircraft

- Identify any usable airports or suitable helicopter landing sites in the disaster zone.

- Determine the local availability and cost of helicopters and/or fixed wing aircraft.

- Estimate their capacity.

- Identify the owners/agents.

- Determine the availability and cost of fuel.

4. Seaports

- Identify the port being assessed by:
  - Name and location.
  - Current description of the condition of the facilities.
  - Whether the port is fully operational. Daylight hours only?
  - Security fences/facilities.
  - Percentage of port losses reported.
  - Collection for port losses possible?

- Determine whether the disaster has altered any of the following physical characteristics of the port:
  - Depth of approach channels.
  - Harbor.
  - Turning basin.
  - Alongside piers/ wharves.
  - Availability of lighters.

- Determine whether the disaster has blocked or damaged port facilities:
  - Locks.
  - Canals.
  - Piers/wharfs.
  - Sheds.
  - Bridges.
  - Water/fuel storage facilities.
  - Communications facilities.
  - Customs facilities.

- Describe the berths:
  - Number.
  - Length.
  - Draft alongside (high tide and low tide).
  - Served by rail? Road? Sheds? Lighters only?
  - Availability.
  - Check the availability and cost of fuel.
  - Determine what cargo handling equipment is available, including condition, fuel, and operators.
  - Heavy lift cranes (number, capacity).
  - Container and pallet handling (with port equipment? with ship's gear only?).

- Outline what storage is available:
  - Covered?
  - Hardstand space?

- Capacity?
- Quality?
- Security?

- Find out if pilots, tugs, and line handlers are available.

- Specify the working hours for the port.

- Specify the working hours for customs.

- Determine whether arrangements can be made with the port and host-country authorities to obtain priority berthing for vessels delivering disaster relief shipments.

- Identify an adequate number of personnel to tally and document cargo as it is received and transshipped.

- Check the history of turnover time. What effect has the disaster had on turnover time?

- Determine what repairs and/or auxiliary equipment would be needed to increase the port's capacity. How soon can local authorities be expected to restore service?

5. Transfer Points

- Identify transfer points by location.

- Determine whether surface transportation for cargo is available from airports and seaports:
  - Road?
  - Railroad?
  - Canal/river?

- Estimate the capacity of transfer points, including handling.

- Outline what storage is available.

- Describe security arrangements.

- Identify an adequate number of personnel to receive and document cargo for transshipment.

6. Trucking

- Describe damage to the road network as it relates to the possibility of delivering relief supplies by truck.

- Indicate any restrictions, such as weight, width, length, or height limitations at bridges, tunnels, etc.

- Determine whether it is possible to bypass damaged sections of the road network and what weight restrictions would apply.

- Determine whether containers can be moved inland.
  - 20-foot or 40-foot container sizes?
  - To the disaster site or to a transfer point?

- Check the availability and cost of trucks owned by the government of the affected country.

- Check the availability and cost of UN/PVO/NGO/IO-owned or operated vehicles.

- Check the availability and cost of commercial vehicles.

- Determine the types, sizes, and number of commercial vehicles available.

- Judge whether the relief program could or should contract for any of the above trucks. What would be the freight rates per ton? What about collection for losses?

- Ascertain that maintenance facilities and spare parts are available.

- Outline measures to provide for security of cargo in transit.

- Check the availability and cost of fuel.

7. Railroads

- Identify and locate any railroads in the disaster-stricken area. Assess their current condition.

- Describe any damage to the electrical power system.

- Identify any interdictions—damaged bridges and tracks, fallen trees, etc.

- Judge the reliability of the rail system.

- Determine whether cars can be made available for relief shipments on a priority basis.

- Determine the capacity and cost of rail shipments.

- Outline security measures to protect cargo in transit.

8. Warehousing

- Identify undamaged or damaged but usable warehouses located in reasonable proximity to the disaster site.

- Determine the capacity of these warehouses.

- Determine their availability over a specific period of time.

- Specify whether the warehouses are government, UN/PVO/NGO/IO, or privately owned.

- Determine whether they are staffed or not.

- Determine the cost per square meter.

- Assess the adequacy of the warehouses' construction:
  - Ventilation.
  - Lighting.
  - Hard floor.
  - Fireproofing.
  - Loading docks.
  - Condition of roof (check during day).

- Describe loading/unloading equipment that is available:
  - Pallets.
  - Forklifts and fuel for them.

- Ascertain that adequate security exists:
  - Perimeter fence.
  - Lighting.
  - Guards.

- Determine whether any refrigeration is available.

- Determine whether sorting and repackaging facilities exist.

- Determine whether fumigation is necessary and if it is available for food, medicines, etc.

- If assessing a functioning warehouse, determine:
  - Accounting and record keeping procedures.
  - Bin/stock cards on piles (they must match the warehouse register.
  - Physical inventory checks at random intervals.
  - Use of waybills.
  - Stacking methods.
  - Spacing system between rows.
  - Cleanliness.
  - Commodity handling system.
  - Reconstitution of damaged goods.
  - Prompt disposal of damaged goods.
  - First in/first out system.

J. Coordination Capacity

- Evaluate the coordination capacity of the following by identifying qualified personnel, reviewing program descriptions, and evaluating past performance:
  - Affected country government. Describe coordination operation among various levels of government and their ability to provide liaison with outside donors.
  - UN/PVO/NGO/IOs. Do UN/PVO/NGO/IOs have sufficient experienced field staff to carry out their present activities effectively and expand them if required? What is their coordination link with the affected government?
  - Local service agencies, for example, credit unions, cooperatives.

- Describe coordination mechanisms in use, including meetings.

- Determine whether a lead agency has been designated.

K. Infrastructure

- Determine the predisaster condition of the infrastructure.

- Ascertain from the affected government the minimum needs for infrastructure recovery.

1. Communications

- Describe where the system's facilities are located.

- Determine the broadcast/reception area or zone of influence (for example, towns serviced by the system).

- Identify the organization/firm that is responsible for operation and maintenance of the system. Is there a disaster response plan with identification of priority facilities, material supply, and priority screening of messages?

- Obtain technical information, such as:
  - Broadcast power.
  - Operating frequencies, call signs.
  - Relay/transmission points.
  - Hours of operation.
  - Standby power sources.
  - Mobile capability.

- Repair/maintenance facilities, including capabilities of manufacturer's local agent.
- Language of transmission.

- Identify key personnel (owners, management, operations, maintenance).

- Determine the degree of integration of military and civilian communications networks.

- Note the source(s) of the above information.

- Determine what communications facilities exist that are operable or easily repaired and could be used to pass on assessment information and assist in coordination of life-saving responses.

- Identify the type of system assessed:
    - Radio.
    - Private ownership.
    - Commercial.
    - Broadcast.
    - 2-way.
    - Amateur.
    - Citizens band.
    - Public systems.
    - Police.
    - Armed forces.
    - Government agencies (which ministries have communications facilities?).
    - Telephone.
    - Cable and wireless.
    - Television.
    - Newspaper.
    - Other.

- Describe specific reasons why a system is not operating.
    - Unavailability of:
        - Personnel.
        - Power.
        - Fuel.
        - Access to facilities.
    - Damage to system:
        - Broadcast/transmission equipment.
        - Antennae.
        - Buildings.
        - Transmission lines.

- Relay facilities.
- Power source.
- Other.

- Note source(s) of the above information.

- Outline options for restoring minimum essential services.

- Identify local/regional suppliers of communications equipment and materials available for repair. Check cost and availability.

- Determine the local/regional availability of technical services available for repair.

2. Electric Power

- Describe the power system, including:
  - Baseload facility.
  - Peaking facility.
  - Number of units.
  - Fuel source.
  - Plant controls.
  - Output capability (specify voltage and cycle).
  - Mobile plants.
  - Other standby capability.
  - Switching facilities.
  - Transmission facilities.
  - Distribution facilities (number of substations).
  - Interconnections.

- Inventory auxiliary equipment that may be available locally (for example, from construction companies).

- Determine why power is not available (that is, at what point the system has been damaged).

- Ascertain the condition of generating units.

- Check the integrity of the fuel system.

- Determine whether towers, lines, and/or grounding lines are down.

- Assess the condition of substations.

- Outline the impact of power loss on key facilities, such as hospitals and water pumping stations.

- Describe the options for restoring minimum essential services.

- Ascertain whether load shedding and/or switching to another grid can restore minimal services.

- Identify local/regional suppliers of equipment and materials. Check the cost and availability.

- Determine the local/regional availability of technical services available for repair.

3. Water/Sewage

- Describe the preexisting systems: that is, for water, the source, treatment facilities, mains, pump stations, and distribution network; for sewage, the treatment facilities and pump stations.

- Estimate the number of people who depend on the water sources by type (for example, river, city water system).

- Determine why water (especially potable water) is not available (that is, at what point the system has been damaged).

- Check the integrity of the water source.

- Assess the condition of water and sewage treatment facilities and of the distribution network. Are pump stations operational?

- Determine whether water mains are broken. Are leaks in the sewage system contaminating the water supply?

- Outline the impact of water loss on key facilities and on individual users. How quickly can the responsible ministries be expected to restore services?

- Describe options for restoring minimum essential services.

- Evaluate the possible alternative water sources.

- Identify local/regional suppliers of equipment and materials. Check cost and availability.

- Determine the local/regional availability of technical services available for repair.

4. Hydro Facilities (Hydroelectric, Irrigation)

- Describe the function of the facilities, their proximity to the stricken area, and their relationship to the disaster itself.

- Identify the host country organization that controls and operates the facilities.

- Identify the suppliers, contractors, and/or donors that built the facilities (that is, what were the equipment and technical sources?).

- Describe any damage to systems.

- Check the soundness of the structures and outlet works. Are the reservoirs watertight?

- Identify any immediate or near-term safety risks (generating and control machinery, structural defects, power to operate gates, etc.).

- Assess the condition of canals or downstream channels.

- Identify any changes in watershed conditions (for example, saturation, ground cover, streambed loading, new impoundments).

- Determine whether water is being contaminated.

- Evaluate the management of the facilities.

- Determine whether storage and outflow quantities are being managed in accordance with prescribed curves.

- Identify preparations for follow-on storm conditions (for example, emergency drawdown of reservoirs).

- Describe the probable impact of discharging on downstream damage and/or relief efforts (for example, depth at river crossings, releases into damaged canals). Is there a need to impound water until downstream works can be repaired?

- Outline the options for restoring minimum essential services.

- Outline the repair plans of the responsible host country officials.

- Check on any proposed assistance from the original donors of the facilities.

- Identify local/regional sources of equipment and technical expertise.

5. Roads and Bridges

- Describe the road networks in the affected area by type. What is the load capacity of the bridges?

- Identify the responsible ministries and district offices and constraints on their operations.

- Describe any damage to the network.

- Determine which segments are undamaged, which can be traveled on with delays, and which are impassable.

- Describe any damage by type:
  - Blockage by landslides, fallen trees, etc.
  - Embankments.
  - Drainage structures.
  - Bridges/tunnels.
  - Road surfaces.

- Identify alternate crossings and/or routes.

- Evaluate the importance of the road network to the relief effort and rehabilitation.

- Outline the options for restoring minimum essential service.

- Determine which elements must be restored first.

- Describe the need for traffic control (police, military, other) on damaged or one-way segments.

- Determine how long the emergency repairs can accommodate relief traffic (size, weight, volume?). Will emergency maintenance and fuel points be needed in remote areas?

- Identify the host country agencies, military, and/or civilian forces that are available to make repairs. Do they have equipment, spare parts, and maintenance support?

- Check whether local or expatriate construction companies can loan equipment and/or expertise.

- Check regional sources of equipment and/or expertise that are available for repair.

- Ascertain that arrangements can be made for standby forces at damaged sections to keep roads open.

Chapter III

Information on
Populations at Risk

INFORMATION ON POPULATIONS AT RISK

The information in this chapter is designed to provide team members a background in understanding terms, concepts, procedures, and measurements used in disaster relief for populations at risk. The information can also be used to assist in evaluating the design, quality, and accuracy of assessments conducted by other specialists, organizations, and governments and for monitoring ongoing programs.

Introduction

This unit provides reference information for dealing with populations that are at risk. This information is useful for Assessment Teams gathering information on the plight and condition of these people or for a Disaster Assistance Response Team (DART) that has been sent to assist in dealing with relief activities targeted at these individuals.

Populations at risk are those groups of people adversely affected by a disaster (natural or manmade) who have been placed in situations where they are at an increased risk. They are at risk because of the disruption or loss of their normal community and social support systems that provide the critical elements of their survival: water, food, immunization, health care, shelter, and sanitation. The negative impacts on populations at risk increase the longer they are displaced from their homes. In some cases, these populations have also traveled great distances from their homes to escape long-term disasters such as famine, drought, and civil strife.

Immediate Response

A. Protection of Displaced Persons (DPs)

The immediate need for displaced persons (DPs) is that they be in a secure location where their safety and human rights are ensured. It is difficult to begin an assistance program in an unsafe location or in an atmosphere of vulnerability.

The International Committee of the Red Cross (ICRC), the United Nations High Commissioner for Refugees (UNHCR), and the United Nations Office for the Coordination of

Humanitarian Affairs (OCHA) often attempt to protect displaced populations from arbitrary actions of outsiders and to provide relief assistance. OFDA Assessment Teams and DARTs should support the efforts of the ICRC, UNHCR, and OCHA. However, Assessment Teams and DARTs should not assume any responsibility for the protection of DPs.

B. Organizational Considerations

Once the situation and needs have been assessed and the protection of individuals has been secured, the priority will be to provide vital immediate assistance to the displaced population. To do so, key organizational and planning decisions must be made, which may determine the future of the whole operation. These decisions involve the issues summarized below. If the following issues are not addressed quickly and correctly, they will be difficult to resolve later:

- The location of the DPs will have a major influence on all sectors of assistance. If the DPs are not already concentrated in settlements, they should not be relocated to settlements unless compelling reasons exist for breaking their present pattern of spontaneous informal settlements. New arrivals should be diverted elsewhere. On the other hand, if they are already in settlements that are unsatisfactory, they must be moved. Particular attention should be paid to the special needs of women and children. The difficulty in moving DPs from an unsuitable site increases markedly with time.

- Reception or transit centers are generally recommended when an influx is likely to continue.

- Control at campsites: A determination of the optimum population should be made in advance to plan for new campsites accordingly. Careful control of the population in a camp should be exercised as people arrive, so that sections prepared in advance are filled in an orderly manner.

- Numbers and registration: An accurate estimate of numbers is a prerequisite for any effective assistance. Delivery of help to all in need will require at least family registration and a fair distribution system. The sooner this is established the better.

C. Material Assistance

The specific types and amounts of emergency assistance required will depend on standards established for each situation. These standards are as follows:

- The general condition of the displaced population (people in extreme distress will need extraordinary measures).

- The immediately available resources (for example, unfamiliar food may have to be used if there is nothing else).

- The normal customs of the DPs and the local population.

The standards established for emergency assistance must be consistent with the aim of ensuring the survival and basic well-being of the displaced population, should be fairly applied to all, and must be respected by all involved.

The first priority in an emergency is to provide the organizational capacity required to meet the needs of the emergency. The affected country and UN/PVO/NGO/IOs must be mobilized within the framework of a plan for immediate action. The organization of the logistical capacity necessary to deliver the assistance will be of critical importance.

Once the organizational capacity has been established, the immediate needs of the displaced population must be met. The following is a list of needs in the order of their importance.

- **Water**—Protect existing water sources from pollution. Establish maximum storage capacity with the simplest available means. Transport water to the campsite if the need cannot otherwise be met.

- **Food**—Ensure that at least the minimum need for energy is met (a full ration can follow). Set up special feeding programs if there are clear indications of malnutrition. Establish storage facilities.

- **Immunization for Measles**—The first preventative health measure to be taken in any large DP situation is to institute a measles immunization program for all children between 6 months and 5 years of age, even if resources are scarce. In some situations the upper age level may be increased depending on the prevalence of measles in the population. If significant malnutrition is present, it is absolutely essential to implement a measles immunization program as soon as possible! After diarrhea, measles is the highest cause of death among children under 5 years of age in DP situations.

- **Health Care**—Provide the necessary organizational assistance, health personnel, basic drugs, and equipment in close consultation with national and local health authorities. Although the immediate need and demand may be for curative care, preventative, reproductive, and particularly environmental health measures should not be neglected.

After the primary needs have been addressed, the focus will be on providing secondary needs. They are as follows:

- **Emergency Shelter**—Use local supplies and services, when possible, to meet shelter needs for roofing and other materials. Request outside supplies (for example, plastic sheeting, tents) only if absolutely necessary.

- **Sanitation**—Isolate human excreta from water sources and inhabited areas.

Promote self-sufficiency in the displaced population from the start. Involve the displaced in the planning for their welfare. This may be difficult, but if it is not done the effectiveness of the emergency assistance will be severely reduced, and an early opportunity to help the displaced population to start recovering from the psychological effects of their ordeal may be missed.

The remaining sections in this unit provide an indepth review of the needs of a displaced population, focusing on water, food and nutrition, health, displaced persons camps, and sanitation and environmental health issues.

Water

A. General

People can survive much longer without food than without water. Thus, the provision of water demands immediate attention from the start of a DP emergency. The aim is to ensure the availability of enough safe drinking water to allow unrestricted distribution.

Adequate storage capacity and backup systems for all water supplies must be ensured, because interruptions in the water supply may be disastrous. To avoid contamination, all sources of water used by displaced populations must be separated from sanitation facilities and other sources of contamination.

Availability will generally be the determining factor in organizing the supply of sufficient quantities of safe water. It may be necessary to make special arrangements for water extraction, storage, and distribution. Measures will be required to protect the water from contamination. In some circumstances, treatment will be required to ensure that the water is safe to drink. The safety of the water must be ensured right through to consumption in the home.

Improvements in the existing water supply may take time, particularly if it is necessary to drill or dig wells. In many DP emergencies, only contaminated surface water (standing water, streams, or rivers) is initially available. Immediate action must be taken to stop further pollution and reduce contamination of such water. If it becomes evident that available sources of water are inadequate, arrangements must be made to bring in water by truck. Where even the most basic need for water cannot safely be met from existing sources in the area, and when time is needed for further exploration and development of new sources, the DPs should be moved to a more suitable location.

B. Assessment and Organization

Available water sources must be protected from pollution and contamination at once. Initially, rationing of scarce water may be needed. An influx of displaced people may overburden water resources used by the local population. Rationing will ensure survival of the weak and equity in distribution to the rest of the displaced population. The design, establishment, and function of a water supply and distribution system must be closely coordinated with the site planning and layout, and with health and environmental measures—particularly sanitation.

1. Assessment

Although estimating the immediate need for water does not require special expertise, assessing different sources of supply does. Depending on the situation, sources of water may be identified by:

- The local government.

- The local population.

- The DPs.

- UN/PVO/NGO/IOs.

- The lay of the land (ground water is often near the surface in the vicinity of rivers and in low places generally, or is indicated by richer vegetation).

- Maps and surveys of water resources.

- National and expatriate experts (hydrologists).

- Water diviners.

The assessment of these water sources is the basis for selecting an appropriate supply and distribution system and requires expertise in water engineering, sanitation (testing, purification), and, in some cases, logistics.

Seasonal factors must be carefully considered. Supplies that are adequate in the rainy season may dry up at other times. Local knowledge will be essential.

2. Organization

The water system must be developed and organized with and operated by the displaced people from the start, to the extent possible. The displaced people, particularly those of rural background, may have relevant skills. For example, some individuals from rural communities may be experts at digging and maintaining wells. Others may be familiar with simple pumps or common pump motors. Such skills can and should be fully used in planning, developing, operating, sustaining, and repairing the water system. Displaced people without prior experience should be trained as necessary.

Although special equipment may be required for ground water exploration or surface water treatment, the material and equipment to establish a water supply and distribution system should be found locally. The technology should be kept simple and appropriate to the country, and, again, should draw on local experience. Where pumps and other mechanical equipment are unavoidable, supplies should be standardized, and repair expertise and fuel should be available locally.

For the water system to remain effective, both organizational and technical aspects of the complete water supply system need to be carefully monitored. Use of the system must be controlled, water wastage and contamination prevented, maintenance assured, and technical breakdowns quickly repaired. Basic public health education on such topics as the importance of avoiding polluting the water with excreta and the use of clean containers in the home is essential.

C. Needs

1. Quantity

Minimum water needs vary with each situation but increase markedly with raised air temperature and physical activity. In general, the following amounts of water are desirable:

Individuals:
– Drinking	3–4 liters (L)/person/day
– Food preparation, cleanup	2–3 L/person/day
– Personal hygiene	6–7 L/person/day
– Laundry	4–6 L/person/day
Total individual needs	***15–20 L/person/day***

Feeding Centers:	20–30 L/person/day
Health Centers:	40–60 L/person/day

Table III–1 contains figures on the water needs of large groups of DPs. Additional water may be needed for livestock, sanitation facilities, other community services, and irrigation. Cattle need approximately 30 L of water daily, and small stock require 5 L. Water will also be a factor in deciding on a sanitation system. Water is also necessary for the cultivation and irrigation of food by the displaced people. During the initial stages of an emergency, wastewater may be the only type of water available for agriculture and irrigation, but it can suffice for small vegetable patches. Large-scale irrigation is a matter for expert advice and therefore not addressed here. If possible, however, water sources for large-scale irrigation should be identified and reserved at an early stage.

Care should be taken to avoid pollution or depletion of scarce water sources by livestock. The more convenient the supply, the higher the consumption.

Reduction in the quantity of water available to individuals has many health consequences. Proper supplementary and therapeutic feeding programs will be impossible unless sufficient

Table III–1. Water Needs for Displaced People (1-million-liter increments)

Population	Time (Days)						
	1	30	60	90	120	180	365
500	0.0075	0.225	0.45	0.675	0.9	1.35	2.738
1,000	0.0150	0.450	0.90	1.350	1.8	2.70	5.475
5,000	0.0750	2.250	4.50	6.750	9.0	13.50	27.380
10,000	0.1500	4.500	9.00	13.500	18.0	27.00	54.750
20,000	0.3000	9.000	18.00	27.000	36.0	54.00	108.600
50,000	0.7500	22.500	45.00	67.500	90.0	135.00	273.750
100,000	1.5000	45.000	90.00	135.000	180.0	270.00	547.500
500,000	7.5000	225.000	450.00	675.000	900.0	1,350.00	2,737.500
1,000,000	15.0000	450.000	900.00	1,350.000	1,800.0	2,700.00	5,475.000

Formula: 15 liters × no. of people × days = liters/day.

water is available for preparation of food and basic hygiene. As supplies are reduced, clothes cannot be washed; personal hygiene suffers; cooking utensils cannot be properly cleaned; food cannot be adequately prepared; and, most importantly, the direct intake becomes insufficient to replace moisture lost from the body. Water reduction is also reflected by increased incidence of parasitic, fungal, and other skin diseases; eye infections; diarrheal diseases; and the often-fatal dehydration associated with them. Even individuals who have traditionally lived on less than the normally recommended amount of water, such as nomads, will require more in a DP community because of crowding and other environmental factors.

2. Quality

Water must be safe to drink. Although water may look safe, it may be impure and contain microbiological organisms that cause diseases. "Waterborne" diseases are not usually as serious or widespread as "water-washed" diseases such as skin and eye infections, which result from insufficient water for personal hygiene. *Nevertheless, a large quantity of reasonably safe water is preferable to a smaller amount of very pure water.* The most serious threat to the safety of a water supply is contamination by feces. Once contaminated, it is hard to purify water quickly under emergency conditions.

Where drinking water is scarce, brackish, or even salt water, if available, may be used for domestic hygiene.

New water supplies should be tested before use. Existing supplies should be tested periodically, and immediately after an outbreak of any waterborne disease. The most useful and widely used tests detect and enumerate common fecal bacteria, such as fecal coliforms. Indicators of water quality are:

- *Escherichia coli* or fecal *streptococci* contamination will be indicated by the presence of fecal coliforms.

- *E. coli* and fecal *streptococci* are subsets of fecal coliforms, which are a subset of the total coliforms.

- Both the fecal coliform numbers given and the chlorination concentration mentioned are two primary water-quality indicators.

The actual test used will depend on the availability of local water laboratories and the experience of local sanitarians. The presence of fecal coliform bacteria indicates that the water has been contaminated by feces of humans or other warm-blooded animals. Concentrations of fecal coliforms are usually expressed the fecal coliform count per 100 milliliters (mL) of water. Use the following table as a rough guide.

Fecal Coliforms Per 100 mL	Risk
0–10	Reasonable quality
11–100	Polluted
101–1,000	Very polluted
Over 1,000	Grossly polluted

In cases where water is disinfected by **chlorination,** it is easier and more appropriate to test for the presence of "available chlorine" than for bacteria. The presence of available chlorine at approximately 0.2 milligrams per L (mg/L) at the distribution point indicates that almost all bacteria and viruses have been killed, and that the water is no longer heavily contaminated with fecal or other organic matter. See also the section below on the treatment of water with chemical disinfectants.

Water stored in tanks and tanker trucks should also be tested periodically. Environmental health measures should be taken to protect the water between collection and use.

D. Immediate Response

Measures to meet short-term water emergency needs are appropriate while a longer term supply system is being developed, or pending the move of the DPs to a more suitable site. If the locally available water supply is not sufficient to meet the minimum needs of the displaced, arrangements must be made to bring in water by truck. If this is not possible, the displaced population must be moved from the site without delay.

While the *quantity* of water available may meet initial minimum needs, the *quality* of the water may be the problem: It is likely to be contaminated. Efforts to control and manage the use of contaminated water should be arranged with the displaced community leaders. Otherwise, DPs will use surface water or, less often, ground water (well or spring)—or whatever water is closest, regardless of quality—for their immediate needs. Immediate steps should be taken to prevent pollution by excreta. If the water source is flowing, supplies must be drawn off upstream and a special area set aside for this. Then allocate an area for washing and finally, downstream of the settlement, allow any livestock to water.

Where the source is a well or spring, it must be fenced off, covered, and controlled. Prevent DPs from drawing water with individual containers that may contaminate the source. If possible, make immediate arrangements to store water and to distribute it at collection points away from the source. Not only does this help avoid direct contamination; storage can also make water safer.

From the start, families will need to carry and store their own water at the household level. Suitable containers (10–20 L) are essential. If empty cooking oil containers or the like are un-available, buckets or other containers must be supplied. They must be kept clean.

If immediately available supplies of water are insufficient, priority will be given to rationing supplies and ensuring equi-table distribution. Rationing is difficult to organize. The first step is to control access to sources, using full-time watchmen if necessary. Uncontrolled distributions are open to abuse. Distribution at fixed times for different sections of the camp should be organized. Vulnerable groups may need special arrangements. Every effort must be made to increase the quantity of water available so that strict rationing is unnecessary.

E. Water Source

There are three main sources of water: surface water (streams, rivers, lakes), ground water (underground or emerg-ing from springs), and rainwater.

1. Surface Water

Surface water is collected directly from streams, rivers, ponds, lakes, dams, and reservoirs. Where such a source holds water year-round, the water table in the vicinity can be expected to be near the surface. However, it is rarely pure and is likely to require treatment measures for direct use. Direct access may also cause difficulties with the local population. It is preferable to use ground water that has passed through the natural filter of the soil than to collect water from the surface. However, if the ground is not sufficiently porous to allow extraction of enough water from wells, surface water may be the only op-tion. In such circumstances, emergency treatment measures such as storage, sand filtration, or even chlorination are advised. Control of access to this water is essential.

2. Ground Water

Springs are the ideal source of ground water. Spring water is usually pure at the source and can be piped to storage and distribution points. Spring water should be collected above the camp, if possible, and care should be taken to check the true source of spring water. Some springs may be nothing more than surface water that has seeped or flowed into the ground a short distance away. Once detected, the source of the spring water must be protected against pollution as it flows to a tank or collection point. Care must also be taken to prevent contamination above the takeoff point. The supply of water from a spring may vary widely with the seasons, with supply at a minimum at the end of the dry season.

If water requirements cannot be met by springs, the next best option is to raise ground water by means of tube wells, dug wells, or boreholes. Ground water, being naturally filtered as it flows underground, is usually microbiologically pure. The choice of method to raise ground water will depend on the depth to the water table, yield, soil conditions, and availability of expertise and equipment. Table III-2 and Figure III-1 provide additional information on several methods of digging wells.

Even though wells are often used to access ground water, they have several disadvantages. Without good water resources surveys, preliminary test drilling, or clear local evidence from nearby existing wells, there is no guarantee that new wells will yield adequate supplies of water or water of the right quality. Digging wells can also be expensive. A hydrogeological survey must be undertaken before starting any extensive drilling program. For these and other reasons, it is often better to attempt to improve an existing well with an inadequate yield rather than dig a new one.

Wells, boreholes, and pumps must be disinfected immediately after construction, repair, or installation, as they may have been polluted during work. Wells must also be protected from pollution. They should be located where surface water, seasonal rain, or flood water will drain away from the well head. **Well heads should be located above and at least 15 to 30 meters (m) away from any sanitation facilities and their discharge.**

Table III–2. Characteristics of Different Types of Well Constructions

Well Type / Approximate Maximum Depth	Technique and Comments
Driven tube well / 10–15m	Special small-tipped pipe is hammered into ground. Can be sunk in 1–2 days. Needs special filter "well point" at top of the pipe. Can't be sunk in heavy clay soil or rock.
Auger-bored tube well / 25m	Hole bored by hand using a suitable auger for soil. Can be sunk in 2–3 days. May need imported augers but locally available boring tools can often be used.
Hand-dug well / 30–40m	Requires skilled workers; otherwise dangerous. Speed depends on soil conditions: 210m per week for a team of 4–8. Easily contaminated by misuse or poor workmanship.
Jetted tube / 80m	Water (high volume) is pumped down the well pipe to loosen and carry solid soil back up out of the hole, enabling the pipe to be driven deeper. Usually requires special skills and drilling equipment.
Drilled tube well (bore-hole) / >100m	Large mechanized drilling rig requiring skilled operators, logistical support, and equipment and supplies for the rig. Several days to dig depending on soil and rock conditions.

Note: The yield potential of a well depends on the geological formation in which it is sunk, the contours and gradients of the land, and the well construction. Actual output depends on the pump. If wells are sited too close together, yields will be reduced.

Figure III–1. Methods of Well Construction

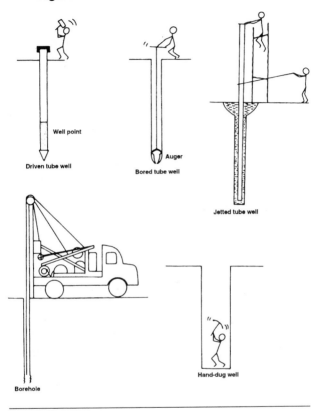

Driven tube well — Well point

Bored tube well — Auger

Jetted tube well

Borehole

Hand-dug well

3. Rainwater

Rainwater may be the major source of water in areas with
adequate and reliable year-round rainfall. Reasonably pure
rain water can be collected from the roofs of buildings or tents
if they are clean and suitable. Collecting rainwater, however, is
unreliable and requires suitable shelter as well as individual
household storage facilities, making it generally impractical for
some DP emergencies. However, every effort should be made
to collect rainwater. Small collection systems, such as using

local earthenware pots under individual roofs and gutters, should be encouraged. Allow the first rain after a long dry spell to run off, thus cleaning the accumulations of dust and sediment.

4. Seawater

Seawater can be used for almost everything but drinking, and thus reduces freshwater requirements.

5. Water Source Considerations

Consider the following when selecting an appropriate water source:

- Speed with which the source can be made operational.

- Volume of supply.

- Reliability of supply (taking into account seasonal variations and, if necessary, logistics).

- Water purity, risk of contamination, and ease of treatment if necessary.

- Rights and welfare of local population.

- Appropriate technology and ease of maintenance.

- Cost.

Take careful account of systems and methods already in use locally. Adopting well-proven and familiar techniques, combined with efforts to improve protection against pollution, is often a sound solution.

In addition to organizational measures to protect the water supply, some form of treatment may be necessary. However, water sources that would require treatment should be avoided if at all possible. The purification of unsafe water, particularly in remote areas, can be difficult and requires trained supervision.

F. Storage

All DP camps must be provided with facilities to store an adequate reserve of water as soon as possible. In nearly all systems it will be necessary to store water in covered tanks between the source and distribution points. Stored water provides an essential reserve and can greatly facilitate distribution, particularly when water is pumped up to elevated tanks. Sedimentation tanks should have the capacity to store an amount of water equal to a day's consumption, thus allowing sedimentation to take place overnight. The size of the reserve will depend on the number of people, the nature of the water supply system, and certain logistical aspects. Using internal dimensions and overflow pipe heights, capacities are calculated as follows:

- Rectangular tanks:
  length × breadth × height (in m) × 1,000 = capacity in L

- Cylindrical tanks:
  height × radius squared (in m) × 3,140 = capacity in L

OFDA provides 3,000-gallon collapsible water tanks and 5-gallon collapsible water containers to disaster victims from its stockpiles. See Chapter VI, "Reference Information," for more information on OFDA stockpile commodities.

In areas with pronounced dry and rainy seasons where alternative sources of water are limited, the construction of a reservoir to collect water should be considered despite dangers from pollution and breeding mosquitoes. An erosion-protected spillway should also be provided. Catchment tanks for the collection of surface water can also be considered in drier parts of the world. Pits can be dug into the ground to catch and hold water that runs off hard ground during heavy storms. Pits need special lining to hold water, and should be covered if possible.

Where the water table is very high and contamination cannot be otherwise avoided, aboveground tanks may be needed. A number of types of simple, air-portable, butyl rubber storage tanks are available. Some can be supplied together with a complete distribution system.

G. Distribution

Water distribution will be an important consideration in the layout of the camp because displaced persons must have easy and safe but controlled access to water. Experience shows that persons forced to get water from considerable distances tend to either not collect enough to limit water-washed diseases or to collect water from closer but contaminated sources. **Ideally, no dwelling should be located further than 100 m or a few minutes' walk from a**

distribution point. Distribution points should not be located in low-lying areas. The area around the distribution point should be paved with stones or gravel or protected by boards, with a runoff to allow proper drainage.

Water can be distributed to individuals in a number of ways depending on local conditions. Uncontrolled access by individual consumers to primary water sources must be avoided. *A distribution system should have a sufficient number of taps or outlets relative to the size of the population to ensure that people do not wait for long periods to have access.* Equity in the distribution of water is an extremely important consideration. Water for domestic use should flow between source/storage and distribution point in pipes to protect its quality. Pipes must be watertight; leaking pipes suck in pollution when the pressure drops or when the system is turned off. Pipes may be made of metal, cement, plastic, or bamboo. Bamboo is unlikely to be suitable in the majority of emergencies. Plastic pipes are often the cheapest and easiest to lay. They are available in both lengths of coiled, flexible pipe and in rigid lengths, (commonly 3 m). Pipes should be buried for protection, and sections of the system should have isolated valves.

Standpipes and push taps are recommended where possible as outlets for water. Taps, however, are very vulnerable and often require spares, which must be available. Where water supplies are limited and the camp is crowded, valve distribution points that can be chained shut may be the only effective solution. **There should be one tap per 200–250 displaced persons. The more people using a single source or outlet of water, the greater the risk of pollution or damage.**

A certain amount of wastewater will be generated in the community, both at the individual and communal service level. Although it must be prevented from becoming a danger to public health, wastewater may be reused for livestock or vegetable gardens, or to flush latrines.

H. Treatment

Water may contain pathogens, particularly certain viruses, bacteria, protozoal cysts, and worm eggs, that are transmitted from feces to mouth. Although water contamination by human feces is the major concern, animal feces in water may also transmit disease. Water contamination by urine is a significant threat only in areas where typhoid and urinary schistosomiasis (*Schistosoma haematobium*) is endemic. By far the greatest risk associated with polluted drinking water is the spread of diarrhea, dysentery, cholera, and infectious hepatitis (hepatitis A). Diarrhea and dysentery are caused by a variety of viruses, bacteria, and protozoa. The numbers of viruses and protozoa in water will always decrease with time and most rapidly at warm temperatures. Bacteria behave similarly, but in exceptional circumstances, they may multiply in polluted water. The infectious dose of viruses and protozoa is typically very low, whereas the dose of bacteria needed to establish an infection in the intestine may be high, or as in the case of cholera, very low.

Determining how to treat water on a large scale is best done by experts. If possible, professional engineering advice should be sought. However, simple and practical measures can be taken before such help is available. All methods require regular attention and maintenance.

In addition to protecting water at its source and initially disinfecting wells and boreholes (usually by chlorine), there are four basic methods of treatment: storage, filtration, chemical disinfection, and boiling. These can be used singly or in combination.

1. Storage

Leaving water undisturbed in containers, tanks, or reservoirs improves its quality. Storage kills some pathogens and settles any heavy matter in suspension (sedimentation). If water supplies cannot be assumed to be safe, immediate action must be taken to provide maximum water storage capacity. Storage of untreated surface water for 12 to 24 hours will considerably improve its quality. The longer the period of storage and the higher the temperature, the greater the improvement. The clarification of cloudy water can be greatly speeded up by the addition of aluminum sulfate. A two-tank system is often used, with the first tank used as a settling tank and the second used to store the clarified water. Treatment can be done in the second tank as well, and a third used for storage if necessary. While clear water may only require chlorination, turbid surface water will usually require sedimentation and/or filtration before chemical disinfection. Even so, greater doses of chlorine may be required.

Great care should be taken to prevent the pollution of stored water. This can be done by covering storage tanks. In addition, the storage area should be fenced off and guarded to prevent children from playing or swimming in the water.

Long-term storage can help control schistosomiasis (bilharzia) by killing parasites by preventing them from reaching the freshwater snail within 24 hours of excretion by an infected person, or by preventing the parasites from reaching a human or animal host within 48 hours of leaving infected snails. Thus, 2 days' storage would provide an effective barrier to transmission of the disease, if snails do not enter the tank.

2. Sand Filtration

Sand filtration can also be an effective method of treatment. A proper, slow, sand filter works in two ways. First, the passage of the water through the sand physically filters out solids. Second, and more importantly, it causes a thin and very active layer of algae, plankton, bacteria, and other forms of life to develop on the surface of the sandbed. This organic matter is called the "schmutzdecke." The rate of filtration depends on the surface area, depth, and type of sand through which the water is passed, and the pressure of the water. The average range size of sand is 0.3–1 millimeters (mm). In general, the slower the rate of filtration, the higher the quality of the water.

A packed drum filter can be used for sand filtration and is a good way of providing limited quantities of safe water quickly (for example, for a health center). If a packed drum filter is used, water should pass down through sand on a 5-centimeter (cm) layer of gravel and be drawn off at a rate not to exceed 60 L per hour for a 200-L drum. If a tap is used, unfiltered water equal to the amount drawn off should be added to the top. Other types of sand filters include horizontal sand filters and riverbed filters (suitable only where the bed is permeable). These can be used to treat larger amounts of water but are likely to be more difficult to set up quickly and effectively. To filter water from a river, a well may be dug close to the bank. However, remember the water is river water, and though it will have been filtered through the bed and bank, further treatment may be necessary (for example, chlorination).

3. Coagulation and Flocculation

This is a water treatment process by which finely divided suspended and colloidal matter in water is made to join together and form flocs. These flocs then settle to the bottom and can be removed.

4. Chemical Disinfection

Chemical disinfection for water treatment on a large scale is recommended when storage and/or filtration cannot meet the need. It will be required to disinfect wells, sand filters, pumps, and piped water systems. Both iodine and various forms of chlorine can be used, although chlorine is more widely used, cheaper, and often more readily available. The most generally suitable form of chlorine for DP emergencies is calcium hypochlorite powder.

Expert advice is essential for large-scale chlorination. All systems require regular attention and will be of little value if not fully reliable. Chlorination should take place after any sedimentation or filtration process. It requires at least 30 minutes to act.

Care must be taken to ensure strict control of any chemical disinfection process. Water should be tested for chemical residual levels after each disinfection and before distribution.

After chlorination, at least 0.2 parts of available chlorine per million (0.2 mg/L) should still exist in the water to kill bacteria and viruses. The amount of chlorine required to achieve this is usually a broad indication of the level of pollution. If the amount of available chlorine is above 0.5 parts per million at the distribution point, people may not want to drink the water. Overchlorinated water tastes unpleasant and will be useless if people prefer untreated water. *Chlorine and iodine water purification tablets are available, but are rarely suitable to treat water for large populations. Tablets, however, may be useful to treat water used in health or supplementary feeding centers.*

5. Boiling

Boiling is the surest and perhaps simplest method of water sterilization but is only practical or possible for small displaced populations. At low altitudes, bringing water to a boil will destroy all pathogens transmitted by drinking water. (Boiling should, however, be increased 1 minute for every 1,000 m of altitude above sea level, as the boiling temperature reduces with altitude). Prolonged vigorous boiling is often recommended but not necessary to destroy the fecal-orally transmitted pathogens. In fact, prolonged boiling wastes fuel and increases the concentration of nitrates, which are dangerous for very young babies. In the longer term, domestic fuel supplies may be the determining factor, as boiling requires about 1 kilogram (kg) of wood per liter of water. However, if the displaced people have traditionally boiled their water, they should be encouraged to do so. This may make the need for other types of treatment less urgent.

Food and Nutrition

A. General

1. Food Security

The food and nutritional needs of any population at risk is based on its level of food security. Food security is defined as the point when all people at all times have both physical and economic access to sufficient food to meet their dietary needs for a productive and healthy life. There are three distinct variables that are central to the attainment of food security: availability, access, and utilization.

a. Food Availability is achieved when sufficient quantities of food are consistently available to all individuals within a country. Such food can be supplied through household production, other domestic output, commercial imports, or food assistance.

b. Food Access is ensured when households and all individuals within them have adequate resources to obtain appropriate foods for a nutritious diet. Access depends on income available to the household, the distribution of income within the household, and the price of food.

c. Food Utilization is the proper biological use of food, requiring a diet providing sufficient energy and essential nutrients, potable water, and adequate sanitation. Effective food utilization depends in large measure on knowledge within the household of food storage and processing techniques, basic principles of nutrition, and proper child care.

2. Assessing Needs

The types of feeding programs required to meet the food security needs of the displaced people will be determined by the initial needs assessment. Continuous monitoring will ensure adjustments to reflect changing conditions. Coordination of the feeding programs with health and other community services is essential.

Assistance must be culturally acceptable and appropriate to the nutritional needs of the displaced people. Foods prepared locally with local ingredients are preferable to imported foods. Infant feeding policies require particular attention.

Infants, children, pregnant and lactating women, the sick, and the elderly are very vulnerable to malnutrition and have special needs. Since the population has already probably suffered a prolonged food shortage, many will be malnourished by the time of the first assessment of their condition and needs.

If the displaced people are already suffering the effects of severe food shortages, immediate action must be taken to provide whatever food is available to them. *The first priority is to meet the energy requirements of the population rather than protein needs. Supplying bulk cereal is the first objective of the general feeding program.*

Displaced people must be involved from the start in the organization and management of the feeding programs. Special training for some displaced people may be necessary.

Simple nutrition education is important when unfamiliar foods or new methods of cooking and preparation have to be introduced to the population. This should be organized with other health education activities to provide guidance on proper infant feeding, feeding of sick children, treatment of diarrhea, basic food hygiene, and the preparation of available foods for maximum nutritional benefit.

Particular attention must be paid to the provision of cooking fuel. A lack of cooking fuel can quickly lead to destruction of the vegetation around the camp and friction with the local population. On average, a family will use 5 kg of wood per day to cook on a simple wood stove.

B. Nutritional Assessment and Surveillance

Initial nutritional assessments should be completed by nutritional specialists, if possible. The information in this section is designed to inform the team member on the methodologies of conducting a nutritional assessment and followup surveillance activities, not to teach him or her how to conduct these activities.

Followup surveillance of the population as a whole should be done by gathering information about the nutritional status of the children, using the Weight-for-height (WFH) or Weight-for-length (WFL) comparison method. Children are the first to show signs of malnourishment during a food shortage. Their nutritional status is an indicator of the amount and degree of malnutrition in the population as a whole. Using the WFH or WFL comparison method on a random sample of children will enable you to assess the nutritional status of the population as a whole.

When using the WFH or WFL method in a surveillance program, a random sample of children from 6 to 59 months of age (under 5 years of age) or less than 110 cm tall are weighed and measured regularly. Children less than 85 cm tall are measured supine (WFL) and children above 85 cm tall are measured standing up (WFH). (See also *Weight-for-height (Weight-for-length)* later in this section of this chapter for additional information on assessing malnutrition using this method.). In a given population, 18 to 20 percent will be under 5 years of age. For a small displaced population (2,000 to 3,000), all the children, about 400 to 500, should be measured. For larger populations, there are two methods of surveillance that are most applicable: *systematic random sampling* and *cluster sampling*.

1. Systematic Random Sampling

Systematic random sampling, in which an interval of every *Nth* shelter or household is sampled and all children under 5 years in that household are measured, is recommended where populations are living in an organized or structured setting as a refugee camp. To undertake a systematic random sampling, one needs to know the total number of households, the average number of children under 5 years of age in a household, and the total population. The recommended sample size for a systematic random sampling is 500 children. This sample size will ensure 95 percent probability that the sample is representative.

To calculate the *Nth* interval, first calculate the number of households to be visited in order to measure 500 children. Use the following equation, $500/(A \times P)$, where A = (average household size) and P = (proportion of children under 5 years of age in the total population).

For example, if the average household size is six persons and the proportion of children under 5 years of age (110 cm in height) is 17 percent, then $500 / (6 \times 0.17) = 490$ households to be visited in order to measure 500 children.

If there are 10,000 households in the population, the *Nth* sampling interval would equal 10,000 / 490 households to be visited = 20. Therefore every *20th* household should be visited, until 500 children under 5 years (110 cm) are measured.

2. Cluster Sampling

Cluster sampling, in which random "clusters" of households are measured, is used in populations that are not in even or structured settings but are spread unevenly over a large geographic area. The cluster sample method is most often used because, in the initial stages of emergencies, people are rarely living in a structured pattern. The sample size needed to obtain 95 percent probability is 900 children. For reliable results it is important to examine *at least* 30 clusters and *not less* than 900 children or "30 clusters of 30."

In a rapid assessment, the area of interest should be divided on a map into sections of equal size. Each section should have at least 300 inhabitants. The total number of clusters, drawn from a list of all sections and their population estimates, is divided by 30 to obtain the cluster interval *K*. Starting at a random selected interval, every *Kth* cluster is selected.

For example, suppose that there are a total of 210 clusters. This total number of clusters is divided by 30 to obtain the cluster interval (210 / 30 = 7). Starting from a randomly selected cluster, every 7th cluster on the list is selected until 30 survey clusters are chosen.

During the survey, the team starts at the center of the cluster and chooses a direction (by spinning a bottle or pen). The survey is then started at the next nearest household or shelter in that direction. All the eligible children in the household are

measured. The team moves to successive houses until
30 children have been examined.

Initially, such surveys should be conducted every 2 months.
When conditions have stabilized, a survey once every 3 to
6 months is sufficient. Any change or trend in nutritional status
can thus be detected and adjustments made in the relevant
feeding programs.

If the initial assessment indicates a need for supplementary or
therapeutic feeding, individuals with these requirements
should be identified and registered for appropriate programs.
Their individual progress should be monitored through more
frequent weighing at feeding centers.

3. Assessing Malnutrition

Malnutrition can be recognized by certain clinical signs (for
example, marasmus, kwashiorkor, and marasmic-kwashiorkor)
and body measurements (see the section on *Nutritional Diseases* under the heading *Common Diseases* in the *Health*
section of this chapter for definitions). Body measurements
are required for objective assessment of nutritional status and
comparison with regular surveillance data.

a. Weight-for-Height (Weight-for-Length). The **weight-for-
height (weight-for-length)** method, which is expressed either
as a **percentage of a reference median** or as a **Z-Score**, is
preferred for nutritional surveillance and for measuring individual progress in emergencies. If a **percentage** is used, it
indicates the weight of the child expressed as a percentage of
that of a well-nourished child of the same height as given in
international reference tables. **If a Z-Score is used, the "Z"
represents the median for children and a Z-Score represents the number of standard deviations above or below
the median (since the population is normally distributed,
the median equals the population mean).** Children with less
than 80 percent weight-for-height or with a Z-Score of less
than –2 are classified as malnourished; those with less than
70 percent weight-for-height or with a Z-Score of less than –3
are considered severely malnourished. Without special feeding
programs, severely malnourished children will die. *Abbreviated
reference tables with weight-for-height and weight-for-length
comparisons and Z-scores are located in Tables III–3, III–4,
III–5, and III–6.*

Table III–3. Weight-for-Length Expressed as a Percentage of Median Weight (length assessed supine up to 85.0 cm., sexes combined)

Length (cm)	Median Weight (kg)	80%	75%	70%	60%
65.0	7.0	5.6	5.3	4.9	4.20
66.0	7.3	5.9	5.5	5.1	4.38
67.0	7.6	6.1	5.7	5.3	4.56
68.0	7.9	6.3	5.9	5.5	4.74
69.0	8.2	6.6	6.1	5.7	4.92
70.0	8.5	6.8	6.3	5.9	5.10
71.0	8.7	7.0	6.5	6.1	5.22
72.0	9.0	7.2	6.7	6.3	5.40
73.0	9.2	7.4	6.9	6.5	5.52
74.0	9.5	7.6	7.1	6.6	5.70
75.0	9.7	7.8	7.3	6.8	5.82
76.0	9.9	7.9	7.4	6.9	5.94
77.0	10.1	8.1	7.6	7.1	6.06
78.0	10.4	8.3	7.8	7.2	6.24
79.0	10.6	8.4	7.9	7.4	6.36
80.0	10.8	8.6	8.1	7.5	6.48
81.0	11.0	8.8	8.2	7.7	6.60
82.0	11.2	8.9	8.4	7.8	6.72
83.0	11.4	9.1	8.5	7.9	6.84
84.0	11.5	9.2	8.7	8.1	6.90

Table III–4. Weight-for-Height Expressed as a Percentage of Median Weight (height assessed by standing from 85.0 cm., sexes combined)

Height (cm)	Median Weight (kg)	80%	75%	70%	60%
85.0	12.0	9.5	9.0	8.4	7.20
86.0	12.2	9.8	9.1	8.5	7.32
87.0	12.4	9.9	9.3	8.7	7.44
88.0	12.6	10.1	9.5	8.8	7.56
89.0	12.9	10.3	9.7	9.0	7.74
90.0	13.1	10.5	9.8	9.2	7.86
91.0	13.3	10.7	10.0	9.3	7.98
92.0	13.6	10.8	10.2	9.5	8.16
93.0	13.8	11.0	10.3	9.7	8.28
94.0	14.0	11.2	10.5	9.8	8.40
95.0	14.3	11.4	10.7	10.0	8.58
96.0	14.5	11.6	10.9	10.2	8.70
97.0	14.8	11.8	11.1	10.3	8.88
98.0	15.0	12.0	11.3	10.5	9.00
99.0	15.3	12.2	11.5	10.7	9.18
100.0	15.6	12.4	11.7	10.9	9.36
101.0	15.8	12.7	11.9	11.1	9.48
102.0	16.1	12.9	12.1	11.3	9.66
103.0	16.4	13.1	12.3	11.5	9.84
104.0	16.7	13.3	12.5	11.7	10.02
105.0	16.9	13.6	12.7	11.9	10.14
106.0	17.2	13.8	12.9	12.1	10.32
107.0	17.5	14.0	13.1	12.3	10.50
108.0	17.8	14.3	13.4	12.5	10.68
109.0	18.1	14.5	13.6	12.7	10.86
110.0	18.4	14.8	13.8	12.9	11.04

FOG Version 3.0

Table III–5. Weight-for-Length and Associated Z-Scores (length assessed supine up to 85.0 cm., sexes combined)

Length (cm)	Median Weight (kg)	−2SD Z	−3SD Z
65	7.0	5.6	4.9
66	7.3	5.9	5.2
67	7.6	6.1	5.4
68	7.9	6.4	5.7
69	8.2	6.7	5.9
70	8.5	6.9	6.1
71	8.7	7.2	6.4
72	9.0	7.4	6.6
73	9.2	7.6	6.8
74	9.5	7.8	7.0
75	9.7	8.1	7.2
76	9.9	8.3	7.4
77	10.1	8.5	7.6
78	10.4	8.6	7.8
79	10.6	8.8	8.0
80	10.8	9.0	8.1
81	11.0	9.2	7.4
82	11.2	9.4	8.5
83	11.4	9.6	7.8
84	11.5	9.7	8.8

Table III–6. Weight-for-Height and Associated Z-Scores (height assessed by standing from 85.0 cm., sexes combined)

Height (cm)	Median Weight (kg)	–2SD Z	–3SD Z
85	12.0	9.8	8.7
86	12.2	10.0	8.9
87	12.4	10.2	9.1
88	12.6	10.4	9.3
89	12.9	10.6	9.5
90	13.1	10.8	9.6
91	13.3	11.0	9.8
92	13.6	11.2	10.0
93	13.8	11.4	10.2
94	14.0	11.6	10.4
95	14.3	11.8	10.5
96	14.5	12.0	10.7
97	14.8	12.2	10.9
98	15.0	12.4	11.1
99	15.3	12.6	11.3
100	15.6	12.8	11.5
101	15.8	13.0	11.7
102	16.1	13.3	11.9
103	16.4	13.5	12.1
104	16.7	13.7	12.3
105	16.9	14.0	12.5
106	17.2	14.2	12.7
107	17.5	14.5	12.9
108	17.8	14.7	13.2
109	18.1	15.0	13.4
110	18.4	15.2	13.6

FOG Version 3.0

b. Mid-Upper-Arm Circumference (MUAC). Another method
used when a rapid screening of young children is necessary is
the **mid-upper-arm circumference (MUAC)** measurement. It
is less sensitive than the weight-for-height method but can be
done more quickly. It measures the part of the arm whose
circumference does not normally change significantly between
the ages of 1 and 5, but which wastes rapidly with malnutrition. The technique is not suitable for monitoring the progress
of individual children. Professional help should be used for the
arm circumference method.

**Before being measured, the child should be checked for
edema, the swelling associated with kwashiorkor.** Press a
finger against the front of the child's foot for about 3 seconds.
A dent (pitting) indicates that the child has edema and therefore should not be measured. It should be recorded that the
child has edema and is severely malnourished.

If there is no sign of edema, the mid-upper-arm circumference of
the child should be measured, using a custom-made measuring
tape. The tape should be wrapped closely, but not tightly, around
the arm, midway between the elbow and the point of the shoulder. The arm should be hanging loosely, with the tape measure
circled around the arm. The tip should be inserted back-to-front
through the narrow slit at the white end of the tape. The arm
circumference should be read to the nearest 0.1 cm between the
vertical arrows at the center of the large opening. The arm circumference of normal children between 1 and 5 years of age
changes very little. Therefore, children of these ages can be
included in a nutrition survey using the same standards.

The arm circumference tapes have colored bands representing different nutritional states:

Status Arm	Circumference	Color
Normal	13.5 cm or greater	Green
Mild malnutrition	12.5 to 13.4 cm	Yellow
Moderate to severe malnutrition	Less than 12.5 cm	Red

If custom-made measuring tapes are not available, a thin strip
of plastic (about 30 cm in length) should be used with marks
clearly indicated at the zero point, 12.0 cm, 12.5 cm, and
13.5 cm.

Each arm circumference has an approximate equivalent to a weight-for-height percentage. They are:

- 13.5 cm or greater—approximately equivalent to over 85 percent weight-for-height.

- 12.5 to 13.4 cm—approximately equivalent to 80 to 85 percent weight-for-height.

- Less than 12.5 cm—approximately equivalent to under 80 percent weight-for-height.

The amount and degree of malnutrition can be calculated as percentages of the sample. The percentage of children with edema (kwashiorkor) should also be reported.

C. General Feeding Program

Every effort should be made to provide familiar foodstuffs and to maintain sound traditional food habits. Expert advice on the appropriate food ration is essential and should take full account of local availability. Staple foodstuffs should not be changed simply because unfamiliar substitutes are readily available. Providing unfamiliar foods often leads to wastage and malnutrition and lowers the morale of the population.

The amount and quality of food provided must satisfy energy and protein requirements. A **Survival Ration** should provide at least **2,100 Kcal (and 60 g of protein)** per person per day. This is based on the Institute of Medicine's 1995 report on *Estimated Mean per Capita Energy Requirements for Planning Emergency Rations.* Active adults may require considerably higher energy intakes, especially if part of the relief plan includes a Food-for-Work Program. Although there is a marked difference between the needs of a young child and an active adult, it is strongly recommended that a standard ration be provided for each displaced person without distinction. **A typical daily ration providing sufficient calories and protein should include selections from *each* of the following categories of food:**

Food Category	Example	Daily Ration
A staple food that provides the bulk of the energy and protein requirement	Cereal	400–450 g
An energy-rich food	Vegetable oil	20–30 g
A protein-rich food	Pulses	30–60 g

Fortified foods may also assist meeting micronutrient needs but should be combined with local foods and supplements.

Tables III–7 and III–8 provide information on examples of food rations in protracted crisis situations and planning figures to determine bulk food requirements during these situations.

If grains must be milled, the population will require an increased ration, because a portion must be given to the miller and because of loss during milling. Vitamin B is also lost in the milling process.

Other items such as vegetables, sugar, spices, condiments, fruits, and tea should be provided according to cultural and nutritional needs, if possible. However, absolute priority must be given to the delivery of the staple food. *The assured delivery of a few staple items is better than no delivery of hard-to-find items.*

Essential vitamin and mineral requirements must also be met. Where adequate quantities of certain nutrients cannot be provided in the diet, the inclusion of seasonally available vegetables will usually prevent vitamin and mineral deficiencies. When possible, the population should be encouraged to grow home gardens of vegetables for personal use or shop at local food markets.

Particular attention must be paid to vitamin and mineral deficiencies prevalent in the local area. Two deficiencies are commonly seen among displaced people: vitamin A deficiency and anemia. **Vitamin A deficiency** *in malnourished populations, especially children, leads to increased morbidity, blindness, and death.* **Anemia** *is commonly associated with certain parasitic diseases such as schistosomiasis and hookworm or an insufficient intake of iron and folate.* In the most severe cases, anemia can lead to cardiac failure and death. Both deficiencies are preventable with a proper diet. Efforts must be made to include food items that are rich in the needed nutrients. The distribution of multivitamin tablets to the entire population may be useful to prevent some deficiencies but is expensive, labor intensive, and not effective for all deficiencies.

However, vitamin A should be given once every four months to children under 5 years of age. *Infants less than 6 months should receive no vitamin A* because of possible toxicity.

Table III–7. Examples of Survival Food Rations for Populations in Protracted Crisis Situations (quantity in grams, based on 2,100 Kcal/person/day)

Commodities	Ration Option 1	Ration Option 2	Ration Option 3
Rice/wheat flour/cornmeal	430	430	430
Pulses (beans/peas)	45	0	0
Pulses (lentils)	0	30	0
Vegetable oil	25	25	25
Corn-soya blend	35	0	35
Wheat-soya blend	0	35	0
Canned fish	0	0	30
Sugar	0	15	15
Salt (iodized)	5	5	5
Total grams:	*540*	*540*	*540*
Approximate food value			
Energy (kcal)	2,100	2,100	2,100
Protein (g)	50	60	50
Fat (g)	30	30	30

Note: Fresh fruits and vegetables, cereals and legumes, and condiments or spices should be made available whenever possible. Fortified cereal blends, such as wheat-soya blend and corn-soya blend, are good sources of micronutrients. The addition of quantities of various micronutrients, through the inclusion of such fortified cereals and local fresh foods, is highly desirable.

Table III–8. Example of Planning Figures to Determine Food Needs for Survival Food Rations for Populations in Protracted Crisis Situations (food quantity in MTs, based on 540 g/person/day [2,100 Kcal option])

Population	Time (days)						
	1	30	60	90	120	180	365
250	0.135	4.05	8.1	12.15	16.2	24.3	49.275
500	0.270	8.10	16.2	24.30	32.4	48.6	98.550
1,000	0.540	16.20	32.4	48.60	64.8	97.2	197.100
5,000	2.700	81.00	162.0	243.00	324.0	486.0	985.500
10,000	5.400	162.00	324.0	486.00	648.0	972.0	1971.000
20,000	10.800	324.00	648.0	972.00	1296.0	1944.0	3942.000
50,000	27.000	810.00	1620.0	2430.00	3240.0	4860.0	9855.000
100,000	54.000	1620.00	3240.0	4860.00	6480.0	9720.0	19710.000
500,000	270.000	8100.00	16200.0	24300.00	32400.0	48600.0	98550.000
1,000,000	540.000	16200.05	32400.0	48600.00	64800.0	97200.0	197100.000

Formula: No. of persons per day × .540/1,000 kgs.

Infants from 6 to 11 months should receive the equivalent of 100,000 international units (usually one half of a capsule). Children from 1 to 5 years of age should receive the equivalent of 200,000 international units (usually one capsule). Women of reproductive age should not receive concentrated doses of vitamin A. Women should receive vitamin A through other strategies mentioned above such as vitamin-rich food or, in areas with a known dietary deficiency, a supplement not to exceed 25,000 international units per week.

The need for a fair, efficient, and regular ration distribution cannot be overemphasized. Normally, rations are issued in 7- to 14-day intervals. Distribution intervals must be continually reviewed based on continuing assessment of the displaced population. An accurate census is needed and a monitoring system must be established to ensure that the food is actually reaching every person as intended. Some waste, diversion, and corruption are inevitable, but if these problems are severe they may lead to discontent and unnecessary suffering by the population.

1. Types of Food Distribution

There are two types of food distribution: dry rations and cooked or "wet" rations. Whichever is used, it is important that those distributing the food have exact instructions on the size of the rations. If scales are not available or become an inconvenient way to measure out food, cans or containers with a known weight/volume comparison for each commodity should be used. The distribution of food as prepackaged rations is an unsatisfactory solution and should be avoided.

a. Dry Ration Distribution (Take Home). This method has major advantages over cooked food distribution. Dry ration distribution allows families to prepare their food as they wish, permits them to continue to eat together as a unit, and is generally more culturally and socially acceptable. This method also assumes that the family units have access to potable water.

Distribution is usually made at 7- to 14-day intervals. Where an accurate census is available and families have food distribution cards, some form of group distribution is possible. A designated family member or group leader becomes responsible for distributing the food. This method is fast and relatively easy to monitor. In the initial stages, however, the best way to guarantee a fair distribution may be to have every individual present.

The food distributor is responsible to the people and camp authorities. A standard measure (for example, a can) should be used for distribution. Each person should understand how much he or she should receive.

Groups should remain fixed to a piece of ground when they first register to prevent multiple registrations. Simultaneous food distributions will prevent people from moving from one distribution session to the next.

In addition to cooking pots, fuel, and utensils, displaced people must have containers and sacks (for example, empty cooking-oil tins and grain sacks) to protect and store their food rations. Depending on the type of food distributed, there may be a need for grinding and milling facilities.

Food distribution to dispersed populations may present problems. For example, if the displaced camp is located in a food-deficit area, the local population may become intermingled with the displaced population. The local government may try to prevent a census that might cause the local people to be excluded from the food distribution. One solution to overcome this problem is to have the traditional leaders of the displaced population do the distribution. Another solution is to have a separate food distribution system in the local community located away from the displaced settlement. This should keep the local population out of the settlement. While it will cause a certain diversion of commodities, this is an acceptable loss considering the alternatives. Food distributions may also interfere with original planning assumptions. If the affected population is in a village, it may have access to other food sources. Relief managers should take this into account and provide only a portion of their food requirements.

In providing food to dispersed populations, one must be very careful not to destroy local markets and marketing systems. Two methods for food distribution can be used: providing food directly or using the food-for-work or cash-for-work methods. There can also be village-based or nutrition-based distributions. The village-based method counts the number of people requiring food, determines the amount of food needed, and then gives that amount to everyone. This method is easy but expensive because there is no targeting. These programs are difficult to end, and the local markets are disrupted by them. Nutrition-based food distribution programs target distribution to vulnerable groups and then decrease as the area's nutrition level improves. Although this is a good system, it is complicated and staff-intensive. It requires home visits, good records, nutrition-monitoring equipment, and trained people to administer the program.

The quality and quantity of rations should be discussed regularly with the displaced people, and complaints should be investigated. It is also important to check that food is being properly distributed and used at the family level. Food basket monitoring, measuring the ration amount from a random selection of recipients just after they have received their ration, is a useful tool to ensure equitable and efficient distributions. Nutrition education can help with some problems and may prevent improper storage or spoilage. This is especially true if the population is not accustomed to the type of food in their ration.

b. Wet Ration Distribution. This method requires centralized kitchens with adequate utensils, water, fuel (although obviously less than the amounts required for family cooking), and trained, healthy personnel. At least two meals must be provided per day, and the efficient organization of wet ration distribution for large numbers is difficult. Such distribution may be necessary during the initial stages of an emergency, especially when families have insufficient cooking utensils or fuel.

D. Selective Feeding Programs

When malnutrition exists or the needs of vulnerable groups of infants, children, pregnant and lactating women, the sick, and the elderly cannot be met from the general ration, special arrangements are required to provide extra food. The vulnerability of these groups stems from the increased nutrient requirements associated with such factors as growth, production of breast milk, repair of tissues, and production of antibodies. Selective feeding programs fall into two categories: Supplementary Feeding Programs (SFP), designed to meet the extra nutritional requirement of vulnerable groups, and Therapeutic Feeding Programs (TFP), lifesaving feeding programs designed to treat severe malnutrition.

Planning and implementation of SFPs and TFPs is a step-by-step process. It is important to be flexible given the circumstances of each emergency. Clear criteria and cutoff points for admission to SFPs and TFPs should be set up in agreement with all the local and humanitarian assistance organizations carrying out SFP and TFP programs.

1. Supplementary Feeding Programs

Small children are particularly susceptible to the cycle of infections and malnutrition. *Sick children must eat and drink, even if they have no appetite, are vomiting, or have diarrhea. They must receive additional, "supplementary" food whenever possible.*

A Supplementary Feeding Program (SFP) requires strong advocacy among the population. Its purpose must be clearly understood, otherwise some will question why the weak and sick are being fed when there are children who are healthy and need food.

Factors to consider when determining the need for an SFP include:
- General rations average less than 1,500 Kcal/person/day.
- 10 to 20 percent of the children are malnourished (children under 5 years old exhibit under 80 percent weight-for-height or less than –2 standard deviation Z-score).
- Severe public health hazards exist.
- Significant diseases, especially measles, are prevalent or imminent.

The aim of an SFP is to provide extra high-energy, high-protein, low-bulk extra meals once or twice a day to those who need it. The number of meals depends on the nutritional status of the population, the nutritional value of the general ration, and the age of the beneficiaries. The size of the supplement also depends on the nutritional status of the beneficiaries. However, at least 400 Kcal and 15 g protein per day should be provided.

These programs usually take two forms: wet or dry rations. In addition to the criteria listed above for wet and dry general rations, supplemental dry rations should always be given priority in emergencies. Dry rations are easier to organize, less costly, lower the risk of communicable diseases, decrease the time mothers have to spend in centers, improve accessibility, and support local customs and household structures.

Wet rations should be considered if there are is a lack of fuel or cooking facilities in the households, if women are put at risk from carrying and storing a supplementary ration, or if there is a strong indication that children will not receive a ration in the household.

Supplementary meals should be prepared as porridge or soup, which are easily digestible and can be eaten by people of all ages. The food is generally based on cereal and legume blends with edible oil added to increase the energy content. Other ingredients (for example, sugar, vegetables, fish, and milk) can be added to provide additional nutrients and a variety of flavors. There are some prepackaged cereal/legume blended meals available through UN agencies (for example, CSB [corn-soya-blend], WSB [wheat-soya-blend], etc.) that may be useful at the start of an emergency feeding program if ingredients are familiar to the population. However, local foods should be substituted as quickly as possible and prepared in a more traditional and appropriate way. **High energy and protein biscuits** are also used *sometimes* early in the program. These biscuits are specially blended to be a high-protein and high-energy food supplement in a dry, easy-to-distribute form. However, their use is not encouraged for supplementary feeding because they serve a special niche, where cooking facilities are unavailable for an emergency feeding program or for distribution as a supplementary food source for a displaced population on the move.

Supplementary feeding programs are usually implemented either as targeted or blanket programs, depending upon the objectives and available resources for the program.

a. Blanket SFP. Blanket SFP distributions are implemented to reduce or prevent the deterioration of a precarious nutritional situation. Blanket SFPs are those in which all vulnerable groups receive a supplementary ration (usually a dry ration of a blended food). In addition to pregnant and lactating women and sick and elderly persons, blanket SFP programs usually include all children under 5 years of age and do not use anthropometric measurements (weight and height) to define vulnerability.

b. Targeted SFPs. If food resources are limited, then a more restricted (targeted) program is most likely. Targeted SFPs establish anthropometric criteria for those "targeted" to receive a supplementary ration. *Targeted SFPs must be based on the active identification and followup of those considered vulnerable.* This requires a regular house-by-house or family-by-family assessment, usually made by public health workers operating through a referral system. In addition to encouraging those in need to participate in the SFP and ascertaining the reasons for nonparticipation, continued home-visiting is required to monitor the progress of infants and children. Those identified for the program should be registered and issued a numbered identity bracelet or card to facilitate followup. An SFP that does not actively identify those in need, but operates on an open "come-if-you-wish" basis, is unlikely to benefit those in greatest need and is a very poor use of food and organizational resources.

The criteria for admission to a targeted SFP will depend on the condition of displaced people and resources available. The SFP order of priority is:

1. Any malnourished child (less than 80 percent weight-for-height or a Z-Score of less than −2).

2. Women during the last 3 months of pregnancy and the first 12 months of lactation.

3. Medical referrals and the socially vulnerable.

Children should not be discharged from the SFP until they have maintained more than 85 percent weight-for-height for at least 1 month.

2. Exit Criteria

Once begun, SFPs must be considered necessary until an appropriate general ration is provided that meets the needs of the vulnerable and as long as living conditions remain hazardous. *SFPs should be phased out if surveillance results reflect sustained improvement and global malnutrition prevalence is less than 10 percent among children less than 5 years of age, the mortality rate is low, and there is no anticipated seasonal deterioration of the nutritional status (for example, a rainy season).* As children improve, they should be excluded from the program. Otherwise, the SFP becomes too large and unmanageable.

3. Supplementary Food Quantities

The typical daily supplementary ration is illustrated below along with the amount of food required for supplementary feeding of 1,000 beneficiaries over a month (approximately 3.6 metric tons).

Typical Daily Ration with Monthly Totals

Commodity	Amount (g)	Energy (kcal)*	Fat (g)	Protein (g)*	Metric Tons
Cereal (rice)	50	180	0	4	1.50
Vegetable oil	10	89	10	0	0.30
WSB**	55	204	3	11	1.65
Salt	5	0	0	0	0.15
Total	**120**	**473**	**13**	**15**	**3.60**

* Meets minimum levels of 350 kcal of energy and 15 grams of protein/person/day.
** Wheat-soya-blend.

4. Organization and Management of an SFP

Any SFP must be closely integrated with a community health care program, since the SFP will identify health problems. Certain daily medications (for example, iron, folate) may best be given in the course of the supplementary feeding.

Feeding centers and kitchens must be well organized and kept clean. Long waiting periods must be avoided and the schedule must not clash with family mealtimes or other essential community activities. Mothers may have to be fed with children to ensure that vulnerable children receive special feeding. Parents must be made to understand that the SFP is given in addition to the normal meal. Otherwise, parents will think that young children are fed at the center while older children must eat at home. Utensils, bowls, scales, fuel, water, storage facilities, and other equipment will be required. These can generally be obtained locally. Some of these supplies are available with an OXFAM Feeding Kit.

One SFP center can usually handle up to 500 beneficiaries. The centers should be run by trained displaced persons. An experienced nurse should be able to supervise four to five centers. If different organizations establish separate SFP centers, central coordination and standardized procedures for all centers are very important. Programs must avoid dependence on outside assistance to prevent their collapse when individuals or organizations leave.

E. Therapeutic Feeding Programs

Therapeutic feeding reduces deaths among infants and young children with severe **protein-energy malnutrition (PEM)**. *The forms of PEM (marasmus and kwashiorkor) are described in* Nutritional Diseases *in the* Health *section, later in this chapter.* The main causes of death in severe PEM are dehydration, infection, hypothermia, hypoglycemia, cardiac arrest, and severe anemia. If severe PEM exists, therapeutic feeding will be the most important way to save lives. However, if the startup of an SFP is delayed because resources, particularly trained personnel, are concentrated on a Temporary Feeding Program (TFP), there may be a sudden deterioration in other less-malnourished children. The lifesaving achievements of a TFP will be overtaken by the life-threatening consequences of not having an adequately functioning SFP benefiting more people.

Food is the treatment for PEM. Unlike SFPs, TFPs are used solely for curative measures and should be administered only as short-term programs. The need for its continuation will depend on the effectiveness of general and supplementary feeding programs as well as the nutritional conditions of new arrivals.

The usual criteria for admission to a TFP is if a child under the age of 5 years suffers from bilateral edema on the feet (kwashiorkor), or severe marasmus (weight-for-height less than 70 percent or a Z-Score of less than −3). If persons older than 5 years are to be admitted, nutritional status should be assessed clinically, since clear anthropometric criteria does not exist. Patients should remain on a TFP until they are free from illness, at least 80 percent of weight-for-height, and without edema. Only upon recovery should patients be discharged to the SFP.

Therapeutic feeding should take place on an inpatient basis whenever possible, as food must be given every 3 to 4 hours. Boiled water mixed with a dried skim milk/oil/ sugar mixture and appropriate mineral and vitamin additives can be used to initiate treatment. A mixed diet is introduced once the patient's condition starts to improve (usually after 4 to 5 days).

There are now three products produced as "ready to use" sachets for the treatment of severe malnutrition. A special oral rehydration solution for use for the malnourished; a formula for the severely malnourished during the first few days (phase one) of treatment called F75; and a formula for rapid growth (phase two) called F100. They are produced by Nutriset in France and by Compact in Denmark. These products not only include the appropriate protein and caloric mix for safely refeeding the severely malnourished but also include essential vitamins and minerals that are usually missing in feeding mixtures using dried skim milk.

Infection and dehydration are the major causes of death. Patients must be closely watched for medical complications. If weight does not increase quickly at a properly run TFP, it is likely that the individual also has an illness that must be treated. *The immunization of children against measles is a priority because of the high mortality associated with this disease in a malnourished population.* All children admitted to a TFP should be given a full course of vitamin A, with doses on days 1, 2, and 7 of admission.

TFPs must be run by experienced and qualified personnel. One center can usually handle about 50 children and will require two experienced supervisors working full-time. Doctors and nurses with little training in nutrition or experience in treating severe PEM must be given necessary guidance. Displaced people and mothers of patients, in particular, should be involved in running the therapeutic feeding center.

Treatment of severe PEM is divided into two phases, a 24-hour care unit (phase one) and a day-care unit (phase two). Ideally, the TFP begins with an intensive first phase where medical complications are treated and nutritional treatment begins; the patient is cared for on a 24-hour basis. The second phase includes continued feeding on a day-care basis in which the child will receive four to six meals a day. This situation is often unattainable because of security issues, staff resources, or overwhelming numbers of patients.

1. Phase One (24-Hour Care)

Phase one usually lasts up to 7 days. The objective of phase one is to restore metabolic functions and address medical complications. In phase one, there is feeding of 8 to 10 meals a day of **high-energy milk (HEM)** *with the addition of appropriate minerals and vitamins* (available in a packaged form called CMV) at 100 Kcal/kg body weight/day. Because severe PEM is almost always accompanied by diarrhea, oral rehydration should be started immediately. However, caution should be taken as children with severe marasmus and kwashiorkor have an electrolyte imbalance with an excess of sodium, therefore standard oral rehydration salts (ORS) should not be used, as they can provoke a heart attack. A physician should monitor children in phase one.

HEM is made of 80 grams/liter dried skim milk, 60 grams/liter vegetable oil, and 50 grams/liter sugar mixed in clean, boiled, and cooled water. This mixture gives approximately 100 kcal/100 ml solution. Although HEM is practical and very effective in most settings, its one limitation is that it does not contain sufficient potassium. It is important to add the CMV package.

2. Phase Two (Day Care)

In phase two, children should arrive at the TFP early in the morning and return home in the late afternoon. The objective of phase two is to gain weight and appetite as quickly as possible. The phase two diet should provide at least 200 Kcal and 5 grams of protein/kg body weight/day. For practical reasons, the rule of thumb is to provide a standard ration of 350 ml HEM per feeding. Porridge may be alternated with the HEM feeds. Children should be able to eat a family-type meal by the time they leave the feeding program.

F. Infant Feeding and Milk Products

Human milk is the best and safest food for infants and children under 2 years of age. Breast feeding also provides a secure and hygienic source of food, as well as antibodies that protect against some infectious diseases. *Therefore, every effort must be made to promote lactation, even among sick and malnourished mothers.* In some cases, mothers may need to receive extra food to encourage breast-feeding and provide the additional calories and nutrients required. This should be done through the SFP.

Problems associated with using infant formula and feeding bottles are exacerbated in a displaced population situation. Clean, boiled water is essential but rarely available to dilute the formula. Careful dilution of the formulas is also difficult to control as mothers are unlikely to be familiar with the use of infant formula and instructions are often in a foreign language. Infant formula, if unavoidable, should be distributed from health or feeding centers under strictly controlled conditions and proper supervision. *Infant feeding bottles must never be distributed or used*; they are almost impossible to sterilize and to keep sterile under such conditions. Babies should be fed by a clean cup and spoon if necessary.

Milk should not be distributed if it is not a traditional part of the displaced people's diet. Some populations may even have lactose (milk sugar) intolerance.

The use of dried milk powder also has major practical problems. Both hygiene and proper dilution are difficult to ensure. Also, powdered milk mixed with unsafe water or exposed to dust or flies can easily become contaminated and provide an ideal environment for bacterial growth. For these reasons *milk should not form part of the general ration*, unless milk was used as a normal source of protein for the displaced population.

In addition to infant formula, products commonly offered in emergencies include dried whole milk (DWM), dried skim milk (DSM), sweetened and unsweetened condensed milk, and evaporated milk. Their appropriateness must be ascertained before acceptance. *It should be noted that if the DSM is vitamin A fortified, the vitamin A has a shelf life of 6 months.*

Milk products are useful in SFPs and TFPs when administered under supervision and controlled and hygienic conditions. For example, milk can be added to SFP cereal mixtures to boost their protein content. Milk powder is the usual basis for early stages of treatment in therapeutic feeding.

G. Basic Facts about Food and Nutrition

1. Nutrients

Foods are made up of *five basic types of nutrients*: carbohydrates, fats, proteins, vitamins, and minerals. **Carbohydrates** are a source of energy and consist mostly of starches and sugars of vegetable origin, such as cereals and tubers. **Fats and oils** provide the most concentrated source of energy, having more than twice the energy content per weight of carbohydrates and proteins. In most poor countries, most energy is derived from staple foods, especially cereals, with fats accounting for a much smaller portion. *Table III–9 lists the approximate nutritional values of various commodities.* **Note however that several of the commodities listed on the table are not available through P.L. 480 Title II.** If more information is desired on these commodities, contact the

Table III–9. Approximate Nutritional Values of Commodities (per 100 grams edible portion)

Commodity	Energy (Kcal)	Protein (g)	Fat (g)
Cereals			
Wheat	330	12.3	1.5
Wheat flour	350	11.5	1.5
Bulgur wheat	350	11.0	1.5
Maize	350	10.0	4.0
Maize meal	360	9.0	3.5
Sorghum	335	11.0	3.0
Rice	360	7.0	0.5
Rolled oats	380	13.0	7.0
Blended Foods			
Instant corn-soya blend	365	12.2	4.0
Corn-soya blend	380	18.0	6.0
Wheat-soya blend	370	20.0	6.0
Soya-fortified bulgur wheat	350	17.0	1.5
Soya-fortified corn meal	360	13.0	1.5
Soya-fortified rolled oats	375	21.0	6.0
Soya-fortified wheat flour	360	16.0	1.3
Pulses			
Dried peas and beans	335	22.0	1.5
Ground nuts	330	15.0	25.0
Milk, Cheese, and Eggs			
Dried skim milk	360	36.0	1.0
Dried whole milk	500	26.0	27.0
Cheese	355	22.5	28.0
Dried eggs	575	45.5	43.5

Table III–9. Approximate Nutritional Values of Commodities (per 100 grams edible portion) (contd.)

Commodity	Energy (Kcal)	Protein (g)	Fat (g)
Meat and Fish			
Canned meat	220	21.0	15.0
Dried salted fish	270	47.0	7.5
Canned fish in oil	305	22.0	24.0
Fish protein concentrate	390	75.0	10.0
Oils and Fats			
Vegetable oil	885	0	100.0
Butter oil	860	0	98.0
Margarine	735	0	82.0
Edible fat	900	0	100.0
Fruits and Beverages			
Dried fruit	270	4.0	0.5
Dates	245	2.0	0.5
Jam	265	0	0
Tea	0	0	0
Coffee	0	0	0
Miscellaneous			
Sugar	400	0	0
Iodized salt	0	0	0
Pasta	365	12.5	1.2
Freeze-dried meat	480	65.0	25.0
Minestrone	500	22.5	27.0
Protein-enriched ration	450	16.7	15.5
Milk biscuits (whole milk)	470	23.4	10.4
Milk biscuits (skim milk)	375	24.0	1.5
High-energy protein biscuit	450	15.0	20.0

Office of Food for Peace. **Proteins** are bodybuilding substances required for growth and tissue repair. Protein is found in foods of animal origin, cereals, and legumes. **Vitamins and minerals** are needed in small quantities for the adequate functioning of the body. Individual vitamins and minerals or combinations are found in all foods in variable amounts.

2. Energy and Protein Intakes

If the energy intake is inadequate, some protein in the body will burn to provide energy instead of promoting body growth or repair. That is, it will be used in the same way as carbohydrates or fats. No less than 10 percent of the energy requirement should be supplied from fats and oils. They also greatly enhance the palatability of the diet and increase energy density, which is important for younger children. Energy requirements vary widely, even among normal individuals, and increase with physical activity. *Much higher intakes are required for the treatment of malnutrition,* when the aim is rehabilitation rather than maintenance.

3. Food and Diets

Diets in most countries contain adequate amounts of nutrients required for good health *if enough of the diet is taken to satisfy the individual's energy requirements.* Even a growing, healthy child requires no more than 10 percent of the calories to be supplied from protein sources.

Health

A. General

Health services provided to displaced people should be based on the concept of primary health care. This strategy strongly emphasizes preventive rather than curative care, because curative care places a much heavier burden on response resources. The majority of the population is generally more influenced by public health measures than by individual care.

The exception to the rule of emphasizing preventive care over curative care occurs in sudden onset disasters, such as earthquakes or civil strife, where there can be initially a significant need for trauma care within the population. Positions are identified within the DART and can be filled as needed to deal with trauma care situations.

The level of health care provided will be determined by the condition of the DPs and resources available. In theory, the peak of curative medical care should be during the early stage. This is when DPs are most vulnerable to their new environment and before it has been possible to complete any major public health improvements in the sectors of shelter, water supply, and sanitation. In practice, however, the medical staff often arrive later and begin to build up curative services at the same time the overall health status of the DPs is improving. The emphasis of health care, however, should be placed instead on preventive care. Once immediate health problems are controlled, the level of health care provided should be appropriate for the local population and at a level that can be maintained. Services and levels of care available to the displaced people should be standardized.

B. Initial Health Assessment, Mortality Rate, and Morbidity Rate

The aim of the initial health assessment is to identify mortality rates, morbidity rates, and health needs and to establish responses, recommendations, and priorities.

1. Health Assessment

Factors contributing to health or disease in the displaced population must be determined by establishing the pattern of disease, the effect of cultural and social influences on the population's health, and the effectiveness of any existing health services.

The key to an effective assessment and surveillance program is good information. Information can be collected by observation or from health workers. Sample surveys reveal symptoms and disease patterns and indicate distribution in the community. When possible, mass screening on arrival is the most effective method. Mass screening and can sometimes be conducted at a camp during the registration process.

The initial assessment should be done by field-experienced persons who have an understanding of epidemiology. If OFDA takes on this responsibility, it normally requests these services from the Centers for Disease Control in Atlanta.

A centrally coordinated surveillance system must be established quickly to identify problems in time for preventive action.

For example, the incidence of diarrheal diseases may be an important indicator of environmental problems.

Records on individuals and on the community as a whole serve important purposes. Individual record cards are used for recording immunizations and the treatment of illnesses. These cards should be kept by the displaced, and in the case of young children, by the mother. Experience shows that these cards are generally well-cared for by their owners.

Community reporting has a different purpose. It is an essential tool for the planning of services and monitoring of disease patterns. National health authorities may also require specified "notifiable" communicable diseases to be reported at once. To be fully effective, surveillance requires rapid access to laboratory services. Very simple lab services at the camp level are usually adequate.

2. Mortality Rate

The *mortality rate* (death rate) is the single most important indicator of serious stress (for example, illness, malnutrition) in a DP population. Knowing the causes of death is crucial because it helps set priorities for appropriate relief interventions. In addition, deaths are indicators/events of obvious interest and concern to the displaced population, relief administrators, and the media.

In displaced populations served by well-run relief efforts, overall *mortality rates should not exceed 1.5 times those of the host population*. An elevated mortality rate signals an ongoing problem and should prompt an immediate investigation of the situation. In general, even initially high mortality rates should fall to or below 1 per 10,000 per day within 4 to 6 weeks of beginning a basic support program that provides sufficient food and water, immunizations, simple health care, and other immediate needs. Rates above 1 per 10,000 after 4 to 6 weeks should be a cause for concern. *Mortality rates exceeding 2.0 per 10,000 population per day indicate a serious situation*. Immediate actions should be taken.

For comparison, in most developing countries, in nonemergency times, the average mortality rate for all ages is 0.5/10,000/day. In children less than 5 years old, the rate is between 1 and 2/10,000/day. So anything that doubles these rates is considered an emergency situation.

Because the number of deaths fluctuates from day to day, death rates should be calculated over an extended period, ranging from 1 week to 1 month. For example, take the number of deaths occurring each day over a 7-day period and average the total; the resulting average daily number is used in analyses. Surveys of death rates should be conducted on a regular basis. *Remember, in an emergency the critical task is to get the death rate down. It is also the measure by which the effort will be judged!*

Procedures for calculating mortality rates

$$\text{Mortality rate} = \frac{\text{No. of deaths} \times 10,000}{\text{No. of days} \times \text{population}} = \text{deaths/10,000/day}$$

Example: If 21 deaths have occurred over a 7-day period in a displaced population of 5,000 people, the death rate would be calculated as follows:

$$\text{Death Rate} = \frac{21 \times 10,000}{7 \times 5,000} = \frac{210,000}{35,000} = 6$$

which is expressed as 6.0 deaths per 10,000 per day.

3. Morbidity Rate

Morbidity rates measure the frequency of illness or morbidity within specific populations. Time and place must always be specified. The most commonly used morbidity rates include **prevalence** (point and period), **incidence,** and **attack rates.** Prevalence and incidence are covered in the following section. An attack rate is an incidence rate usually expressed as a percentage. It is used for particular populations and observed for limited periods of time, as in an epidemic.

C. Epidemiology and Disease

OFDA often calls upon U.S. Public Health Service epidemiologists to assess the health issues in complex disasters with large numbers of displaced persons. The following health information on epidemiology and disease is provided to give the Assessment Team or DART member a basic understanding of what the epidemiologist takes into account as he or she assesses the epidemiologic condition of a displaced population.

1. Epidemiology Concepts

Epidemiology is the study of the occurrence, distribution, and determinants of diseases and injuries in human populations. An epidemiologist is concerned with the types and frequencies of illnesses, injuries, and other health-related conditions or problems in groups of people and with the factors that influence their distribution. The overall goal of the epidemiologist is to discover the factors essential for diseases to occur within groups and then to find the best methods to reduce or prevent those factors and other conditions detrimental to the health of communities.

a. The Epidemiologic Triangle. The epidemiologic triangle consists of three components, with the **Host** at the top point and the **Agent** and the **Environment** at the other two points of an equilateral triangle. Each component must be analyzed and understood to comprehend and predict patterns of disease. Changes in any component will alter the existing equilibrium to increase or decrease the frequency of a disease. In a steady state of the triangle, each leg of the component is affecting and being affected by the other components. If a change occurs in any of the components sufficient to affect the steady state, changes will occur in one or both of the other components.

b. Epidemiologic Definitions

Agents. Specific living or inanimate objects that can cause health problems to hosts. Examples of living agents are microbes (bacteria, viruses) and certain plants (poison ivy, plants that are poisonous when eaten). Examples of inanimate agents are poisons, pesticides, and severe heat or cold.

Clinical Infection. The state in which the host has symptoms, feels ill, or dies. *Clinical infection* and *disease* are terms often used as synonyms.

Contamination. The state of things in the environment (like water, air, or food) when the agent is found to exist in a state capable of reproducing (for a living agent) or in a state capable of causing symptoms in hosts if they are exposed (for a toxin or poison).

Disease. This is the point at which an abnormal condition within the host impairs normal physiologic functioning.

Disease Cycles. Cycles are named for each specific condition under study. For example, there are diarrhea cycles, typhoid fever cycles, malaria cycles, etc. Each cycle is made up of specific factors in hosts and agents within a specific environment such that if all the factors are present, then diseases or conditions of poor health will occur. Notice that the definition of hosts and agents include some common terms. For example, animals can be hosts agents. However, for a specific disease cycle, animals must be defined either as hosts, agents, or part of the environment through which the agent is transmitted. Describing specific disease cycles can help epidemiologists solve problems related to the health and well-being of displaced populations. The disease cycle helps explain how people get ill and suggests ways to prevent illness in a specific population. It does not matter whether a disease cycle is constructed with animals as host or as agent, as long as the result of the study is a better understanding of how the health problem occurs and how it might be prevented.

Endemic. The disease or condition of ill health that is always present in about the same percent of the population (hosts). See *epidemic.*

Epidemic. This is a very general and somewhat vague expression that means a greater number of hosts have been found to be ill than one would expect to find during a period of time within a certain population. An epidemic is any unusual excess amount of disease or injuries within a population. This idea is most useful when contrasted with the term *endemic.*

These same terms, *epidemic* and *endemic,* are also used to classify agents as either endemic or epidemic. Whether an agent is classified as endemic or epidemic does not consider the seriousness of the condition to the hosts. Conditions can be epidemic in one population while they are endemic in another. An endemic illness can become epidemic under certain conditions where there is a change in the behavior or immunity of the host population. The reverse situation also occurs.

Environment. The physical surroundings of the hosts and agents such as altitude, climate, geography, dust, amount of sunlight, etc. Time can also be considered as an environmental factor, including season of the year or the time of day, week, or month that illnesses or deaths occur.

Hosts. Groups of living organisms (people, animals, and plants) that, under certain circumstances, may become unhealthy.

Incidence. The probability that healthy people will develop a disease during a specified period of time (that is, the number of new cases of a disease in a population over a period of time). Incidence measures the rapidity with which a disease occurs or the frequency of addition of new cases of a disease. These new cases of disease occur either through onset of the disease in current members of the population or by immigration into the population of persons already ill. The formula for determining incidence rates is:

Incidence rate =
$$\frac{\text{No. of new cases during a given period}}{\text{Population at risk during the same period}} \times 10^n$$

Prevalence. The number of people in a population who have a given disease at a given period of time.

The formula for determining prevalence rates is:

Prevalence rate =
$$\frac{\text{All new and preexisting cases during a given time period}}{\text{Population at risk during the same time period}} \times 10^n$$

Note: It is important to remember that the rates for both incidence and prevalence include a factor of 10 such as per 100 or per 1,000. (Rate is usually expressed per 1,000.) The value of n depends on the relative frequency of a given disease.

The major distinction between prevalence and incidence is that prevalence includes both *old* and *new* cases.

For prevalence and incidence to be useful in the evaluation of the effects of control programs, they must be precisely defined and the time periods clearly designated. Incidence is the preferred count for disease such as measles, mumps, rubella, and conditions such as poisonings.

Both incidence and prevalence counts are important for the control of malaria and tuberculosis. Prevalence counts are important for planning services for the treatment of disease.

Incubation Period. The time from first contact with an infectious agent until symptoms appear in the host. This is an important fact to consider when a group is ill. Epidemiologists often calculate the average incubation period for the group and then look back in time to see when exposure could have occurred.

Infection. This occurs only when a living agent causes any observed effect in a host. The concept of infection implies that the agent has invaded the host tissues and has reproduced to a point where tests or symptoms reveal its presence. Such agents are called pathogenic for the hosts.

Infectiousness or Communicability. The ability of the infected host to interact with the agent so that the agent is transmitted to another host and causes infection. By definition, the contaminated host-agent states are not infectious. However, contaminated articles in the environment can be infectious.

Latent Period. The time from first contact with nonliving agent until symptoms appear (cold, heat, irradiation, poisons, toxins, etc.).

2. Definitions of Environmental Characteristics

Environmental factors can influence the relative strength (resistance and immunity) of the host or the relative strength of the pathogenic organisms (pathogenicity and virulence) so that either the host or the pathogen is favored. When the pathogen benefits from environmental conditions, disease spread is more likely. Likewise, when conditions benefit the host, disease is less likely. Environmental conditions may include many things, such as overcrowded living conditions, presence or absence of pathogens, food supplies, and air quality.

Contamination. The state of things in the environment like food, water, or air, when the agent is found to exist in a state capable of reproducing (for a living agent) or in a state capable of causing symptoms in hosts if they are exposed (for a toxin or poison).

Fomite. An inanimate object that is contaminated with infectious agents.

Epizootic. An condition of outbreak of disease in animals. Environmental health specialists and epidemiologists watch carefully for epizootic conditions that may be transmitted to humans so they can take early action to prevent human disease. Examples include rabies in wildlife, encephalitis in birds or horses, and plague in rodents.

Pollution. The existence of certain abnormal amounts of toxic chemicals or dust within an environmental category such as air, water, food, or soil.

Reservoir. Living organisms or inanimate matter (such as soil) in which an infectious agent usually lives and multiplies. Reservoirs of infection consist of human beings, animals, and environmental sources.

Routes of Transmission. Some agents are transmitted through the environment or through society by many different ways. Others can be transmitted by only one method. Listed below are some ways to describe methods by which an agent can be passed to another host.

- **Direct person-to-person contact** with the skin or bodily fluids of a diseased person. Examples are dysentery, boils, and several airborne diseases (see below).

- **Fecal-oral transmission** is the usual route of transmission of **enteric diseases**. Enteric diseases are diseases that affect the gut and other abdominal organs such as the liver. Infectious agents present in stools of infected persons are transmitted to uninfected persons through contaminated food or water that is ingested by mouth. Examples are cholera, typhoid, dysentery, botulism, staphylococcal food poisoning, polio, hepatitis A and E, polio, and amebiasis.

- **Mucus-to-mucus** contact by kissing or sexual intercourse. Examples include sexually transmitted diseases (STDs), infectious mononucleosis, and hepatitis B.

- **Direct contact with the skin, flesh (raw or not thoroughly cooked), saliva, or other bodily fluids of domestic or wild animals.** Examples are rabies, plague, anthrax, tularemia, and trichinosis.

- **Indirectly through inanimate fomites (objects).** Examples are staphylococcal infection, streptococcal infection, colds, hospital-acquired wound infections through use of improperly sterilized items.

- **Indirectly through the air** (sneezes, tobacco smoke, coughs, dust). Examples are colds, influenza, measles, mumps, chicken pox, and pneumonia.

- **Blood contamination indirectly by arthropod vectors.** Examples are malaria, typhus, plague, African sleeping sickness, encephalitis, yellow fever, and dengue fever.

Vector. An arthropod or other invertebrate organism that conveys the agent from a person or an animal to another person or animal.

Vehicle of Transmission. The matter, usually inanimate, in which pathogenic agents are present and survive until there is physical contact (including ingestion) with susceptible persons (hosts). Bodily discharges including blood, pus, saliva, urine, and feces may contain such agents. Hands, eating utensils, toilet articles, water, air, sewage, clothing, or milk and other foods may be the vehicle of transmission.

3. Disease Cycle Intervention

The interaction of host, agent, and environment makes up the disease cycle. Although the agent must be present for a disease to occur, it alone is not a sufficient cause. The cycle must be completed for the disease to occur or conversely, the cycle must be broken to control the disease. Listed below are some intervention concepts used for disease control programs.

- **Surveillance programs** are designed to detect early cases of disease among hosts.

- **Monitoring programs** are like surveillance activities but are for hosts known to be infected with agents transmissible to others. The same term is used for routine testing of the environment for pollution.

- **Eradication programs** are aimed at the reservoir of infection for the purpose of completely removing the agent. Eradication programs, when applied to certain small niches in a controlled environment, are often successful. An example would be an effort to eradicate a reservoir of an agent in a community water supply.

- **Immunization programs** are directed toward the host to provide specific antibodies against agents. They are usually directed at those individuals at the highest risk from the agent.

- **Behavior modification programs** are aimed at changing the actions of the host that add to the level of risk of disease, allowing the host to enter environments where the agent is located. Health education is a method often tried in displaced persons camps.

D. Disease Control

The risks of communicable (infectious) diseases are increased by overcrowding, poor environmental conditions, and the often poor initial state of health of the population. The infectious organism, however, must first be present to spread. For example, if no one is carrying typhoid, it will not suddenly appear.

Measures to improve environmental health conditions are, therefore, very important. These measures include providing enough safe water and soap, properly disposing of excrement and garbage, controlling rodents and vectors, and educating the population on general public health issues.

1. Immunization

The **priority** *immunization required during the early weeks of an emergency is for young children against measles. This is a high priority even when resources are scarce.* The next priority immunization would be for meningitis if there is an epidemic. All other necessary immunizations (for example, diphtheria-tetanus-pertussis (DTP), polio, and BCG (tuberculosis)) should be given later, once facilities allow, and to the extent possible within the framework of the government's own expanded program of immunization (EPI).

In DP situations, rumors of epidemics in camps often are rampant. Rumors should be confirmed by responsible experts, and information disseminated to the displaced population.

Infections that cause much disease and death in DP camps are often aggravated by malnutrition. These infections cannot be effectively prevented by mass immunization programs, and the programs are labor-intensive and require controlled handling and careful supervision.

It should be remembered that vaccines *prevent* diseases; they do not cure them. Therefore, these diseases must be anticipated and detected early.

2. Common Diseases

The most common symptoms and diseases among displaced people are those normally to be expected in any community in a developing country: diarrhea, measles, nutritional deficiencies, respiratory infections, malaria, parasites, and anemia. However, crowded conditions among the displaced people are likely to increase the occurrence of these diseases, in particular diarrhea. Diarrhea, due to the new environment, overcrowding, and poor environmental services, usually poses the major threat to displaced people's health in the first weeks of living in a camp. It remains a major health risk should there be a sudden deterioration in some aspect of the communal services, such as contamination of the water supply.

The following provides information on diseases common to DP emergency situations. It includes information on the symptoms, transmission, and possible curative and/or preventive measures that can be introduced for these diseases.

An important point to note is that among the diseases listed, 80 to 90 percent of all deaths in displaced populations are caused by five killer conditions: malnutrition, measles, acute respiratory infections, diarrheal diseases, and malaria. Most of these diseases are caused by protozoa, bacteria, or viruses.

Protozoa are mainly single-celled organisms that are part of the animal kingdom. When they cause diseases in the body they are often referred to as parasites. Protozoa are responsible for diseases such as malaria, amebic dysentery, giardia, leshmaniasis, and trypanosomiasis.

Bacteria are considerably smaller than protozoa. Bacteria produce toxins in the system that kill the cells. They can stimulate the body's immune system to overwork itself by producing huge amounts of its own immune cells into the system, which will eventually overdose the body with its toxins. The immune system will then start to destroy the body's own cells and organs. The immune system can also generate so many cells in the blood vessels that the vessel's lining will rip. Plasma leaks out of the blood stream, causing blood pressure to drop, organs to fail, and shock to the system.

Antibiotics and penicillin are used to kill off bacteria in the body, but drug-resistant strains have evolved. These strains have the ability to make enzymes that destroy or are resistant to the effects of antibiotics.

A **virus** is the smallest of the three pathogens. Whereas protozoa and bacteria are both living organisms that are able to take in nutrition and reproduce asexually, viruses cannot live or reproduce on their own. Viruses only contain a shell of protein and some DNA and RNA genetic makeup materials. To reproduce, the virus invades a cell in a host and uses the cell to produce more of itself. The virus destroys the cells or takes over cell spaces and the nutrients needed for the cell's survival. Viruses such as AIDS take over and destroy the immune cells, leaving people defenseless against other diseases. Viruses are also responsible for diseases such as measles, yellow fever, hepatitis, and some cancers.

Viruses are the hardest of the three microbes to fight once an infection starts, because the drug that kills the virus can also harm the cells. There are small amounts of antiviral drugs to fight the infection. The best prevention against viruses is vaccination.

Acute Respiratory Infections (ARIs). Acute respiratory infections (ARIs) are caused by a variety of viruses and bacteria. They are marked by cough, fever, and shortness of breath. They may be mild or may progress rapidly to death, especially among malnourished children. ARIs are favored by cold rain, inadequate blankets and clothing, poor ventilation, and crowding. The best preventive strategy is to provide adequate space, shelter, clothing, blankets, and ventilation. For severe cases, the treatment consists of antibiotics.

Cholera. Cholera is an acute intestinal disease characterized by sudden onset of profuse, watery stools with occasional vomiting. In some cases, diarrhea can be so severe that it can lead to dehydration and even death. Many infected individuals, however, have mild diarrhea or even no symptoms at all. The recommended treatment is rehydration with appropriate electrolyte solutions, by mouth if possible.

Transmission occurs through ingestion of water contaminated with feces. To a lesser extent, food contaminated by water, soiled hands, and even flies can spread the disease. Person-to-person spread generally does not occur.

The incubation period for cholera is usually 2 to 3 days, but can be from a few hours to as long as 5 days.

Patients generally carry the cholera bacteria in their stools only while they are having diarrhea and for a few days after recovery. Although long-term carrier states have been described, the incidence is quite rare.

Both oral and injectable cholera vaccines are now available but they have not been tried in DP emergencies. The World Health Organization does not recommend cholera immunization during the emergency phase but it may be appropriate during the stable phase of a DP crisis.

If cholera is suspected, the following measures should be taken:

1. Report suspected cases to national public health authorities.

2. Confirm the diagnosis by culturing stool samples from suspected cases. Regional public health laboratories or a hospital lab in the capital city should be able to help confirm this diagnosis by testing the samples.

3. Check the hygiene loop to be sure water is safe and protected from sewage contamination (the source of the infection in most cases).

4. Remember: *The vaccine does not prevent the spread of the cholera organism!*

Dengue Fever (Breakbone Fever). Dengue fever/dengue hemorrhagic fever is a viral disease transmitted by urban *Aedes* mosquitoes. There are four infectious dengue viruses. Dengue viruses are found in most tropical countries.

Dengue fever is a flulike illness that is characterized by sudden onset, high fever for 3 to 5 days (rarely more than 7), severe headaches, joint and muscle pain, anorexia, gastrointestinal disturbances, and rash. The rash appears 3 to 4 days after the onset of fever. Dark-skinned races frequently have no visible rash. Recovery may be associated with prolonged fatigue and depression. Epidemics are explosive, but fatalities (with the exception of dengue hemorrhagic fever) are rare. There is no vaccine or specific treatment available; prevention of mosquito bites is important.

The mosquito that causes dengue fever is usually found in or near human habitations. There are two peaks of biting activity, in the morning for several hours after daybreak and in the later afternoon for several hours after dark. The mosquito may feed at any time during the day, and especially indoors, in shady areas, or when it is overcast. Larval habitats include artificial water containers such as discarded tires, barrels, buckets, flower vases/pots, cans, and cisterns.

Children usually have milder effects from the disease than adults. The incubation period is about 3 to 14 days, commonly 7 to 10 days.

The dengue disease is not directly transmitted from person to person. Patients are usually infectious for mosquitoes from the day before to the end of the fever period, an average of about 5 days. The mosquito becomes infective 8 to 12 days after the blood meal and remains so for life.

Diarrheal Diseases. Diarrheal diseases are one of the most common fatal childhood diseases worldwide. *Malnourished individuals are particularly prone to diarrhea. Complications among young children can result in dehydration and shock.* If untreated, diarrhea is frequently fatal in already malnourished children. Diarrhea is transmitted through contaminated food and water. There are several diseases that manifest themselves as diarrhea, for example, dysentery (viral, bacterial, and amebic) and giardia.

Antibiotics can shorten the duration of symptoms in some cases. Diarrheal diseases generally are self-limited and, if fluids and electrolytes (water, salt, bicarbonate, potassium, etc.) can be replaced by mouth, the illness will run its course and the patient will usually survive. There are still fatalities, even with rehydration, especially in cases of shigella dysentery. While packets containing the proper mixture of electrolytes (**oral rehydration salts** [ORS]) are available, homemade fluids containing the most important minerals can easily be produced (see "3" below).

If diarrhea other than cholera or typhoid is suspected to be a major problem, the following measures should be taken:

1. Confirm the prevalence of the problem by reviewing morbidity and mortality data. Additional information, such as the location of patients in the camp, the length of time in

the camp, and the source of family water supplies, can help pinpoint the source of infection.

2. Check the adequacy and purity of the water supply to determine if there is any actual or potential contamination of water supplies by human feces.

3. Stress the importance of **oral rehydration therapy.** If packets containing the proper mixture of electrolytes are not available, the most suitable fluid is a sugar-salt solution containing the following ingredients in 1 liter of water:
   - Sodium chloride (table salt)   3.5 g
   - Sodium bicarbonate (baking soda)   2.5 g
   - Potassium chloride   1.5 g
   - Glucose (sugar)   20.0 g

4. Remember: Intravenous fluids are rarely preferable to oral rehydration and are used only if the child cannot drink.

Diphtheria (D), Tetanus (T), Pertussis (P, also known as whooping cough)

Diphtheria is generally not a problem in tropical countries. It is usually characterized by a patch or patches of a grayish membrane in the throat.

Tetanus is a severe infection characterized by painful muscular contractions, especially of the jaw and neck muscles. In developing countries, this disease is almost always fatal.

Tetanus is transmitted through spores introduced into the body during injury, usually a puncture wound contaminated with soil or feces, but also through burns and trivial wounds. Neonatal (infant) tetanus continues to occur in large numbers in developing countries because of unsterile cutting of the umbilical cord or ritualistic covering of the cord stump with unsterile items (for example, cow dung). *Tetanus cannot be transmitted person-to-person.*

The incubation period for tetanus is about 10 days.

Whooping Cough **(pertussis)** is a bacterial disease common in children throughout the world. It begins with a runny nose and an irritating cough. The cough gradually becomes worse over 1 to 2 weeks and lasts for 1 to 2 months. Whooping cough can be a severe disease and fatal, especially in nonimmunized malnourished children less than 1 year of age.

Diphtheria and whooping cough are transmitted through the air from respiratory secretions of infected patients.

The incubation period for both can last from 7-10 days. The period of communicability is the first 3 weeks of illness.

DTP (diphtheria-tetanus-pertussis) vaccine is available and highly protective against these three diseases. The vaccine must be given in three separate injections at least 4 weeks apart. The vaccine can be given to children as young as 1 to 2 months. DTP vaccinations can be delayed until after the emergency phase of a DP operation. An essential part of a tetanus vaccination program is administering two doses of tetanus toxoid vaccine to women in their last 4 months of pregnancy (who should receive two doses 4 to 6 weeks apart).

There is a high incidence of minor reactions to the DTP vaccine, especially to the pertussis component. These reactions, which are generally of short duration and not serious, include fever, muscle aches, irritability, and aching at the site of injection.

Intestinal Parasites. Intestinal parasites are extremely common in developing countries. A majority of the population can be infected with one or more parasites, of which the most common are usually hookworm, *Ascaris,* giardia, and *Trichuris* (whipworm). Many of those infected will appear perfectly healthy; however, fever, anemia, abdominal pain, vomiting, and exacerbation of malnutrition can occur with heavy infestations. These parasites are usually transmitted when people walking barefoot step on soil contaminated by feces. Intestinal parasites are not spread from person to person.

Intestinal parasitic infections should assume a *very low priority* in the emergency phase of a DP operation. Because reinfestation after treatment is an indicator of poor sanitation, correction of sanitary deficiencies is likely to abate the parasite problem and other, more serious diseases.

Lassa Fever. Lassa fever is a severe, often fatal, hemorrhagic fever that occurs in rural areas of West Africa, and is caused by a virus transmitted from infected rodents to man. Treatment with the antiviral drug ribavirin may be lifesaving. There are no vaccines currently available.

Leprosy. Leprosy is a chronic infectious disease characterized by progressive deterioration of the skin and occasionally other tissues. Despite adequate treatment that is now available, leprosy still carries serious social stigma in many cultures. Leprosy primarily occurs in tropical regions and in the lowest socioeconomic groups. The incubation period for leprosy is 1 to 20 years, but 90 to 95 percent of those "infected" never develop any manifestations of the disease.

In most DP camps in developing countries, a few cases of leprosy may be encountered. Identified cases should be treated. However, since leprosy is *a chronic disease and is not very contagious*, low priority should be given to identifying new cases and establishing a control program, especially in the early phases of an emergency. But because of the social stigma attached to the disease, efforts may be needed to calm the fears of other displaced people and workers in the camp.

Malaria. During the last decade, malaria has had an upsurge in many developing countries. This is due to the decreased number of mosquito control programs and an increased resistance of the malaria parasite to the usual treatment. There are four types of malaria, but *vivax* and *falciparum* are the most common. Vivax is generally not a life-threatening disease, but falciparum can be rapidly fatal and requires prompt treatment. The usual symptoms of malaria are fever, chills, headache, and sweats that can progress to kidney and liver failure, shock, and even coma. In an area known to have falciparum malaria, fever, delirium, disorientation, or coma should be assumed to be malaria and treated promptly.

Those who have already been exposed to malaria have some immunity to the disease and may either remain without symptoms or have a mild attack if reexposed to malaria. The major threat to health arises in nonimmune populations who may be forced to flee from a setting where malaria is not a problem (especially urban areas) to jungles, swamps, or other areas where malaria transmission is occurring and where they can contract the disease.

Measles. Measles is a highly contagious viral infection characterized initially by fever, cough, running nose, and red eyes. This is followed in 3 to 7 days by a dusty red, blotchy rash that begins on the face and then extends over the rest of the body and lasts for 4 to 6 days. *Measles is a disease that can result in very high mortality, especially in an undernourished population.*

Measles outbreaks are highly contagious and are common causes of death, especially among children. Outbreaks are due to low immunization coverage, malnutrition, and vitamin A deficiency. Measles can lead to weak immune systems, which may make patients susceptible to xerophthalmia, blindness, and premature death.

Measles is spread by airborne contact with nasal or throat secretions or by contact with articles freshly soiled with secretions from the nose and throat. The incubation period is about 10 days from exposure to disease to onset of first symptom.

The infected individual can infect others from the first appearance of symptoms until 4 days after the appearance of a rash. However, once a person has had measles, he or she will develop a lifelong immunity and cannot again be a carrier.

The measles vaccine should ideally be given as soon as the DPs can be assisted, that is, before an outbreak occurs or during emergency phases of a DP crisis, defined as a crude mortality rate higher than 1/10,000/day. If significant malnutrition is present, it is absolutely essential to implement a measles vaccination program as soon as possible.

Generally only one injection is necessary, but if a child receives a dose between 6 to 9 months, he or she should receive a second dose as soon as possible after reaching 9 months of age. The vaccine should be administered to all children between 6 months and 5 years of age. If vaccine supplies are limited, the top priority is to vaccinate *all malnourished and hospitalized children.* The next priority is to vaccinate 6-month to 2-year-old children, regardless of nutritional status. If vaccine supplies are ample, all children to age 12 should be vaccinated. The age limit may be extended to 14-year-old children, depending on the prevalence of measles in the area. The vaccine should not be given to pregnant women, persons with high fevers, or those with severe egg allergies.

Because measles is such a highly contagious disease, by the time several cases have been reported, it is likely that most susceptible individuals have been exposed and are incubating the disease. Measles immunization programs should not be stopped or postponed because of the presence of measles in the camp or settlement. On the contrary, immunization efforts should be accelerated. Among persons who have already been exposed to the measles virus, measles vaccine may provide some protection or modify the clinical severity of the disease if administered within 3 days of exposure.

About 5 to 15 percent of those receiving measles vaccines will develop a temperature greater than 39.4° C (103° F), generally between the 5th and 12th day after vaccination. The fever usually lasts 1 to 2 days. Transient rashes have also been reported in approximately 5 percent of vaccine recipients.

Initial emergency efforts to control the spread of measles consist of vaccination, and an EPI plan should be implemented as an ongoing, long-term health program. Measles immunization should start as soon as the necessary personnel, vaccines, cold-chain equipment, and other supplies are available. It cannot be delayed until measles cases have been reported or other vaccines become available.

Isolation of patients with measles is not necessary during an emergency camp setting. Measles vaccination can somewhat protect or change the severity of the disease if administered within 3 days of exposure to the measles. Measles vaccination programs should continue after the disease has calmed or settled. In fact, the immunization effort should increase.

Responsibilities for each aspect of the immunization program need to be explicitly assigned to agencies and persons by the coordination agency. The national EPI should be involved from the outset of the emergency. National guidelines regarding immunization should be applied in DP settings. A preimmunization count should be conducted to estimate the number of children eligible for vaccination. This should not be allowed, however, to delay the start of the vaccination program. In large, dense DP camps, large outbreaks can occur even if the vaccine coverage rate exceeds 80 percent.

Children exposed to measles should have their nutritional status monitored and be enrolled in a feeding program. Children with measles complications should be administered standard treatment, for example, ORT for diarrhea and antibiotics for acute low respiratory infection (ALRI). If they have not received vitamin A during the previous month, all children with clinical measles should receive 200,000 international units (IU) of vitamin A orally. Children less than 12 months should receive 100,000 IU. This should be repeated every 3 months as part of the routine vitamin A supplementation schedule.

Meningitis. Meningitis is characterized by fever, stiff neck, and headaches. If left untreated, it can progress rapidly to confusion, delirium, coma, and death. Meningitis can be caused by bacteria, viruses, and parasites, including malaria.

Some types of meningitis are contagious, especially those due to certain bacteria (*meningococcus* and *hemophilus*). The level of contagion is low, but occasionally *meningococcus* can occur in outbreaks and become a serious cause of morbidity and mortality. Finding the specific cause of meningitis is often very important because with meningococcal meningitis it may be appropriate to vaccinate, or perhaps treat, high-risk groups with an antibiotic.

Meningococcal Disease. Meningococcal disease (bacterial meningitis) is a bacterial infection in the lining of the brain or spinal cord. Early symptoms are headache, stiff neck, rash, and fever. The bacteria are transmitted through respiratory droplets when an infected person sneezes or coughs on someone. There is a seasonal risk of meningococcal disease in parts of West Africa, primarily during the dry season from December through June.

Nutritional Diseases

Protein-Energy Malnutrition (PEM). Protein-energy malnutrition (PEM) can refer to either acute or chronic malnutrition. Because children between 6 months and 5 years of age (especially at the time of weaning) are among the most acutely affected by malnutrition, assessment of this age group by physical measurement is usually done to determine PEM prevalence in a population. In general, acute malnutrition results in wasting and is assessed by an index of weight-for-height (WFH); however, edema of the extremities may also be associated with acute malnutrition, in which case a clinical assessment is necessary. Chronic malnutrition produces stunting and typically results in a diminished height-for-age index.

The prevalence of moderate to severe acute malnutrition in a random sample of children less than 5 years of age is generally a reliable indicator of this condition on population. Because weight is more sensitive to sudden changes in food availability than height, nutritional assessments during emergencies focus on measuring WFH. Also, WFH is a more appropriate measurement foregoing monitoring of the effectiveness of feeding programs. As a screening measurement, the mid-upper-arm-circumference (MUAC) method may also be used to assess acute malnutrition. The *Food and Nutrition* section of this chapter contains information on how children under 5 are measured for PEM.

PEM is a problem in many developing countries, even under normal conditions. Severe PEM is usually precipitated by low food intake associated with infection. Displaced people are particularly vulnerable to PEM. *PEM has three forms, which are described below:*

- **Nutritional marasmus** is the most frequent form of PEM in cases of prolonged food shortage. The main sign is a severe wasting away of fat and muscle that have been expended to provide energy. Affected children become very thin, may have an "old man or old woman" face, and loose folds of skin. However, they may appear relatively active and alert. Marasmus can be confused with dehydration; very often children suffer both. Dehydrated children appear more sick, have a very rapid pulse, usually have a fever, and are usually very thirsty.

- **Kwashiorkor** is seen most commonly in areas where the staple food is mainly carbohydrate, such as tubers and roots like cassava. It is precipitated, however, by many factors other than protein deficiency. The main sign of kwashiorkor is edema, a swelling that usually starts at the lower extremities and extends in more advanced cases to the arms and face. Edema must be present for the diagnosis of kwashiorkor, but edema can also occur in other diseases. Where there is gross edema, the child may look "fat" and be regarded by the parents as well-fed. To check for edema, press the area on the back of the foot and see if the dent remains after you remove your finger (often called pitting edema). Associated signs of kwashiorkor, which do not always occur, include hair changes (color becomes lighter, curly hair becomes straight, hair comes out easily with a gentle pull) and skin changes (dark skin may become lighter in places, skin may peel off, especially on the legs, and ulcerations may occur). Children with kwashiorkor are usually apathetic, miserable, and withdrawn, and often refuse to eat. Profound anemia is a common complication of kwashiorkor.

- **Marasmic kwashiorkor** is a mixed form of PEM, with edema occurring in children who are marasmic, and who may or may not have other associated signs of kwashiorkor. Mixed forms will often be seen.

Micronutrient Deficiency Diseases. In addition to PEM, micronutrient deficiencies play a key role in nutrition-related morbidity and mortality. Following are common micronutrient deficiencies.

- **Vitamin A Deficiency (VAD).** The most common deficiency syndrome in displaced populations is caused by a lack of vitamin A. Vitamin A deficiency is also known as xerophthalmia. It can cause night blindness in early stages and permanent eye damage and blindness in later stages. Famine-affected and displaced populations often have low levels of dietary vitamin A intake before experiencing famine or displacement, and therefore may have very low vitamin A reserves. Furthermore, the typical rations provided in large-scale relief efforts lack vitamin A, putting these populations at high risk. In addition, some diarrheal diseases rapidly deplete vitamin A stores. Depleted vitamin A stores need to be adequately replenished during recovery from these diseases to prevent the disease from becoming worse. Vitamin A is stored in the liver, and after initial treatment, supplemental doses can be as much as 3 months apart.

- **Vitamin C Deficiency (Scurvy).** Although scurvy rarely occurs in stable populations in developing countries, many outbreaks have occurred in displaced and famine-affected populations, primarily because of inadequate vitamin C in rations. Scurvy is marked by spongy gums, loosening of the teeth, and a bleeding into the skin and mucous membranes. Fortification of foods with vitamin C is problematic because vitamin C is unstable and cannot be stored in the body. The best solution is to provide a variety of fresh foods either by including them in the general ration or by promoting access to local markets. In addition, local cultivation of vitamin C-containing foods should be encouraged. Patients with clinical scurvy should be treated with 250 mg of oral vitamin C two times a week for 3 weeks.

- **Niacin Deficiency (Pellagra).** Pellagra is caused by a severe deficiency of biologically available niacin in the diet. It is endemic where people eat a maize-based diet with little protein-rich food. It is marked by dermatitis, gastrointestinal disorders, and central nervous system problems. Treatment of maize flour with lime (which converts niacin into a biologically available form of niacin) and the inclusion of beans, peanuts (ground nuts), or fortified cereals in daily rations increases the total intake of available niacin and will prevent the development of pellagra.

- **Anemia.** Anemia is caused by a lack of hemoglobin and indicates a lack of iron in the diet. Diets that are lacking in vitamin C or are high in fiber reduce iron absorption. It is marked by a lack of energy. Severe anemia in a displaced population can be a major cause of mortality for young children and pregnant women. Treatment for anemia includes a daily administration of iron/foliate tablets and vitamin C. Supplementary feeding of high-risk groups with corn-soya-milk (CSM) will also help reduce the likelihood of anemia (CSM contains 18 g iron per 100 g).

- **Thiamine Deficiency (Beriberi).** Beriberi is caused by an inability to assimilate thiamine. It occurs where people have to exist on a starchy staple food such as cassava or polished white rice. It is marked by inflammatory or degenerative changes of the nerves, digestive system, and heart. Sources of thiamine include dried peas and beans and whole-grain cereals. One major problem is that thiamine is destroyed during cooking.

Polio. Polio is an acute viral infection characterized by fever, malaise, headache, nausea, vomiting, and stiffness of neck and back, with or without paralysis. Polio can range in severity from an apparent infection without any symptoms or meningitis, to paralytic disease and even death due to paralysis of the muscles or respiration. The incidence of an apparent infection or "minor" illness usually exceeds that of paralytic cases by more than a hundred fold.

The paralysis of polio is typically asymmetrical (that is, involving only one leg or one arm). In DP situations, the diagnosis is generally made on symptoms alone, since laboratory diagnosis involves the difficult task of isolating the virus from feces or saliva.

Polio is spread by close contact with infected individuals, but rarely by food or water. In developing countries, older children and adults are usually immune to polio, having had contact with the virus during childhood.

The incubation period for polio is from 3 to 21 days, but commonly 7 to 12 days.

The polio virus persists in the throat for about 1 week, and in the feces for 3 to 6 weeks or longer. Cases are most infectious for 1 week before and after onset of symptoms. One should assume that fever followed by asymmetric (one-sided) paralysis is polio. Even a few cases of paralytic polio indicate an epidemic and should be treated by a mass childhood vaccination campaign with oral polio vaccine. Oral polio vaccine is safe, inexpensive, has few side effects, and is easy to administer. Inactivated polio vaccine is available in injection form, but the easiest and most effective way to administer the vaccine is orally.

Shigellosis (Bacillary Dysentery). Shigellosis is an acute bacterial disease characterized by diarrhea accompanied by fever, nausea, and sometimes toxemia, vomiting, and cramps. In typical cases the stools contain blood, mucus, and pus (dysentery). About one-third of the cases present with a watery diarrhea. Convulsions may be an important complication in young children. Mild and asymptomatic infections occur. Illness can last several days to weeks, with an average of 4 to 7 days. The severity of morbidity and mortality rate are functions of the age and state of health of the victims.

Diagnosis is made by isolation of *Shigella* from feces or rectal swabs. Infection is usually associated with the presence of pus cells in the stool.

Worldwide, two-thirds of shigellosis cases, and most of the deaths, are in children under 10 years of age. Illness in infants under 6 months is unusual. Outbreaks commonly occur under conditions of crowding and where personal hygiene is poor. Shigellosis is endemic in both tropical and temperate climates. The only significant reservoir/host is man.

Transmission is by direct of indirect fecal-oral transmission from a patient or carrier. Infection may occur after the ingestion of *very few* (10 to 100) organisms. Water transmission may occur as the result of direct contamination. Flies may transfer organisms into a nonrefrigerated food item, in which they can multiply to an infectious dose.

The incubation period is 12 hours to 1 week.

The communicability period occurs during acute infection and until the infectious agent is no longer present in feces, usually within 4 weeks after illness. Asymptomatic carriers may transmit infections. Appropriate treatment usually reduces the duration of the illness to less than 1 week.

There are no commercial vaccines available to prevent shigellosis.

There is a potential disaster implication if personal hygiene and environmental sanitation are deficient.

Skin Infections. Scabies is a common displaced person skin infection, especially for those living in crowded conditions with inadequate water supplies for washing. Scabies is caused by a mite and is characterized by intense itching and small sores caused by the mite burrowing under the skin.

Impetigo (streptococcal infection of the skin) is another contagious skin infection common in displaced people.

Skin infections are generally a low priority in the emergency phase of the relief operation, but these infections may be an indication of deficiencies in the supply of soap and water and of overcrowding. **If soap does become available, the recommended amount is 200 gm/person/month.**

Tetanus (see *Diphtheria*)

Tuberculosis (TB). Tuberculosis (TB) is usually not an illness that needs to be considered in the first few weeks of a displaced person emergency. The disease can take years to develop after original exposure. It is a chronic, progressively debilitating disease most commonly involving the lungs that is characterized by fever, cough with sputum (phlegm) production, and weight loss. TB is usually not a rapid fatal disease except in very young children who can die rapidly of disseminated TB or TB meningitis. Various treatment regimens have been developed, but even the shortest regimen requires 6 months of continuous treatment. Although TB may not be a first priority in an emergency, it should not be forgotten. Crowded camps housing debilitated displaced people provide a fertile ground for transmission of the disease. Two arguments are often raised to justify not instituting a TB control program:

- TB requires prolonged treatment that is unlikely to be completed in an emergency displaced person situation.

- Inadequate short-term treatment may cause the development of resistant TB strains.

These are not always valid arguments in DP situations for the following reasons:

- Ill individuals have difficulty traveling and are unlikely to leave a safe haven where food and water are available. In addition, secure camps tend to remain in existence for more than 6 to 9 months; that is, displaced person situations tend to exist much longer than desired or anticipated).

- Short-term treatment with adequate TB combination therapy regimens is unlikely to develop resistance and may actually prevent the spread of TB in a crowded camp.

Typhoid. Typhoid is characterized by fever, headache, malaise, and occasionally a mild rash on the trunk. Constipation occurs more commonly than diarrhea.

Typhoid is spread by food or water that has been contaminated by feces or urine from a patient or carrier of the disease. Flies can also transmit the disease.

The incubation period is 1 to 3 weeks.

Usually the typhoid bacteria are excreted in the stool while the patient is sick. About 70 percent of patients will excrete bacteria for 3 months, and 2 to 5 percent will become permanent carriers.

As with cholera vaccine, typhoid immunization is not recommended in displaced person situations or following natural disasters. The vaccine requires two shots 1 month apart to be effective. The vaccine is associated with a high incidence of side effects such as 1 to 2 days of localized pain around the injection site, fever, malaise, and headache.

In an outbreak situation, vaccination programs can be harmful because they divert scarce resources and attention that should be directed at ensuring safe food and water supplies.

Typhus Fever. Several distinct rickettsiae (a parasite carried by ticks, fleas, and lice) cause a disease known as typhus in humans. All cause disease with similarities of fever, headache, and rash. Treatment of all forms of typhus consists of similar antibiotics. Antibiotics result in rapid resolution of fever, and relapses are infrequent. **Murine typhus** is relatively common throughout the world and is transmitted by fleas. The highest incidence of cases occurs during the summer months when rats and their fleas are most active and abundant. **Epidemic typhus** is rare except during periods when municipal services are disrupted, such as during wars or natural disasters. Epidemic typhus is passed from human to human by the body louse. Incidents of epidemic typhus occur during the winter months when laundering of louse-infested clothing is absent and person-to-person spread of lice is common. Epidemic typhus exists in highland populations in Africa and South America. **Scrub typhus** is a common cause of fever among susceptible persons who engage in occupational or recreational behavior that brings them in contact with larval-mite-infested scrub brush habitats. Incidence is highest during the spring and summer when the activity of humans brings them in contact with mites seeking animals hosts. The disease is limited to Pacific islands and southeast and east Asia. **Tick typhus** is actually a form of **Spotted fever** in Africa and the Indian subcontinent. Prompt removal of attached ticks and use of repellents to prevent tick attachment provide the best prevention against disease.

Whooping Cough (see *Diphtheria*)

Yellow Fever. Yellow fever is a mosquito-borne viral disease that occurs only in parts of Africa and South America. Illness varies in severity from a flulike syndrome to severe hepatitis and hemorrhagic fever. Yellow fever is preventable by a safe and effective vaccine. In addition, vaccination precautions against exposure to mosquitoes when traveling in areas with yellow fever transmission should be taken.

Doses of yellow fever vaccine are listed below:

Dose	Dose volume	Comments
Primary: 1	0.5 mL	> 9 months of age
Booster	0.5 mL	1 dose every 10 years

D. Displaced Person Health Care

Displaced person health care must include preventive and curative measures. Although the amount of curative measures needed will vary with each emergency, it is often dependent on the amount and quality of preventive care that is achieved.

Particularly where several organizations are involved, close attention must be paid to ensure a common standard of appropriate health care. *Standardized treatment schedules are essential.* In situations where qualified personnel are scarce and a confirmed diagnosis is not possible, standard treatment should be given for presenting symptoms. Unless treatment is administered immediately, clear oral and written guidance on the dosage and schedule must be given to each patient in his or her native language. In addition, organizations should work together to ensure a fair distribution of available services at all displaced person camps.

Treatment inappropriate to both the needs of the people and their circumstances may be not only useless and wasteful, but can also have a negative effect on the displaced people's attitude toward health care and preventive measures in general.

1. The Provision of Health Care

Displaced people must be given responsibility for their own health. Outside health workers must understand the population's own concepts of health and disease. Services should be operated *with, rather than for*, the displaced people. If not, health care services will be less effective, may be distrusted by the population, and are likely to collapse when key outside personnel leave.

Strong emphasis should be placed on the training and upgrading of the medical skills of selected displaced people, particularly in their former roles within the community (for example, traditional healers and midwives). Even a displaced person with no prior experience can be a very effective health worker following basic on-the-spot instructions in a few relevant tasks.

As a general principle, the order of preference for selecting health personnel in cooperation with the national services is displaced people first, experienced nationals or residents next, and, finally, outsiders. Most emergencies will require some combination of these sources. *An important consideration may be the government's attitude toward foreign medical personnel*, including the recognition of qualifications and authority to practice medicine.

In a major emergency, a health coordinator may be assigned responsibility for planning and developing appropriate health care programs, establishing standards, monitoring the quality of services, and ensuring proper liaison and coordination among the health ministry and other international organizations on health matters.

DPs must have easy access to appropriate treatment. Unless treatment is provided at the right level, hospitals or major health centers will be swamped by DPs demanding treatment for simple conditions. What is required, therefore, is a community-based health service that identifies those in need of health care and provides it at the appropriate level.

The first level of health care for DPs is the community health worker, who is responsible for a section of the population and works among them to provide outreach services such as home visits, case finding, and followup. He or she is also responsible for basic communitywide preventive measures, including public health education. The community health worker should be a DP with appropriate training who can identify health and nutritional problems and refer patients to a clinic if simple on-the-spot treatment is not possible. While DPs may go to clinics without referral, it is important to remember that not all those who are most in need will go to a clinic. The diseases of those who do, therefore, may not reflect the most common problems in the community.

As a general rule, one clinic should be established for every 5,000 DPs . The clinic should be staffed by one nurse and 2 to 3 displaced people or national health workers. The clinic should provide both preventative and curative services and supervise community health workers' outreach services. Water and sanitation are essential services at all health facilities.

The next level would be a *health center for each displaced person settlement with limited beds for overnight stays at a ratio of approximately one bed per 5,000 displaced people.* The health center should be staffed by 2 doctors and 8 to 10 nurses per 20,000 displaced people. One doctor should work in the center, and the other should cover clinic-level activities. Health centers are responsible for supervising settlement health services, including training health workers and implementing selective feeding programs, treating/referring cases not handled at the clinic level, providing reproductive health services, and controlling, distributing, and administering drugs.

There may also be a regional/district hospital with a staff assisted by one doctor and two nurses from the emergency organization that handles complicated maternity cases and surgical emergencies on referral from the settlement.

If possible, special hospitals for DPs should be avoided. Special hospitals are skilled-labor-intensive, provide only curative services, rarely continue to be properly run once outside support is withdrawn, and are inappropriate for long-term needs. Once established, they are extremely difficult to close. Such hospitals, therefore, should only be provided if a clear and continuing need exists that cannot be met by existing or strengthened national hospitals. If the need for such a special hospital exists, the number of beds required would depend on the condition of the population. For example, one bed might be required per 2,000 DPs in the early stages of an emergency, requiring 2 doctors and 6 nurses plus auxiliary support. Temporary hospitals constructed with local materials may be appropriate for cholera treatment.

"Portable field hospitals" have several disadvantages, including the complicated logistics of transporting and setup, cost, and inappropriate systems and equipment that are overly sensitive and dependent on outside power. Field hospitals are rarely satisfactory for meeting continuing needs. Unfortunately, donors sometimes encourage such hospitals, even when unsuitable, because of their great public relations value.

2. Medical Supplies

Emergency medical supplies should draw on in-country resources to the greatest extent possible. Special arrangements may be necessary, however, to respond to initial needs for adequate quantities of basic drugs and strict control of unsolicited donations.

a. WHO Emergency Health Kit. The World Health Organization has a standard list of essential drugs and medical supplies for use in an emergency. They are included in the **New Emergency Health Kit,** which has been accepted by many organizations and national authorities as a reliable, standardized, inexpensive, and quickly available source of essential drugs and health equipment urgently needed in an emergency situation. **Its contents are calculated to meet the needs of a population of 10,000 persons for 3 months.**

The kit consists of two different units of drugs and medical supplies: the **Basic Unit** (10 per kit) and the **Supplementary Unit** (1 per kit).

To allow for distribution to smaller health facilities on site, the quantities of drugs and medical supplies in the Basic Unit has been divided into 10 identical Basic Units for 1,000 persons each. The 10 Basic Units contain drugs, medical supplies, and some simple equipment for use by basic health care workers with limited training. **Each Basic Unit is weighs 45 kg and occupies 0.2m³.** It contains 12 drugs, none of which are injectable. Simple guidelines have been developed to help the training of personnel in the proper use of the drugs.

The Supplementary Unit is designed for a population of 10,000 for 3 months and is to be used only by professional health workers or physicians. It contains drugs, essential infusions, supplies, and equipment. It does not contain any drugs or supplies from the Basic Units and therefore to be operational, the Supplementary Unit should be used together with the 10 Basic Units. **The Supplementary Unit weighs 410 kg and occupies 2m³.**

The total New Emergency Health Kit including the 10 Basic Units and the one Supplementary Unit weighs about 860 kg and occupies 4m³. An entire kit can be strapped into the back of a pickup. It should be noted that these kits are designed to meet only initial needs pending the establishment of a regular system for medical supplies.

Medical supplies can also be ordered through the *UNICEF supply warehouse* in Copenhagen that has a stockpile of prepackaged drugs and supplies. These supplies must be ordered through OFDA/W, not directly from the field.

b. Vaccines. Vaccines should be borrowed from local stocks if available. If vaccines are to be provided from overseas supplies, special considerations must be taken. Most vaccines require refrigeration and careful handling to remain effective. *Without a "**cold chain**" (the refrigerated transportation system for vaccines from manufacturer to individual), the immunization program will be ineffective.* Time and temperature-control cards should be posted on cold storage facilities. Temperatures should be checked twice daily and noted on cards accompanying the vaccine. Storage facilities located at the central (capital city) and regional level should have temperature alarms and backup (emergency) generators. Vaccines should be stored on central shelves and *not in refrigerator doors*. Take into account also the time needed to clear customs.

c. Donations of Unsolicited Drugs. Donations of unsolicited drugs may present a problem, as their quantity and quality may vary greatly. Unsolicited drug donations may consist of small quantities of mixed drugs, free samples, expired medicines, inappropriate vaccines, and drugs identified only by brand names or in a foreign language.

3. Health Education

The importance of health education is widely accepted. It is a difficult task, however, and one that outsiders may not understand, to convince and persuade at-risk populations to change long-established habits that increase their health risks. *During the emergency phase, priority topics of any health education program should be directly related to immediate public health problems, such as the disposal of human excreta and refuse.* Trained teachers from the population and respected elders are likely to be more effective than outsiders in communicating basic principles and practices of health to their own people.

Displaced Person Camps:
Site Selection, Planning, and Shelter

A. General

Although circumstances may make displaced person camps unavoidable, the establishment of displaced person camps must be a last resort, because of the attendant problems of camps discussed throughout this chapter. The location of a displaced person camp may range from a spontaneous settlement over a wide area, to an organized rural settlement, to a concentration in a very limited area. A solution that maintains and fosters self-reliance among the displaced is always preferable.

If no prospects are in sight for a resolution to the displacement, planning for the displaced population's needs should assume a long-term outlook. Temporary arrangements can be very difficult to change once established. Site selection, planning, and the provision of shelter have a direct bearing on the provision of other assistance. They are important considerations in the overall assessment of needs and the planning of emergency response.

Decisions must be made as part of an integrated approach taking into account advice from experts, and views of displaced people.

Expertise may be required in the fields of geology, settlement, planning, engineering, and public health. Familiarity with local conditions in both the displaced population's area of origin and the present location of the displaced is important, as is previous experience in similar emergency situations.

There may be a need to set up a reception or transit center through which displaced people pass on the way to a longer term settlement site. These centers must have the same considerations as those relevant to long-term settlements.

B. Criteria for Site Selection

1. Social Needs

If possible, the social and cultural backgrounds of the displaced should be considered when determining a camp location. However, in most circumstances the choice will be limited, and any land that meets even minimum standards may be scarce. Once a site is located, it is wise to determine why the site was not already in use and examine whether the reason (for example, no water or because it floods in the monsoon period) would exclude use by displaced people.

2. Water

The single most important site-selection criterion is the availability of an adequate amount of water on a year-round basis. It is also commonly the most problematic. A site should not be selected on the *assumption* that water can be acquired merely by drilling, digging, or hauling. Drilling may not be feasible and may not provide adequate water. No site should be selected where the hauling of water will be required over a long period. Professional assessment of water availability should be a prerequisite in selecting a site.

Where water is readily available, drainage often becomes the key criterion. For effective drainage therefore, the entire site should be located above flood level at a minimum of 3 m above the water table, preferably on a gently sloping area. Flat sites can present serious problems for the drainage of waste and storm water. Marshes or areas likely to become marshy or soggy during the rainy season should be avoided. The watershed of the area may be a consideration.

3. Open Space

The site must provide a sufficient amount of usable space for the displaced population. *WHO recommends a minimum of 30 m² per person, plus the necessary land for communal and agricultural activities and livestock.* Of this, 3.5 m² is the absolute minimum floor space per person in an emergency shelter. Because there is always the possibility that more people may arrive, the site should be large enough to allow for major expansion.

If the population has been displaced because of civil strife, the site should be removed from areas of potential conflict.

4. Accessibility

The site must be accessible by vehicles and close to communication links and sources of supplies and services such as food, cooking fuel, shelter material, and national community services.

5. Environmental Considerations

The area should be free of major environmental health hazards such as malaria, onchocerciasis (river blindness), schistosomiasis (bilharzia), or tsetse fly. Climatic conditions should be suitable for habitation throughout the year. For instance, a suitable site in the dry season may be unusable during the rainy season. While a daily breeze is an advantage, strong winds may damage emergency and temporary housing, especially tents. To the extent possible, displaced people should not be settled in an area where the climate differs greatly from that to which they are accustomed.

6. Soil and Ground Cover

The soil should allow for water absorption and the retention of human waste. Rocky or impermeable sites should be avoided. If possible, land suitable for vegetable gardens and small-scale agriculture should be selected for the site.

The site should have a good groundcover of grass, or bushes, or trees, as covering vegetation provides shade and reduces erosion and dust. During construction of the camp, care should be taken to cause as little damage as possible to the vegetation and topsoil. Bulldozers, if used, should avoid scrapping topsoil off the site, as often occurs. *If wood must be used for domestic cooking fuel, it should not be taken from vegetation on the site.* Alternative sources of fuel must be found as soon as possible to avoid irreplaceable loss of surrounding wood.

7. Land Rights

The land should be exempt from ownership, grazing, and other uses by local populations. This can be a major cause of local resentment. Some authorities proposing the site are unaware of customary rights exercised by local populations. Sites are often provided on public land by the government. Any use of the land must be based on formal legal arrangements in accordance with the laws of the country.

C. Site Planning

Following are some general things to consider when performing site planning:

- At the onset of an emergency, the immediate provision of essential goods and services is more important than efforts to change the way people have already arranged themselves.

- Site planning should take the potential need for expansion into account.

- Site planning should first consider the characteristics and needs of the individual family and reflect the wishes of the community as much as possible, particularly taking into account the needs of female-headed households.

- A DP settlement is not a natural community. Particular care will be required to ensure that special needs are met.

- The overall physical layout of a site as well as other aspects of the site should reflect a decentralized, community-based approach focusing on family, village, or ethnic group.

D. Specific Infrastructure Design Considerations

1. Latrines

Although water requirements often determine site selection, sanitation requirements can dictate the site layout. **If latrines are used, there should be at least one for every 20 persons. They should be located no less than 6 m, and no further than 50 m, from any house. If latrines are too far away, they will not be used.** Sufficient space must also be left for replacement latrines. If communal latrines are unavoidable, they should be accessible by road to facilitate maintenance. To avoid contaminating water sources, latrines should have an effective drainage system that is easy to repair, both for rainwater and wastewater.

2. Water Distribution

Where possible, **the maximum distance between any house and a water distribution point should be no more than 100 m or a few minutes' walk.** Water will often be pumped from the source to an elevated point to allow gravity-feed distribution. Planning of the site should take this into account.

3. Roads and Pathways

The site should be accessible from other sites and contain all-weather roads and pathways connecting the various areas and facilities. Roads should be built above flood level and have adequate drainage. If there will be a significant vehicle traffic on the site, it should be separated from foot traffic.

4. Firebreaks

Within a displaced persons camp, build a firebreak (an area with no buildings) 50 m wide approximately every 300 m of building area. This area can be used to grow vegetables or for recreation. If space allows, the distance between individual buildings should be great enough to prevent collapsing burning buildings from touching adjacent buildings. The direction of the prevailing wind should be a consideration.

5. Administrative and Community Services

At the onset of an emergency, it may be difficult to foresee all the administrative and community services likely to be required. Underestimation of the space required for future communal needs is a common problem in camps of limited area.

Therefore, where adequate space is available, free areas must be allocated for future expansion of these services. The following lists administrative and community services that are often required:

Likely to be centralized:
- Camp administrative office.
- Essential services coordination offices (health care, feeding programs, water supply, education).
- Warehousing and storage.
- Initial registration/health screening area.
- Tracing service.
- Therapeutic feeding center (if required).

Likely to be decentralized:
- Bathing and washing areas.
- Community services (health centers, social service centers).
- Supplementary feeding centers (if required).
- Education facilities.
- Institutional centers (such as for the disabled or unaccompanied children), if required.

6. Physical Layout

The basic principle of any physical layout of a camp is that **it should be organized into small community units or villages made up of approximately five sectors (1,000 people per sector)** containing the decentralized community services mentioned above. These village units are in turn organized around the central core services.

The location of centralized services will depend on the specific situation and in particular the space available. Where space is available, it may be advantageous to have the centralized services located in the center of the camp. Where space is scarce, it may be better if centralized services are located near the entrance to the site. This will avoid trucks having to drive through a densely populated camp. Whatever the layout, warehouses should be located near the administrative office for security reasons.

The linear, or grid, layout, with square or rectangular areas separated by parallel streets, is often used. It has a simple design, is quick to implement, and allows a high population density. It should be avoided, however, because environmental health problems and disease are directly proportional to population density. Furthermore, a rigid grid design makes the creation of community identity difficult, as the displaced people are not usually accustomed to living in such a pattern.

E. Shelter

At a minimum, shelter must provide protection from the elements, space in which to live and store belongings, privacy, and emotional security. Shelter is one of the most important determinants of general living conditions and is often one of the largest items of nonrecurring expenditure. Although the basic need for shelter is similar in most emergencies, other considerations such as the kind of housing needed, what materials and design are used, who constructs the housing, and how long it must last will differ significantly in each situation.

Lack of adequate shelter and clothing can have a major adverse effect on the health and nutritional status of displaced people. Thus, in addition to shelter, the provision of sufficient blankets, appropriate clothing, and possibly heaters will be a high priority.

Neither prefabricated buildings nor specially developed emergency shelter units have proved effective in displaced person emergencies. Both are ineffective because of their inappropriateness, high unit cost, transport problems, and inflexibility. Also, emergency shelter arrangements will already have been constructed before such systems can arrive. For similar reasons, tents are often not an effective means of providing shelter either. They are difficult to live in and provide little insulation from temperature extremes. Tents, however, may be useful for displaced people of nomadic origin and when local materials are not available or are only seasonally available. If tents are used, repair materials should be provided.

The best way to meet emergency shelter needs is to provide materials or shelter similar to those used by the displaced population or the local population. Only if such materials cannot be adequately acquired locally should emergency shelter material be brought into the country. Above all, the simpler the shelter, the better.

Shelter must be available before other services can be developed properly. Emergency materials should be reusable for the construction of improved housing wherever possible.

Where local materials are in short supply or have a short life, consider acquiring more permanent materials. If a continued high density of occupation is unavoidable, fire-resistant materials may be needed.

The key to providing adequate shelter is the provision of a roof. If materials for constructing a complete shelter are inadequate, priority should be given to constructing at least the roof. Walls can be made of earth or other materials found onsite or made locally available.

Housing should meet the cultural and social requirements of a displaced person's home. Similar housing will help reduce the disorientation and emotional stress suffered by the displaced population. To the extent possible, longer term housing must be similar in design and construction to that with which the displaced are familiar, while reflecting local conditions and practice. This will generally mean single-family shelters, unless the displaced are accustomed to multifamily units. Although more costly, the benefits of individual homes for the displaced cannot be overestimated. The risk of communicable diseases increases enormously in communal shelters. If multifamily shelters must be used, no more than 35 persons (approximately 7 families) should be assigned to any one structure. Experience has shown that social and environmental problems may also rise if more people live in multifamily shelters. Also, buildings made from local materials may be approaching their structural limits at this size.

Materials and design should meet the minimum technical standards for the different local seasons. For example, roof material must be strong enough to withstand damage by the sun, rain, snow, and winds. (OFDA-supplied plastic sheeting has been very effective as roofing material. See the stockpile section of this manual for more information). Raised flooring is required in areas of high rainfall. Wall material must afford privacy and protection from the elements. If the site lies in a hazard-prone area (for example, an area subject to earthquakes or cyclones), the design of buildings and their siting should conform to hazard-resistant criteria. In buildings where cleanliness and hygiene are particularly important, the floor should be cement or at least washable.

Even an emergency shelter, including communal buildings, should be built by the displaced people themselves, provided adequate organization and material support is given. This will help to ensure that housing will meet their particular needs. Work by displaced people will reduce their sense of dependence and can cut costs considerably.

Sanitation and Environmental Service

A. General

The disruption and overcrowding of people accustomed to living in different and less crowded conditions make sanitation a critical issue. Indiscriminate disposal of human and other waste poses serious threats to the health of individuals, family groups, and the whole community. In a displaced person emergency, sanitation facilities to which they were accustomed are no longer available. Basic services are often lacking, and habits may have to be changed.

For this reason, an effective environmental system must be established to include the following: the provision of safe water; disposal of human excreta, wastewater, and garbage; insect and rodent control; safe food-handling practices; and site drainage. These services and the provision of health care are interrelated and should be considered together.

An acceptable and practical system for the disposal of human excreta is the key to reducing health hazards. The system must be developed in cooperation with the displaced and be culturally appropriate, even if circumstances necessitate a departure from traditional practices. Even special public health education may be required to ensure that the system will be used by the displaced population.

B. Importance of Organization, Integration, and Selection

Environmental sanitation will be a very important consideration in campsite layout, and its organization and operation must be integrated with other community services. Expert advice should be sought from a public health engineer or sanitarian familiar with the habits of displaced people and the local population, and who is experienced with displaced persons emergencies.

Good sanitation depends to a great extent on attitudes of the community and the people who run the system. The system and services developed should be able to operate effectively with a minimum of outside involvement. Therefore, selected displaced people must be trained to run the sanitation and environmental programs.

*The most common cause of **complete failure** of a sanitation system is the establishment of the wrong system.* This is a result of inadequate discussions with the population and a failure to take all relevant factors into consideration.

*The most common cause of **breakdown** of a sanitation system is inadequate maintenance*, even for properly designed and installed systems. Breakdown of latrines will lead to contamination of the environment and a high risk of infection and disease. Regular inspection and maintenance of the latrines should be enforced. The best guarantee of proper maintenance is the allocation of latrines to individual families.

Even when in working order, latrines will not be used unless they are clean. Individual families should be responsible for the cleanliness of their own units. If communal latrines are unavoidable, special arrangements to keep them clean may be necessary (that is, compensating individuals who are responsible for keeping them clean and operational on a daily basis). Particular attention must be given to the maintenance and cleanliness of latrines serving community facilities such as health centers. It should be noted that disinfectants should not be poured into pits or tanks of latrines that dispose of excreta by biological degradation. Instead, the regular addition of soil, ashes, or oil may be used to control insect breeding and reduce odor.

A public health education program emphasizing the importance of sound environmental sanitation practices should be established. The link between excreta contamination and disease must be clearly understood by all, including children. Children are the main excreters of many pathogens that cause diarrhea. Because children are often frightened by unfamiliar latrines, particular care will be needed to ensure that latrines are safe and physically suitable for children.

C. Disposal of Excreta

Safe disposal of excreta is critical because agents of most infectious diseases are passed from the body in excreta. These excreted infections fall into four main groups: viruses, bacteria, protozoa, and worms (helminths). Excreta, unless properly isolated, can also provide a breeding ground for insects, which act as either direct or indirect transmitters of disease.

Links between diseases, infections, means of transmission, and the sanitation system must be kept under constant surveillance. But the links are not always the most obvious. For example, the most important human link in transmission of an infection is the carrier who shows little or no sign of disease. Conversely, persons in an advanced state of disease may have little or no importance in transmission.

Human waste is more dangerous than animal waste; therefore, the safe disposal of human excreta is more important than the disposal of animal waste. Human feces are much more dangerous than urine. However, in areas of Africa and the Middle East where the *Schistosoma haematobium* species of bilharzia exists, and in all areas where typhoid is common and endemic, disposal of urine requires special attention.

1. Selection of a System—Immediate Considerations

The selection of an appropriate excreta disposal system requires consideration of a number of factors. In an emergency, however, time is the critical factor. Pollution of the environment by excreta, with all its attendant risks, cannot be stopped without immediate sanitation measures. Thus, the range of choices is always much more limited at the very outset of an emergency; weeks or months cannot be lost in waiting for expert advice, construction to be completed, or material to arrive. Temporary systems to meet immediate needs can be improved or replaced later. In an emergency situation, act first and improve later.

Emergency conditions may therefore dictate at least the initial use of trench latrines. These can be dug quickly and need less space than individual family units. While shallow trenches may be an initial quick solution, deep-trench latrines are incomparably more effective. Where space and soil conditions allow, the simplest and most common individual family unit is the pit latrine.

Once a temporary system has been established, more time and care should be expended to establish the most appropriate waste disposal system. Two main factors will affect the choice of an excreta disposal system: the traditional sanitation practices of the displaced people and the physical characteristics of the area, including the geology, availability of water, rainfall, and drainage. Failure to take proper account of either factor can cause the system to rapidly become a health hazard. Above all, cleanliness of latrines and their ease of access will determine whether or not they are used.

First it must be determined how the displaced people can modify their traditional practices to reduce health hazards during the emergency situation. Over one-half the world's population does not use latrines. This and other factors must be considered at the planning stage and will directly affect the type of system to be established. Other cultural factors to consider include:

- Previous sanitation system and practices.

- Method of anal cleaning.

- Preferred position (sitting or squatting).

- Need for privacy.

- Segregation of sexes and other groups or individuals with whom it is culturally unacceptable to share a latrine.

- Cultural practices for children.

- Cultural taboos (for example, avoiding contact with anything that may have touched excreta of others).

- Social factors, including likelihood of community action to ensure proper use of proposed system.

- Need for special orientation (direction) of latrine.

- Systems used locally in neighborhood of site.

In addition to these considerations, arrangements must be made to ensure the availability of appropriate anal-cleaning materials at or near all latrines. This is essential to the maintenance of hygiene. Also, latrines must be safe for children and women and be accessible at night. For individual units, families may provide their own lamps, but some form of lighting should be provided for communal units. In some cases, guards may be needed near the latrines to ensure security.

2. Immediate Action

The first group of displaced people arriving at a site should construct an adequate disposal system. Without proper facilities, displaced people are likely to defecate indiscriminately, contaminating their environment and possibly their water supply. In consultation with community leaders, *the first step is to localize excreta*; that is, control surface defecation. If space allows, designate an area or areas away from dwellings and downwind but accessible and close in proximity. Fence the area(s), ensure privacy, and provide a shallow trench and spades, if possible. Site such areas where the surface runoff during rain will not cause contamination, and protect the area with cutoff ditches.

A publicity campaign will be required to encourage the population to use specified areas and not defecate indiscriminately near dwellings. Measures must also be taken to prevent defecation or urination in or near the water supply. Immediate action in both regards can significantly reduce public health hazards.

If the ground is flooded or marshy or has a high water table, arrangements must be made as soon as possible to physically contain the excreta. Under such conditions, the location of the area, away from dwellings and the water source, is very important. Pending a proper containment system, a simple raised structure (for example, a wooden stage some 50 cm high) can prevent the population from being contaminated by their own excreta. Empty 200-L (45-gallon) oil drums can also be used if one end of the drum is cut out and then inserted open-end down into a hole that is as deep as the water allows, with the last half meter of the drum left aboveground. A small hole should be cut into the aboveground end of the drum to transform it into a squatting plate. These options should be viewed as *very short-term* sanitation interventions.

3. Long-Term Options

For a number of reasons, expert advice is required to develop the most appropriate waste disposal system. The nature of the soil will be important; if it is highly impervious, some systems will be precluded. The availability of water and cultural considerations must also be considered. There are many simple options, if properly constructed and maintained, that will meet all public health requirements. In most emergencies, two main types of latrines will be required, even for displaced people unaccustomed to them. *Trenches, pits, or holes in the ground can be used as dry latrines.* Water-dependent latrines can be flushed. There are also systems based on the composting or cartage of excreta.

In hot, dry climates where sufficient space is available, localized defecation areas located away from dwellings may be the best long-term arrangement, as heat and sunlight render the feces harmless with time. Black rock is the best surface. Under these conditions, potential health hazards in the area (for example, an increased number of rats) should be periodically reviewed.

If the camp is on the coast, displaced people may choose to defecate in the water. While this is less harmful for the displaced people than to indiscriminately defecate on land, it should be discouraged unless there is no other option. The dangers of defecating in the water increase greatly with numbers. Such practices contaminate the high water line, and increase the health hazards of washing in the sea. Defecation in bays, estuaries, or lagoons where fish or shellfish are caught should be greatly discouraged, since this may be a source of infection.

4. Latrine Styles and Considerations

There are three basic *latrine styles*: individual family units, centralized units with each latrine allocated to an individual family, and communal systems. Individual family units are the preferred solution, because people will always make more of an effort to keep their own latrine clean than a communal facility.

To determine the most appropriate latrine style, consideration must be given to a number of factors, such as the number and siting of latrines, population density, soil, available water, drainage, and construction materials.

a. Number and Siting of Latrines. **As a rule, at least 1 latrine (drop hole) should be provided for every 20 people. Latrines should be located at least 6 m from dwellings, 10 m from feeding and health centers, and at least 15 m (and preferably farther) from wells or other drinking-water sources.** Although all these distances depend on latrine and soil type, **latrines should be located no more than 50 m from users.** If people must walk a considerable distance to a latrine, they will defecate in a more convenient location, regardless of the health hazard.

Even when in working order, latrines will not be used unless they are clean. Individual family latrines are generally preferable, because people will always make more of an effort to keep their own latrine clean than a communal facility. Emergency conditions may dictate at least the initial use of trench latrines. The following standards for pit latrines are desirable:

Facility	Standard
Latrines, family	Not more than 4 families per latrine without organized, paid maintenance. Latrines should be located at least 6 m from dwellings, 10 m from feeding and health centers, and at least 15 m (and preferably farther) from wells or other drinking-water sources, but no more than 50 meters from users.
Trench latrines, shallow (for a few days)	30 cm wide by 1 m to 1.5 m deep by 3.5 m long/100 people.
Trench latrines, deep (for a few months)	70 cm to 100 cm wide by 2 m to 2.75 m deep by 3.75 m long/100 people.

b. Population Density. Population density will affect the space available for the excreta disposal system and thus the type of system. If latrines are too close to dwellings, there may be insufficient space for individual units. Overcrowding may cause major health hazards. This must be considered in site planning. The camp layout should be determined, among other things, by the needs of the most suitable sanitation system, not vice-versa. Space must be available for replacement latrines where necessary.

c. Soil. Soil conditions can vary over a short distance of land, thus requiring a thorough survey of the area. The nature of the soil also may exclude certain options. For example, rocky soil may prevent the digging of pit-type systems. Sandy soil will demand special actions to prevent sidewall collapse of pits. Impervious clay soils may exclude any system dependent upon seepage. Account should also be taken of the difference between dry- and wet-season soil conditions. If the ground freezes in winter, the choice of systems may be limited. Where there is a high water table, even only seasonally, care must be taken to ensure it is not contaminated by seepage from the latrines. Excreta must be contained in flood or swampy conditions.

d. Available Water. The amount of available water will determine whether disposal systems requiring water are a possibility. These systems are generally more expensive than those not requiring water. Because displaced persons' situations are often characterized by a lack of reliable water sources, the excreta disposal system should not be dependent on water availability. However, whatever the system, water should be available for anal cleaning.

e. Drainage. Since all camps experience rain from time to time, it is necessary to anticipate where surface runoff will flow and how to divert it by cutoff ditches. The possibility of flooding should also be considered and drainage provided if necessary. If floodwater enters latrines, large areas may be contaminated.

f. Construction Materials. Construction material will be needed to build some types of disposal systems, for example, those with walls and roofs. Displaced people unaccustomed to latrines generally prefer a large enclosure with no roof. There are, however, strong arguments for covering latrines to prevent rainwater from filling the latrine and causing contamination around it or weakening the surroundings. Roofs should provide proper drainage away from the latrine. Special measures will be necessary to manufacture squatting or sitting slabs, U-pipes, and other material for wet systems, if these are not available locally. Where displaced people have an established method of covering latrines (for example, with a wooden lattice) this is generally to be preferred, even if it is less easy to clean than a special plate. There are, however, a number of simple techniques for making the latter onsite, for example, with reinforced cement or fiberglass from mounds. The structure should be made of local materials that are used for reinforcing the pit when necessary. Avoid uncovered wood if possible. *Above all, the latrine must be easy to clean, and the surfaces around the hole must be washable.*

D. Wastewater, Garbage, and Dust

1. Wastewater

Excess water from washing, bathing, and food preparation is considered wastewater. It can be a problem if not drained away: Wastewater will stand in malodorous, stagnant pools that provide breeding places for insects, especially mosquitoes. Wastewater should generally not be permitted to enter the latrine, as this will cause the latrine pit or trench to fill very quickly. However, if latrine pits or trenches are sufficiently large and the amount of water used for bathing is relatively small, displaced people should be allowed to use the latrine area for bathing because it provides privacy and drainage. To avoid problems like these, special separate washing areas with duck-boards or stones and proper drainage should be constructed. Wastewater can also be contained by localizing sources of wastewater and providing local drainage.

2. Garbage

Because all communities generate garbage, established routines for the control, storage, collection, and disposal of garbage will be required. These needs must be reflected in initial site planning. If uncontrolled, the accumulation of garbage is both unpleasant and unhealthy. Rodent- and insect-borne diseases increase with improper garbage disposal. Free-range chickens, goats, and pigs will help control garbage; dogs will spread it.

The following suggestions for garbage storage, collection, and disposal are of particular concern for high-density camps, where the problem and dangers are greatest.

a. Storage. To store garbage, garbage containers made of metal or plastic with a minimum capacity of 50 L should be provided. A 200-L oil drum cut in half is often used. Storage containers should have lids and drainage holes in the bottom. A ratio of 1 container per 10 families has proven to be effective. Containers should be placed throughout the camp so that no dwelling is located more than 15 m from a garbage container.

b. Collection. The collection of garbage from containers should take place on a regular, daily basis, if possible. Daily collection arrangements must be made to collect medical waste and waste from feeding centers.

c. Disposal. Garbage can be disposed by burying it at designated locations on the site or removing it from the site. Open
dumping of garbage onsite should be avoided. If garbage has
to be dumped, it should be dumped far from the displaced
people. The ashes should be covered with a layer of soil after
each burning.

*The safe disposal of all medical waste requires particular
attention.* Needles and scalpels are especially dangerous.
Medical waste must be tightly controlled. It should be collected, transported, and disposed of separately. Medical waste
should always be burned without delay. This should be done in
an incinerator to ensure a hot, complete burning. Designated
areas where medical garbage and/or ashes are to be buried
should be located far from dwellings and fenced to restrict
access.

3. Dust

Large amounts of dust carried through the air can contaminate
food and be harmful to human health by irritating eyes, the
respiratory system, and skin. Dust can also harm some types
of equipment used onsite. The best preventive measure is to
stop the destruction of vegetation on the site. Dust control can
be achieved by spraying roads with water or oil, especially
around health facilities and feeding centers, as well as limiting
or banning traffic from certain areas.

E. Insect and Rodent Control

The environment in a displaced person emergency is condu-
cive to the proliferation of disease-carrying insects and rodents (vectors) that can also destroy or spoil large quantities
of food. Flies tend to breed in areas where food or human
excreta are present, and mosquitoes thrive in stagnant water.
Because the proliferation rate for both is very high (the life
cycle from egg to adult can take less than 2 weeks), the control of flies and mosquitoes is critical. Rats are also a problem
as they live where there is food, garbage, and cover. As a
result of overcrowding and inadequate personal hygiene, lice,
fleas, mites, ticks, and other arthropods may also cause
health problems.

Reducing the numbers of flies, mosquitoes, and rodents
quickly in an emergency may be difficult, but physical screens
can be used to control the immediate problem. The most

effective long-term method of controlling insects and rodents is to make the environment less favorable for the vectors. This is done by improving personal hygiene, sanitation, drainage, garbage disposal, and food storage and handling practices. Practical measures include removing stagnant wastewater, collecting garbage on a regular basis, using oil in latrines, and providing soap and sufficient water for washing. These measures should be integrated into a regularly inspected program with other health measures.

Vector control methods using insecticides and poisons can be dangerous. Like all methods using chemicals, they should be closely followed, monitored by specialists, and supervised. All major efforts to control insects and rodents must be closely coordinated with national programs and practices, especially with the national malaria control program. Although several different methods may be used, insect breeding grounds and the displaced people's dwellings may be sprayed. Since insects may already have, and can quickly develop, a resistance to chemicals, a rotation system using different sprays may be necessary. Local knowledge of existing resistance is required. Poison and traps may be used against rats in food storage and handling areas. Particular care must be taken in disposing of dead rats, which may carry plague-bearing fleas. *Chemical spraying and rodent poisons can be dangerous to humans*.

The body louse, usually found on inner clothing seams, is the only proven vector of louse-borne (epidemic) typhus and epidemic relapsing fever. If there is a serious increase in body louse infestation, quick action is required by properly trained personnel. This generally includes dusting individuals' inner clothing and bedding with an insecticide or fumigating clothing. There is widespread resistance of lice to some insecticides, especially DDT, and expert local advice must be sought. Mass washing of clothing is not recommended as a water temperature of at least 52° C must be maintained to kill the lice.

The following lists vectors and their potential health risks:

Vector	Risk
Flies	Eye infections (particularly among infants and children), diarrheal diseases
Mosquitoes	Malaria, filariasis, dengue, yellow fever, encephalitis
Mites	Scabies, scrub typhus
Lice	Epidemic typhus, relapsing fever
Fleas	Plague (from infected rats), endemic typhus
Ticks	Relapsing fever, spotted fever
Rats	Rat bite fever, leptospirosis, salmonellosis

F. Fires

Displaced person camps are often overcrowded, use light and highly combustible shelter materials, and have many individual cooking fires. For these reasons, they are very vulnerable to major fires. Measures to prevent and control fires must be considered from the start of emergency assistance at displaced person camps.

1. Prevention

The most basic and effective measure to prevent a major fire is the proper spacing and arrangement of all buildings to provide firebreaks. Other measures include allowing individual fires for cooking only and building fires outdoors only, if possible. If cooking must take place indoors, and especially in wooden or wattle-and-daub buildings, the cooking area should be protected with fire-resistant sheeting if possible. If large-scale cooking takes place indoors (for example, in a supplementary feeding center), fire-resistant ceilings and walls are mandatory. Fire retardants can be applied to thatched roofs in dwellings. Proper precaution must be taken when storing and using fuels. Highly flammable synthetic materials should be avoided.

2. Control

When fighting a large fire with scarce resources, the first priority is to contain it, rather than put it out. Fires can be controlled in the first few minutes with modest resources, providing quick action is taken. To control fires, an alarm system, fire fighting teams, and beaters must be organized in advance and plans prepared. Water is generally not available in sufficient quantities or at adequate pressure for the control of major fires; however, sand or other loose mineral soil material can be an effective method of control. The creation of a new firebreak should be done by taking structures down manually or with a bulldozer if available.

G. Disposal of the Dead

Dead bodies present a negligible health risk unless the cause of death is typhus or the plague and the bodies are infested with infected lice or fleas. Nevertheless, suitable arrangements for the disposal of the dead are required from the start of a displaced person emergency. This is important as the mortality rate after a new displaced person influx may be higher than under "normal" conditions. Also, bodies must be protected from rodents, animals, and birds. Authorities should be contacted immediately to ensure compliance with national procedures and provide assistance as necessary. The necessary space for burial should also be considered at the site planning stage, particularly in crowded conditions.

Burial is the simplest and best method of disposal if acceptable to the community. Health considerations provide no justification for cremation, for which sufficient fuel often may not be available. When possible, traditional practices and customary methods of disposal should be used. Material needs such as cloth for shrouds should also be met.

Before burial or cremation, bodies must be identified and, if possible, the cause of death recorded. This is of particular importance for disease control, registration, and tracing. Local government officials may also insist on the issuance of death certificates. If the whereabouts of relatives are known, the most immediate relation should be notified.

Consideration should also be given to the need to relocate bodies from burial sites after the emergency situation is over and the displaced people are able to return to their homes. This may require further involvement with the local government. A burial location map should be kept from the start of the emergency to aid in locating bodies for removal.

Chapter IV

Disaster Assistance
Response Team

Figure IV–1. DART Organization

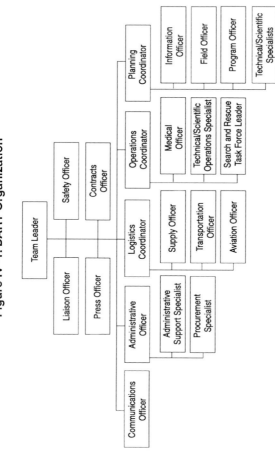

DISASTER ASSISTANCE RESPONSE TEAM

Overview

The U.S. Agency for International Development's (USAID) Office of Foreign Disaster Assistance (OFDA) has developed a response capability called the Disaster Assistance Response Team (DART) as a method of providing rapid response assistance to international disasters, as mandated by the Foreign Assistance Act. A DART provides an operational presence on the ground capable of carrying out sustained response activities. A DART includes specialists trained in a variety of disaster relief skills who assist U.S. Embassies and USAID Missions with the management of the United States Government (USG) response to disasters.

The activities of a DART vary depending on the type, size, and complexity of disasters to which the DART is deployed.

A. Purpose

During fast onset disasters, the focus of a DART is to:

- Coordinate the assessment of the situation and report on the needs.

- Recommend USG response actions.

- Manage USG onsite relief activities (for example, search and rescue and air operations).

- Manage the receipt, distribution, and monitoring of USG-provided relief supplies.

During long-term, complex disasters, the focus of a DART is to:

- Gather information on the general disaster situation.

- Assess the effectiveness of the overall humanitarian response.

- Identify the needs not being met by current overall response efforts.

- Monitor and evaluate the effectiveness of current USG-funded relief activities.

- Review proposals of relief activities for possible future funding.

- Advise USAID/Embassy on disaster issues.

- Make recommendations to OFDA/Washington (OFDA/W) on follow-on strategies and actions.

- Fund relief organizations and procure contractual services when delegated the authority.

During either type of disaster response, DARTs coordinate their activities with the affected country, private voluntary organizations (PVOs), nongovernmental organizations (NGOs), international organizations (IOs), and UN relief agencies and other assisting countries. When U.S. military assets are involved with the disaster response, the DART will work closely with those assets to ensure a coordinated effort by USG resources.

B. Structure

The structure of a DART is dependent on the size, complexity, type, and location of the disaster and the needs of the USAID/Embassy and the affected country. The number of individuals assigned to a DART is determined by how many people are required to perform the necessary activities to meet the strategy and objectives. A description of each DART position is provided in this chapter. Figure IV–1 contains an organization chart of a DART team.

A DART is composed of six functional areas:

1. **Management/Liaison**—Manages overall DART activities, including liaison with the affected country, PVO/NGO/IOs, other assisting countries, and U.S. military, and the development and implementation of plans to meet strategic objectives.

2. **Operations**—Manages all operational activities carried out by the DART such as search and rescue activities, technical support to an affected country, medical and health response, and aerial operations coordination. Most active during rapid onset disasters.

3. **Planning**—Collects, evaluates, tracks, and disseminates information about the disaster. Reviews activities and

recommends future actions. Develops the DART operational (tactical) plan.

4. **Logistics**—Supports the DART with team supplies, equipment, and services. Orders, receives, distributes, and tracks USG-provided relief supplies.

5. **Administration**—Manages fiscal activities of the DART. Procures goods and services required by the DART. Provides cost accounting of DART activities.

6. **Contracting**—Manages grant and contracting activities of the DART for victim needs.

C. DART Activation and Deployment

The decisions on a DART's activation, composition, and mission are made at a disaster response planning meeting held in OFDA. Final approval on deploying a DART rests with the Director of OFDA.

The DART is organized and supervised by a DART Team Leader selected by OFDA. The Team Leader receives a scope of work from and works directly for the Assistant Director of OFDA's Disaster Response Division or his/her designee. The scope of work lists the objectives, priorities, constraints, funding authorities, and reporting requirements for the DART. Based on this information, the Team Leader, in conjunction with OFDA's Assistant Directors, will identify the other positions needed. OFDA's Assistant Director for the Operations Support Division has the responsibility for supporting DART field operations, and ensuring security for the DART throughout the operation.

Prior to departure, the Team Leader will attempt to contact the USAID/Embassy (if present in the affected country) to discuss the situation; review the DART's structure, size, objectives, and capabilities; and identify the areas of support needed by the DART in-country.

Upon arrival in an affected country, the Team Leader reports to the senior U.S. official, or to appropriate affected country officials, to discuss the DART's objectives and capabilities and to receive additional instructions and/or authority. While in the affected country, the Team Leader advises and may receive periodic instructions from USAID/Embassy. Those instructions will be followed to the extent they do not conflict with OFDA policies, authorities, and procedures. The Team Leader maintains a direct line of communications with OFDA/W throughout the operation.

The duration of a DART operation will be determined by USAID/Embassy and OFDA/W after reviewing the disaster situation and the progress of the DART in meeting its objectives.

Figure IV–1 in the front of this chapter portrays the positions and relationships described in this section. The following position descriptions and checklists describe roles and responsibilities for DART members. The position descriptions are grouped according to their functional areas. They are also applicable for defining the roles and responsibilities of members of OFDA Assessment Teams.

There are additional positions under the Search and Rescue Task Force leader; these are described in the Federal Emergency Management Agency's *Urban Search and Rescue Response System Field Operations Guide.*

General Checklist for All DART Members

Predeparture:

- Establish contact with your supervisor and receive a briefing on:
  - The latest situation status of the disaster.
  - DART objectives and priorities.
  - Scope of your assignment within the DART.
  - Organizational structure of the DART.
  - Visa and immunization requirements.
  - Special equipment needs.
  - Functional staffing needs.
  - Travel arrangements and coordination with OFDA.

- Check on availability of local maps.

- Inform supervisor of in-country support needs.

- Contact unit personnel, brief them, and ensure their preparedness.

- Ensure that equipment is acquired, prepared, and ready for shipment.

- Notify Embassy through cable of the type, amount, and serial numbers of all equipment being taken by the team into the affected country.

- Review Individual Team Member and Team Support Checklists in Chapter I, "General Responsibilities and Information."

- Leave family name and contact numbers with OFDA.

- Leave family with power of attorney.

In Travel:

- Acquire and review briefing materials from supervisor, including:
    - USAID/Embassy disaster relief plan.
    - State Department background notes.
    - Disaster history.
    - Lessons learned from previous responses.
    - In-country contact list.
    - Maps.

- Discuss the following with your DART supervisor:
    - Response strategy.
    - Known cultural sensitivities of affected country.
    - Role of USAID/Embassy and affected country officials.
    - Initial work assignment.
    - Daily shift and briefing procedures, including time schedules.
    - Ordering and procurement procedures.
    - Property accountability.
    - Type of documentation required.
    - Reporting requirements by individual and team.
    - Media contact philosophy and procedures.
    - Policy on communicating with family members.

In-Country:

Immediate Actions:

- Perform an initial evaluation of the situation from your functional point of view.

- Discuss the situation with the USAID/Embassy, local officials, other assisting country teams, and UN/PVO/NGO/IOs as appropriate.

- Assess the affected country's and other response organizations' abilities to manage the situation.

- Determine additional requirements (personnel, equipment, facilities, logistical support) and make recommendations to the supervisor.

- Provide inputs to your supervisor for the initial team operational planning process.

- Implement the initial team operational plan.

Ongoing Actions:

- Contribute to the team's operational planning process.

- Provide leadership and technical guidance and resolve any coordination and personnel problems within your function.

- Inform your supervisor and others of the current situation as needed, including:
  - Work accomplishments.
  - Inability to operate as planned.
  - Potential political problems.
  - Internal and external coordination problems.
  - Shortage or surplus of resources.
  - Accidents involving assigned resources.

- Coordinate continuously as directed with affected country local officials, USAID/Embassy, other response teams, and UN/PVO/NGO/IOs.

- Record significant actions and events in the unit log each day and submit it to your supervisor or planning function.

- Constantly critique the operation of the function and recommend changes to your supervisor.

- Evaluate the ability of assigned resources to meet demands.

- Review the need for replacement of supplies, equipment, and personnel. Request more as needed.

- Identify evidence of public health problems.

- Constantly monitor activities to ensure they are carried out safely.

- Monitor team personnel for signs of critical incident stress syndrome.

Demobilization:

- Review staffing and resource requirements and recommend the release of excess personnel and equipment.

- Coordinate demobilization with your supervisor and/or planning function.

- Close out with the affected country and other cooperating organizations as necessary.

- Close out with USAID/Embassy as necessary.

- Account for all your equipment and supplies.

- Prepare nonexpendable items for return shipment, including completion of customs documents.

- Evaluate your function's performance, including:
  - Lessons learned.
  - Individual performance of unit personnel.
  - Concerns.
  - Future training needs.
  - Recommended changes.

- Submit all reports, evaluations, unit logs, and time records to your supervisor or the planning function.

- Review the checklist and make recommendations.

- Prepare for and participate in debriefings as requested.

- Clean up your work area.

Team Leader

The Team Leader manages overall DART activities and is responsible for the liaison with the affected country government, UN/PVO/NGO/IOs, and other assisting countries; ensures the development and implementation of strategic decisions; reports to senior U.S. official in the affected country; and receives a scope of work and any funding delegation of authority from the Assistant Director for OFDA's Disaster Response Division. The DART Team Leader is responsible to OFDA/W.

Following are specific responsibilities of the DART Team Leader:

Predeparture:

- In conjunction with the OFDA Assistant Directors, identify and select DART positions as needed.

- Obtain a copy of the DART scope of work with any funding delegation of authority.

- Receive general briefing from OFDA/W staff. In addition to the general checklist, discuss:
  - DART objectives and authorities.
  - Disaster situation, DART objectives, capabilities, structure, and in-country DART support needs (discussed with USAID/Embassy).
  - Political sensitivities relating to the affected country.
  - Security situation and any potential evacuation strategy.
  - DART-OFDA reporting requirements, including daily telephone calls, situation reporting, and final disaster report.
  - Types of resources that can be requested, resource ordering process, and use of stockpile items.
  - Affected country's disaster response capability.
  - Status of affected country's response to the disaster.
  - Lessons learned from other disasters in the affected country.
  - Lessons learned from other disasters of this type.
  - Other international response to the disaster (countries and organizations).
  - UN/PVO/NGO/IOs with programs in the affected country.
  - Points of contact at USAID/Embassy.
  - Points of contact within the affected country's government.
  - Policies/procedures related to DART members.
  - Staff rotation plans.
  - Exit strategy.
  - Coordination of international response through the UN and points of contact. Other coordination activities among PVO/NGO/IOs and the donor community.
  - Media guidance.
  - Fiscal authorities, restrictions, and reporting.
  - Deployment timeframe.
  - Contractual arrangements with non-direct hire DART members.

- Brief OFDA staff and discuss staffing requirements, in-country support requests, and special travel needs.

- Ensure the acquisition and preparation of team support list items.

- Ensure that adequate communications equipment is ordered for all functions.

- Obtain copies of contracts for non-direct hire DART members.

- Ensure the DART has the capability to fiscally support itself upon arrival in the affected country.

- With Planning Coordinator and OFDA staff, conduct initial DART briefing.

- Designate planning function to take the lead on acquiring all necessary maps.

- Cover all items under "In Travel" in checklists.

In-Country:

Immediate Actions:

- Report immediately to the senior USAID/Embassy official, present DART capabilities and objectives, and receive briefing. Discuss security, disaster, and international response activity update; USAID/Embassy lines of authority and reporting requirements; support capability of USAID/Embassy for personnel, equipment, storage, workspace, and transportation; and in-country procedures related to local laws or customs that might affect DART operations.

- With the Planning Coordinator, formulate an initial team operational plan based on immediate evaluations from all functions and a briefing from USAID/Embassy.

- Notify OFDA/W of the DART's arrival, initial information obtained, and initial actions taken by the DART.

- Locate a DART headquarters and get set up (see also *DART Setup and Closeout Guidelines* in Chapter I, "General Responsibilities and Information"). It should be close to USAID, the U.S. Embassy, or the disaster site.

- With Administrative Officer, meet with key USAID/Embassy officials, including USAID controller and/or Embassy budget and fiscal officer, to discuss OFDA procurement procedures and fiscal requirements of the DART (local currency).

- If the initial operational plan requires an immediate tactical response or logistical support, ensure the deployment of required personnel and equipment.

- Identify potential locations for warehousing, airport staging, storage, and administrative operations.

- Develop a staff work schedule.

- Oversee the development of situation reporting, operational planning, resource tracking, documentation, and commodity consignment systems.

- Establish contact with other assisting country teams and UN/PVO/NGO/IOs.

- Establish contact with the appropriate affected country ministries as necessary.

- Discuss potential safety issues and future technological problems with the Safety Officer and Technical/Scientific Specialists.

- Discuss appropriate media activities with the Press Officer.

- Determine additional requirements (personnel, equipment, facilities, logistical support). Identify these to USAID/Embassy and OFDA and make recommendations.

Ongoing Actions:

- With the Planning Coordinator, conduct regular planning briefing and debriefing sessions. Ensure regular attendance and contributions from all DART members into the team's operational planning process. Review ground rules on press contact and contact with the USAID/Embassy, the affected country, and other organizations.

- Maintain close communication with OFDA. Inform OFDA of the current situation, work progress, problems, planned actions, effectiveness of response, condition, and performance of DART members.

- Review and clear situation reports (sitreps) and DART cables.

- Maintain close communication with senior USAID/Embassy officials. Ask them to explain the mission of the DART to the Country Team.

- Coordinate continuously with affected country representatives, other assisting teams, and UN/PVO/NGO/IOs. Promote coordination among UN/PVO/NGO/IOs and donor communities.

- Conduct a daily, or as needed, critique of all functions for effectiveness, validity of priorities, soundness of objectives, and ability of DART members to carry out assignments. Institute changes as necessary.

- Constantly foster open communications with USAID/Embassy to ensure continued support of the DART and that the DART is meeting their needs. Keep them informed of DART activities and progress.

- Ensure that all DART members maintain daily unit logs as required.

Demobilization:

- Oversee the development of the DART demobilization plan. Review the plan with USAID/Embassy and OFDA.

- Review *DART Setup and Closeout Guidelines* in Chapter I, "General Responsibilities and Information."

- Review all documentation, such as videotapes, pictures, logs, sitreps, and cables.

- Identify additional final disaster report requirements and assign responsibilities as required.

- Participate in writing and reviewing the final disaster report.

- Ensure that all fiscal agreements are concluded.

- Ensure that requested documentation and final disaster report are distributed to the local USAID/Embassy prior to departure.

- Debrief the senior USAID/Embassy officials.

- Notify OFDA of the final demobilization arrangements.

- Prepare and conduct a debriefing with OFDA staff in Washington.

- Submit the final disaster report to OFDA.

- Assist with the preparation and participate in the DART After Action Workshop.

A. Press Officer

The Press Officer manages DART media activities. The Press Officer reports directly to the Team Leader.

Predeparture:

- Contact the Team Leader and receive a general briefing. In addition to the general checklist:
  - Discuss the media philosophy for this disaster, including the level and type of coverage desired, press release guidelines, and press interview guidelines.
  - Arrange in-country Press Officer support needs (for cable to USAID/Embassy).
  - Obtain information on USG response activities to date, including commodities delivered, inroute, and requested from the OFDA Logistics Officer.
  - Obtain information on response actions of other assisting countries and PVO/NGO/IOs (from the OFDA Information Support Unit or INTERACTION).
  - Obtain all press releases pertaining to the disaster.
  - Obtain information on media organizations currently covering the disaster.
  - Coordinate the acquisition and shipping of press function equipment and supplies. Specify weight, cubes, and the number of pieces and arrange for special handling requirements.
  - Organize press coverage at the DART departure site.

In-Country:

Immediate Actions:

- Perform an immediate initial evaluation of the media situation. Discuss current activities with local officials, USAID/Embassy (USIS), other assisting country teams, and UN/PVO/NGO/IOs.

- Meet with USAID/Embassy (USIS) and obtain the following information:
  - Current and planned media activities.
  - Disaster effects on population and property.

- Media management policy (picture taking, filming).
- Current press organization in operation.
- Affected country media sensitivities.
- Support facilities available for briefings.
- Availability of local equipment such as computers, typewriters, copy machines, etc.

- Obtain copies of any new press releases pertaining to the disaster.

- Obtain a list of international and local media presently covering the disaster.

- Obtain and review the USAID/Embassy disaster relief plan and emergency action plan.

- With the Information Officer and Planning Coordinator, establish procedures for press visits to DART headquarters (access to visual displays, maps, situation reports, resource status information).

- With the Operations Coordinator, discuss press visits to worksites.

- Evaluate the need for additional personnel and resources to meet press function needs.

Ongoing Actions:

- Ensure a balanced coverage of team activities.

- Keep the Team Leader informed of all press activities in advance.

- Ensure that proper safety practices are observed during worksite visits.

- Keep DART members informed of U.S. and international news coverage.

- Keep the USAID Legislative and Public Affairs Office informed.

- Coordinate continuously with local officials, USAID/Embassy (USIS), other assisting country teams, and UN/PVO/NGO/IOs.

- Assist the USAID/Embassy (USIS) in arranging and conducting VIP visits.

Demobilization:

- Give a technical debriefing to the USAID Legislative and Public Affairs Office.

B. Safety Officer

The Safety Officer identifies hazards and risks to DART personnel and oversees adherence to safe practices and standards. The Safety Officer reports directly to the Team Leader. Specific responsibilities of the Safety Officer are as follows:

Predeparture:

- Contact the Team Leader and receive a general briefing. In addition to the general checklist:
  - Discuss safety concerns at the disaster site.
  - Meet with the Operations Coordinator to discuss operational issues.
  - Coordinate the acquisition, preparation, and shipment of office and field supplies.

In-Country:

Immediate Actions:

- Perform an immediate initial evaluation of the safety situation. Discuss conditions, security, hazards, and needs with local officials, USAID/Embassy, other assisting country teams, and UN/PVO/NGO/IOs. Determine the best use of the safety function.

- If the plan requires immediate logistics and operations functions activation, begin assessing safety issues of the operation.

- Perform a thorough evaluation of operational areas. Identify, mark, and document potential hazards and unsafe situations. Notify DART members in the area immediately.

- Brief the entire team on unsafe conditions. Recommend protective and preventive actions.

- Ensure that safety standards and practices are observed in all operations.

- Investigate all DART accidents. Document and file.

- Develop a medical evacuation plan with the Administrative Officer, including location of medical facilities, transportation, telephone numbers, and radio frequencies. Give a copy of the plan to the Planning Coordinator, Transportation and Aviation Officers, Logistics and Operations Coordinators, and USAID/Embassy.

- Evaluate the need for additional personnel and resources to safely meet objectives.

Ongoing Actions:

- Continuously monitor DART operations for adherence to safety practices and standards.

- Continuously monitor DART members for signs or symptoms of critical incident stress syndrome. Recommend rest, stress-debriefing, or demobilization as required.

- Provide safety plan information to the planning function for inclusion in the operational plan. The plan can include reviews of air operations, vehicle safety, hazard maps, hazardous materials, safe working practices at worksites, personal and visitor safety (media), reporting of hazards, the emergency medical plan (first aid through medic), reporting of accidents, accident investigation, and scheduling safety meetings.

Demobilization:

See the general checklist at the beginning of this chapter.

C. Liaison Officer

The Liaison Officer coordinates the DART liaison function; serves as the point of contact with the affected country, USAID/Embassy, U.S. military, other assisting country teams, and UN/PVO/NGO/IOs; and identifies the political and operational concerns of these groups. The Liaison Officer reports directly to the Team Leader. Specific responsibilities of the Liaison Officer are as follows:

Predeparture:

- Contact the Team Leader and receive a general briefing. In addition to the general checklist, discuss:

- Liaison concerns and needs at the disaster.
- Relationships among major respondents participating in the disaster relief activities.

In-Country:

Immediate Actions:

- Perform an immediate initial evaluation of the coordination situation.

- Identify yourself as the DART point of contact to USAID/Embassy, affected country officials, U.S. military, other assisting country teams, or UN/PVO/NGO/IOs. Discuss with them disaster needs and coordination issues.

- Obtain the necessary credentials for identification and appropriate security clearances.

- Establish the points of contact with the above groups, including communications links and locations.

Ongoing Actions:

- Respond to requests from DART personnel for interorganizational contacts.

- Monitor disaster operations to identify current or potential interorganizational problems.

- Remain visible and available at the disaster to affected country officials, U.S. military, other assisting countries, and UN/PVO/NGO/IOs.

- Offer methods to coordinate and support disaster response activities among the above groups.

- Maintain a current list of liaison contacts for the above groups and provide it to other DART members as needed.

- Share DART reports and accomplishments with the above groups.

- Document liaison activities.

Demobilization:

See the general checklist at the beginning of this chapter.

Logistics Coordinator

The Logistics Coordinator manages and supervises logistical and aviation support to the DART; ensures the team receives supplies, equipment, and services; and orders, receives, distributes, and tracks USG-donated relief commodities. The Logistics Coordinator reports directly to the Team Leader. Specific responsibilities of the Logistics Coordinator are as follows:

Predeparture:

- Contact the Team Leader and receive a general briefing. In addition to the general checklist, discuss in-country logistical support needs to be communicated to USAID/Embassy.

- Contact the OFDA Logistics Officer and discuss the following:
    - Resource ordering procedures.
    - Current resources requested of USG by the affected country. Obtain a list.
    - Status of OFDA stockpile items and stockpile usage procedures.
    - Availability of in-country support services.

- Contact the logistics function personnel. Brief them and ensure their preparedness.

- Coordinate the acquisition and shipping of team equipment and supplies. Specify the weight, cubes, and number of pieces and arrange for special handling requirements as needed.

In-Country:

Immediate Actions:

- Define and acquire the immediate needs of the DART.

- Perform an immediate evaluation of the logistical situation. Discuss needs with other team members, USAID/Embassy, affected country officials, other assisting country teams, and UN/PVO/NGO/IOs.

- Assess the affected country and other response organizations' abilities to manage the situation.

- Determine whether to activate transportation and supply units.

- If the initial plan requires immediate logistical support, assist in selecting the worksite, setting up equipment, and beginning the operation.

- Set the logistics staff's work schedules.

- Oversee the establishment of an accountability and management system for team equipment and supplies and relief commodities. The system will include receiving, inventory, storing, security, and tracking equipment, supplies, and commodities. Use forms (see Chapter V, "Forms and Instructions") as needed.

- Establish DART logistical support requests process.

- Establish contacts with the USAID/Embassy, affected country, or other groups to obtain the following information:
  - Airport/port operation procedures, capabilities, and conditions, including landing/quay costs, customs inspections, unloading and loading support equipment, storage, security, fuel availability, communications systems in use, and access by ground vehicle.
  - Capabilities, availability, and use of USAID/Embassy transportation.
  - USAID/Embassy supply procedures.
  - Local warehousing capabilities and conditions.
  - Local power source requirements.
  - Availability of local hiring of personnel for logistical support.
  - Reliable local common carriers (trucks, aircraft, ships).
  - Local road conditions.
  - Rail capabilities and conditions, if available.
  - Use of waivers for expediting resources through customs.

- Discuss procurement and contract procedures with the Administrative Officer.

- Establish local contacts for expediting the in-country logistics.

- Oversee the preparation of the DART transportation plan. Submit to the planning function.

- Evaluate the need for more personnel or resources to meet needs.

Ongoing Actions:

- Review resource requests with the Team Leader.

- Ensure that the distribution process gets relief supplies to appropriate recipients.

Demobilization:

- Ensure that logistics and team support equipment is accounted for and prepared for return shipment to United States, including completion of customs documents; and that appropriate documentation is sent to OFDA.

A. Supply Officer

The Supply Officer manages the ordering, receiving, inventorying, storing, issuing, and accounting of OFDA relief commodities. The Supply Officer reports directly to the Logistics Coordinator. Specific responsibilities of the Supply Officer are as follows:

Predeparture:

- Coordinate the acquisition and shipping of equipment and office supplies.

In-Country:

Immediate Actions:

- Perform an immediate initial evaluation of the supply situation.

- Find out the availability of local warehousing, labor, and transportation from affected country officials and USAID/ Embassy.

- If the plan requires an immediate need for supplies, assist in selecting the worksite, setting up equipment, and beginning the operation.

- Obtain the following specific information from USAID/ Embassy:
  - USAID/Embassy transportation capabilities, availability, and use procedures.
  - USAID/Embassy warehousing availability.

- USAID/Embassy supply procedures.
- Use of waivers for expediting resources through customs.

- With the Administrative Officer, locate and contract for warehouse space and equipment and hire local labor as necessary. Discuss the procurement procedures for obtaining local supplies.

- Develop a staff work schedule for the unit.

- Establish locations, facilities, and equipment for receiving, inventorying, storing, and issuing supplies.

- Set up ordering, inventorying, issuing, and tracking systems for team needs and relief supplies. Use forms (see Chapter V, "Forms and Instructions") as needed.

- Ensure that the above systems can provide fast and accurate information as to what is in storage at any one time and in what quantities.

- Obtain a map of the area.

- Establish contact with local customs authorities. Learn country laws, forms, costs, landing fees, and hours of operation of ports of entry.

Ongoing Actions:

- Work closely with the transportation function to ensure the coordination of receipt and distribution of relief supplies.

- Ensure the efficient and accurate receipt of all supplies at storage locations and supervise receipt documentation.

- Take responsibility for both the quantity and quality control of supplies delivered to storage locations.

- Prepare and submit stock inventories as requested.

- Inspect storage facilities as needed to ensure that procedures for stacking, cleaning, and recordkeeping are being adhered to.

- Review the need for replacement parts, equipment, and supplies. Provide information on stock levels and anticipated needs and make requests through the chain of command. Coordinate this activity with other DART members.

- Place USAID logo stickers on all incoming relief supplies containers.

- Ensure that proper safety practices and standards are understood and observed.

- Establish, maintain, and supervise an adequate security system for the warehouse facilities to prevent both theft and damage to team equipment and supplies or relief supplies.

- Brief local labor on the changing situation.

- Take necessary precautions to store and label poisonous or hazardous materials in an appropriate manner.

- Monitor the distribution system to ensure that relief supplies are distributed to the appropriate recipients.

- Organize and file all relevant documentation.

Demobilization:

- With the Administrative Officer, conclude all contracts (personnel and materials) and payments.

- Make arrangements for the disposition of remaining supplies with OFDA and USAID/Embassy.

- Ensure that equipment and supplies returning to the United States are accounted for and prepared for shipment, including completion of customs documents. Send appropriate documentation to OFDA.

- Ensure that requested documentation is distributed to local USAID/Embassy prior to departure.

B. Transportation Officer

The Transportation Officer manages the DART's transportation resources. The Transportation Officer reports directly to the Logistics Coordinator. Specific responsibilities of the Transportation Officer are as follows:

Predeparture:

- Coordinate the preparation and transport of equipment, tools, and relief supplies.

- Obtain transportation system maps.

- Ensure that adequate communications equipment will be available for vehicles.

In-Country:

Immediate Actions:

- Perform an immediate initial evaluation of the transportation situation. Discuss transportation needs with other team members.

- Make an immediate determination on the need to rent vehicles and hire local drivers.

* Obtain a map of the city or region.

- Develop an interim transportation plan if needed.

- If the plan requires immediate vehicle use, arrange for the loan and/or rental of vehicles and establish a base of operations.

- Establish contacts with affected country officials, USAID/ Embassy, other assisting country teams, and UN/PVO/ NGO/IOs to obtain the following information:
  - General road conditions.
  - Locations of hazardous or impassable areas.
  - Fuel availability.
  - Availability of local drivers.
  - List of reliable local common carriers.
  - Availability of local maintenance.
  - Local insurance requirements.
  - Local driving laws and requirements.

- Plan the loading, accounting, dispatching, and tracking system for relief supplies with the Supply Officer.

- Establish locations for maintaining, fueling, and cleaning vehicles.

- Establish a vehicle management process that includes the following: inspection, storage, security, tracking, registration, insurance, mileage recording, and maintenance.

- Ensure an adequate fuel supply system.

- Use DART forms (see Chapter V, "Forms and Instructions") as needed.

- Establish the DART transportation-support-request process.

- Ensure that daily logs are kept on all vehicles to record mileage, tune-ups, oil changes, etc.

- Learn local transportation laws, restrictions, traffic patterns, hours, and customs.

- Establish contact with local customs authorities. Learn country laws, forms, costs, landing fees, and hours of operation of ports of entry.

- Prepare and submit a complete DART transportation plan to the planning function, including routes of travel, time and location of departure and pickup, and assignments of vehicle and driver. Include maps for drivers.

- Control the traffic flow around the supply area and DART headquarters.

Ongoing Actions:

See the general checklist at the beginning of this chapter.

Demobilization:

- Inspect and document rental vehicles after use.

- With the Administrative Officer, conclude all contracts (personnel and vehicles) and payments.

- Ensure that the requested documentation is distributed to local USAID/Embassy prior to departure.

C. Aviation Officer

The Aviation Officer manages the DART's aviation resources. The Aviation Officer may also perform an operational function, such as managing aerial spraying. The Aviation Officer reports directly to the Logistics Coordinator. Specific responsibilities of the Aviation Officer are as follows:

Predeparture:

- Contact the OFDA Logistics Officer and obtain:
  - Copies of aircraft contracts to be used in the disaster.

- List of capabilities and requirements of aircraft that may be used to support the disaster.
- Information on the availability of aircraft and of fuel, oil, and spare parts in-country.

- Contact the OFDA Program Support Division and review aircraft contracts that might be used.

- Coordinate the acquisition and shipping of equipment, tools, and supplies, including maps for air transportation planning, Locust Handbook, spray charts, airport maps, forms, and office supplies as necessary.

- Determine what assistance USAID/Embassy will be giving to the DART, such as customs, overflight clearance, and transportation.

- Determine what other donor countries or UN/PVO/NGO/IOs are operating aircraft in the affected country.

In-Country:

Immediate Actions:

- Perform an initial evaluation of the aviation situation.

- Locate the airport nearest to the disaster site and tour it to determine its adequacy for DART needs.

- Identify the air transportation and air operations needs of the operations and logistics functions.

- Establish contacts with affected country officials, USAID/Embassy, other assisting country teams, and UN/PVO/NGO/IOs to obtain the following information on the airport in the area of the disaster:
  - Length/width of runways.
  - Elevation of runways.
  - Condition of runways.
  - Acceptability of Department of Defense (DOD) aircraft.
  - Landing fees and hours of operation.
  - Limitations and hazards.
  - Use of aircraft for spray and reconnaissance missions.
  - Frequencies in use.
  - Availability of local labor for hire.
  - Customs laws and associated costs.

- Availability of local aircraft, pilots, maintenance personnel, and fuel.
- Aircraft search and rescue plan with local medical facilities and the capabilities of those facilities.

- Determine the need to rent aircraft for DART activities. If the DART operational plan requires immediate air transportation or air operations, set up an air operations office (preferably at the airport) and arrange for rental of aircraft with the Administrative Officer, if necessary, and begin operation.

- Obtain maps of the area for pilots.

- Discuss procurement and contract procedures with the administrative function, including fees, fueling, and support services payment.

- Meet with customs officials and discuss advanced clearance of relief supplies.

- Establish a fueling area away from operations. Ensure the adequacy of quantity and quality of fuel. Mark the area and set up safety equipment.

- Establish an area and procedures for loading and unloading aircraft. Control access to aircraft and loading/unloading and supply areas. If loading pesticides for spraying, ensure that all safety equipment and procedures are used.

- Establish systems for pilot briefings and scheduling, passenger briefings, manifesting passengers and cargo, flight following, transferring information on manifests, receiving supplies, and monitoring contracts. Use DART forms (see Chapter V, "Forms and Instructions") as needed.

Ongoing Actions:

- Ensure that aviation safety is strictly enforced:
  - Adhere to IATA and Federal Aviation Administration (FAA) regulations on packaging and transportation of hazardous materials.
  - Ensure that ATC rules and operators' flight manuals are observed.
  - Establish and maintain continuous radio communications with all aircraft (VHF). Keep a radio watch during flight operations.

- Ensure that proper protective clothing is worn when handling hazardous materials.

- Ensure that proper safety procedures are used when loading, storing, and handling pesticides.

- Transmit all flight plans to civil aviation authorities for approval.

- Ensure that proper aircraft maintenance is conducted.

- Ensure that pilot duty and flight-hour limitations are observed.

- Investigate and document any accidents or spills. Report them to the Logistics Officer.

- Ensure that all flights are manifested and flight-followed.

- Keep daily statistics on aircraft movements, legs, cargo and passengers flown, and fuel consumption for each aircraft. Keep this documentation in a secure, weatherproof location.

- Contribute regularly to the team's operational planning process. Provide input such as aircraft downtime due to maintenance, pilot days off, and poor flying weather.

- Establish and maintain a security system at the airport site to prevent theft and damage to property and supplies.

- Ensure adequate fire prevention.

- Coordinate with the supply and transportation units to ensure safe and effective aircraft loading and off-loading procedures.

- Meet daily with operators of contract aircraft and discuss operation and problems. Document and file meeting results.

- Coordinate continuously with local officials, the airport manager, USAID/Embassy, and other groups.

Demobilization:

- With the Administrative Officer, terminate all contracts (personnel and aircraft) and payments.

- Ensure that requested documentation is distributed to local USAID/Embassy prior to departure.

Communications Officer

The Communications Officer manages DART communications; supervises and trains personnel in the use and operations of equipment and systems; and develops and implements the DART communications plan. The Communications Officer reports directly to the DART Team Leader. Specific responsibilities of the Communications Officer are as follows:

Predeparture:

- Attend general briefings.

- Confer with OFDA Communications Officer. In addition to the general checklists, discuss initial team communications requirements including:
  - Personnel safety and security.
  - Air-to-ground communications needs.
  - Planning of communications setups, personnel requirements, etc.
  - Operational communications (search and rescue, etc.).
  - DART headquarters communications (intraregion) to DART personnel work sites, US Embassy/USAID Mission, affected-country officials, and UN/PVO/NGO/IOs.
  - DART headquarters communications (interregion) to OFDA Washington and other areas outside of region, as necessary.
  - In-country communications support capabilities and availability of:
    - US Embassy/USAID Mission communications.
    - PSTN (local telephone system)/VSAT circuits for voice and e-mail capability.
    - USAID computer net (e-mail).
    - Existing radio frequency networks and authorizations.
    - UN/PVO/NGO/IO equipment and frequencies.
    - AC power, adapters, etc. (or need for generators).
    - Amateur radio networks (ARRL), Military Affiliate Radio System (MARS).
    - Internet access, etc.

- Request US Embassy/USAID Mission to provide latest authorized frequency assignments for HF/VHF/UHF radios, if available.

- Assemble the required documents, manuals, and communications equipment and coordinate packaging for shipment. Specify weight, cubes, and number of pieces and arrange for special handling requirements (radio licenses or authorizations, Air Way Bills (AWB), customs declarations, etc.).

- Acquire local list of communicators.

- Acquire current *World Radio and TV Handbook* or other reference listing of radio frequencies.

In-Country:

Immediate Actions:

- Set up initial communications link to OFDA Washington (typically Satcom, voice/data).

- Establish/utilize existing personnel safety and security radio net (typically VHF/UHF voice).

- Perform immediate initial evaluation of communications situation.

- Obtain information from US Embassy/USAID Mission on frequency uses, call signs and authorizations, available personnel, communications facilities, and USAID Computer Net availability.

- Select communications site with considerations given to highest available elevation with appropriate clearing for radio and satellite terminal antennas.

- Set up Communications Center at DART Headquarters, suboffices, and residences, as required.

- Develop interim communications plan.

- Instruct DART members on use of equipment.

Ongoing Actions:

- Continually review and revise communications plans as conditions change.

- Assist and train DART personnel in the efficient and proper use of communications equipment.

- Keep OFDA informed of communications methods, procedures, and links.

- Ensure the proper use of radio protocols and frequencies.

- Keep radio logs as necessary.

Demobilization:

- Review communications requirements and recommend the release of excess equipment and communications personnel.

- Maintain adequate equipment and support personnel to support DART Team until departure.

- Ensure equipment is accounted for.

- Ensure equipment being released for shipment is properly packaged and documents are properly prepared (Air Way Bill, manifests, Customs Declarations, etc.).

- Compile communications After Action Report and prepare or provide documentation for the team after action report.

- File radio logs if maintained.

Operations Coordinator

The Operations Coordinator manages tactical operations such as search and rescue, medical/health, technical support, and aerial operations coordination. The Operations Coordinator reports directly to the Team Leader. Specific responsibilities of the Operations Coordinator are as follows:

Predeparture:

- Contact the Team Leader and receive a general briefing. In addition to the general checklist, discuss:
  - In-country operational support needs to be communicated to USAID/Embassy.
  - Operational response activities by the affected country.
  - Operational response activities pending or in progress by other assisting countries and the UN.
  - Type of onsite operational coordination occurring among the affected country, assisting countries, and UN/PVO/NGO/IOs.
  - Technical or scientific specialists required for the mission.

- Ensure that adequate communication equipment is ordered to support anticipated team operations.

In-Country:

Immediate Actions:

- Assess the affected country's and other response organizations' abilities to carry out relief operations. Make a determination on the best use of operational resources.

- If the plan requires an immediate tactical response, assist in selecting a worksite, setting up equipment, and beginning the operation.

- With the Communications Officer, determine communications needs, develop a communications plan, and submit it to the Planning Coordinator.

- Develop a staff work schedule considering the need for 24-hour operation.

- With the Press Officer, establish onsite media management procedures.

- If the operational plan does not require an immediate tactical response, offer technical assistance to existing tactical operations.

Ongoing Actions:

- Contribute regularly to the team's operational planning process by recommending tactics to meet team objectives.

- Update the Team Leader, planning function, and appropriate staff on the current situation, including potential or impending life-threatening situations for team members or victims.

- Coordinate with the logistics function to ensure that operational requirements are being met.

- Keep operations staff briefed on the changing situation.

- Conduct frequent debriefings with key staff to review problems and work accomplishments.

- Coordinate continuously with the affected country's response organization, other assisting country response teams, and any onsite coordination organizations such as an Onsite Operations Coordination Center (OSOCC). Complement ongoing activities.

Demobilization:

See the general checklist at the beginning of this chapter.

A. Medical Officer

The Medical Officer manages medical care operations. This position will be filled on the DART when DART operations include assisting disaster victims directly with medical care. The Medical Officer reports directly to the Operations Coordinator. Specific responsibilities of the Medical Officer are as follows:

Predeparture:

- Contact the OFDA/W Health Officers and obtain information on the following:
  - Medical capabilities in the affected country and at the disaster site.
  - UN/PVO/NGO/IOs working in the affected country and the types of programs currently being conducted.
  - Types of USG-sponsored medical personnel and material assets available for disaster response and methods of obtaining them.
  - Any medical responses being planned or carried out by other assisting countries or organizations.

- Ensure that any specialized equipment is properly prepared for shipment.

- Contact medical personnel, brief them, and ensure their preparedness.

In-Country:

Immediate Actions:

- Perform an immediate initial evaluation of the health and medical situation. Discuss needs with local health officials, USAID/Embassy, other assisting country response teams, and UN/PVO/NGO/IOs.

- Assess the affected country's and other response organizations' abilities to manage the situation. Make a determination on the need to activate a medical unit immediately.

- Determine the local medical capabilities and contacts.

- If the plan requires immediate patient care, assist in selecting the worksite, setting up equipment, and beginning operation (if such resources are a part of the DART).

- Develop the staff work schedule.

- Establish medical priorities. Validate the triage process.

- Provide leadership and technical guidance and resolve any coordination and personnel problems within the unit.

- Provide backup support and consultation to the Safety Officer, including monitoring and management of critical incident stress syndrome.

- If the operational plan does not require immediate patient care, offer technical assistance to the existing medical operations.

Ongoing Actions:

- Ensure that proper medical and health practices and standards are observed.

- Coordinate continuously with the search and rescue medical team manager, local Ministry of Health, USAID/Embassy, other assisting country response teams, and UN/PVO/NGO/IOs.

Demobilization:

See the general checklist at the beginning of this chapter.

B. Search and Rescue Task Force Leader

The Search and Rescue Task Force Leader manages search and rescue (SAR) operations, and reports directly to the Operations Coordinator. Additional information on SAR operational response activities is located in FEMA's Urban Search and Rescue Response System *Field Operations Guide.* Specific responsibilities of the Search and Rescue Task Force Leader are as follows:

Predeparture:

- Contact the Operations Coordinator and receive a general briefing. In addition to the general checklist, discuss:

- Type and quantity of communication equipment for SAR operations.
- Construction techniques used in the affected country.

- Contact SAR personnel, brief them, and ensure their preparedness. SAR teams should be self-contained and able to function for 72 hours without resupply.

- Coordinate the acquisition and shipping of equipment. Ensure that engines are purged and air bottles bled. Specify the weight, cubes, and number of pieces and arrange for special handling requirements.

In-Country:

Immediate Actions:

- If the plan requires immediate SAR response, assist in selecting the worksite, setting up equipment, organizing SAR teams, and beginning operation.

- Develop a staff work schedule for the task force, considering the need for 24-hour operation.

- With the Press Officer and Operations Coordinator, establish an onsite media management protocol and brief the unit leaders.

- If the operational plan does not require an immediate tactical response, offer technical assistance to existing SAR operations.

Ongoing Actions:

- Coordinate closely with the Technical/Scientific Operations Specialists.

- Ensure that proper safety practices and standards are observed. Immediately shut down any life-threatening SAR activity.

Demobilization:

See the general checklist at the beginning of this chapter.

C. Technical/Scientific Operations Specialists

Technical/Scientific Operations Specialists provide DART with technical and scientific expertise pertaining to the disaster.

Specialists assigned to the team may be from several different fields, including shelter/housing, volcanology, geology, structural engineering, fire suppression, or hazardous materials (hazmat). These specialists should not be confused with specialists specifically assigned to the DART planning function to provide assessments in technical and scientific areas (see *Planning Coordinator*).

When assigned to the operations function, Technical/Scientific Operations Specialists are expected to perform operational activities such as working with the affected country and other organizations in teaching the proper use of USG-supplied relief commodities, taking measurements and samples, monitoring geologic activities, or providing technical advice in fire suppression and hazmat handling. These specialists report directly to the Operations Coordinator. Specific responsibilities of Technical/Scientific Operations Specialists are as follows:

Predeparture:

- Contact the Operations Coordinator and receive a general briefing. In addition to the general checklist, discuss:
  - In-country support needs.
  - Current technical resources and relief commodities requested of USG by the affected country. Obtain a list.
  - Affected country's technical/scientific capabilities to use resources and commodities.
  - Status of OFDA stockpile items and stockpile usage procedures.
  - Availability of in-country support services.
  - Contact list for technical/scientific government officials and organizations in affected country.

- Coordinate the acquisition and shipping of equipment.

- Consider the need for specialized equipment or adapters for the affected country.

- Specify the weight, cubes, and number of pieces and arrange for special customs clearance requirements.

In-Country:

Immediate Actions:

- Establish contacts with USAID/Embassy and local counterpart experts. Share information on the disaster and predicted technological occurrences.

- Assess the affected country's and other response organizations' abilities to use technical/scientific resources and commodities provided by USG, and where resources and commodities would be best used.

- If emergency shelter is required, work with the logistics function to:
  - Perform a thorough damage and needs assessment of the shelter situation.
  - Move plastic sheeting as close as possible to the area of victims' needs.
  - Establish a location for distribution, such as a large gym or soccer field. Ensure security and prevent distribution to inappropriate recipients.
  - Establish a system of tracking and accounting with local officials or UN/PVO/NGO/IOs.
  - Conduct training on the best use of plastic sheeting, distribute instructions, and provide assistance.
  - Coordinate closely with local housing authorities and USAID/Embassy specialists on the local shelter situation.

Ongoing Actions:

- Ensure the acquisition and shipping of appropriate technical/scientific equipment and relief supplies, including such items as OFDA plastic sheeting and seismic monitoring devices. Specify the weight, cubes, and number of pieces and arrange for special handling requirements as needed.

- Advise the Operations Coordinator of technological or scientific problems.

- Coordinate with the Safety Officer (if he/she is on the DART) on a medical evacuation plan and health and safety issues for DART members.

- Offer assistance to existing technical and scientific operations.

Demobilization:

See the general checklist at the beginning of this chapter.

Planning Coordinator

The Planning Coordinator manages DART planning, assessing, reporting, personnel tracking, information analysis, and documentation activities and makes recommendations based on an analysis of information. The Planning Coordinator reports directly to the Team Leader, and serves as the acting Team Leader, during his/her absence. Specific responsibilities of the Planning Coordinator are as follows:

Predeparture:

- Contact the Team Leader and receive a general briefing. In addition to the general checklist, discuss:
  - Reporting guidelines, procedures, formats, and timeframes for DART cables, situation reports, and final disaster reports.
  - Points of contact for reporting information to USAID/Embassy, OFDA/W, UN, and affected country.
  - Types and frequency of assessments required by objectives.
  - Types (if any) of USG-funded grants and/or contracts currently in place in the affected country.
  - Level of monitoring/assessment of present grants and/or contracts to be performed by DART.
  - Level of review expected for new proposals for relief activities.

- Discuss the guidelines, procedures, formats, and timeframes for information reporting with the OFDA/W information specialist responsible for the disaster relief effort.

- Ensure the acquisition and shipping of special supplies for the planning function.

- Ensure that adequate telecommunications equipment is ordered, considering requirements for conducting assessments, tracking resources, updating current events, and conveying information back to Washington.

- With the Team Leader and OFDA staff, conduct the initial DART briefing. Cover all items under "In Travel" checklists and provide a security briefing, travel advisory alert, public health bulletin, and a list of do's and don'ts.

- Ensure that the planning staff obtains copies of USG-funded relief activity grants and/or contracts that the DART will be monitoring in the affected country.

- Obtain a copy of OFDA's guidelines for grant proposals.

- Ensure that adequate maps of the affected country and mapping supplies are obtained.

In-Country:

Immediate Actions:

- Locate the affected country's emergency management organization and/or onsite operations coordination center; report the DART's capabilities, requirements, and objectives; and receive work area assignments (if the DART has an operational component).

- Set up an initial team briefing. Set the time, place, and list of attendees for future planning meetings.

- Supervise the formulation of an initial team operational plan based on immediate evaluations from all functions.

- Establish a DART headquarters and begin operation.

- Oversee the damage and needs assessment process and the development of a map of the affected area showing location of DART activities and of grants/contracts activities.

- At the DART headquarters, oversee the setup of information displays, including organization charts, resource tracking systems, maps, chronologies of major events and team activities, and situation reports. (See also *DART Setup and Closeout Guidelines* in Chapter I, "General Responsibilities and Information.")

- Develop a staff work schedule for function.

- Establish an operational plan development process with contributions from DART members. Decide if the plan will be given verbally or in writing to DART members. The plan should include:
  - Operational strategy and objectives (Team Leader and Planning Coordinator).
  - Tactical actions (Operations Coordinator).

- Work assignments (Operations and Planning Coordinators).
- Communications plan (Communications Officer).
- Transportation plan (Transportation Officer).
- Commodity distribution plan (Logistics Coordinator).
- Work maps (Information Officer).
- Medevac plan (Safety Officer or Admin Officer).
- Demobilization plan (Planning Coordinator).

- Determine a daily DART briefing and debriefing procedure and time schedule and inform the Team Leader.

- With the Press Officer, establish procedures for press visits to command post (access to visual displays, situation reports, resource status information).

- Establish liaisons with UN/PVO/NGO/IOs, assisting country teams, donor countries, and the affected country to share information related to the disaster.

Ongoing Actions:

- Conduct regular planning briefing and debriefing sessions. Ensure that:
  - Appropriate DART members submit information on time.
  - Sessions are objective oriented.
  - Strategy and tactics are developed and understood.
  - Sessions are brief, conducted on time, and have proper attendance.
  - Information is well-documented.
  - Displays and maps are used for illustration and are available as needed.

- Ensure the satisfactory completion and reporting of assessments.

- Ensure the monitoring of USG-funded relief activities as required.

- Identify and request Technical/Scientific Specialists as needed. Brief and supervise these specialists when deployed with the DART.

- Ensure that DART members regularly submit updates on situation status, work progress, resource location, and significant events.

- Oversee the situation and cable reporting-and-distribution process.

- Oversee the proper documentation of all DART activities.

- Conduct a daily critique of the operational plan's effectiveness, analyze information gathered by the planning staff, and make recommendations to the Team Leader:
  - Recommend alternative team objectives.
  - Recommend an increase or decrease in the resources/activities needed to complete team objectives as objectives change.
  - Ensure the collection of unit logs from team members.

Demobilization:

- Supervise the development of the demobilization plan.

- Ensure that all DART members have submitted the necessary information for the final disaster report.

- Submit a draft of the final disaster report to the Team Leader for review.

- Complete a final disaster report and present it to the Team Leader.

- Submit all reports, evaluations, unit logs, and personnel time records to the Team Leader.

- Compile information (lessons learned, points of contact, reports, etc.) that would be useful for the After Action Workshop.

A. Information Officer

The Information Officer collects, analyzes, documents, and distributes information on DART activities; prepares all situation reports and assists with the preparation of cables, briefing papers, the DART operational plan, maps, and final disaster report; tracks DART resources; and coordinates information-gathering and reporting activities with UN/PVO/NGO/IOs, other donor countries, and the affected country. The Information Officer reports directly to the Planning Coordinator. Specific responsibilities of the Information Officer are as follows:

Predeparture:

- Contact the Planning Coordinator and receive a general briefing. In addition to the general checklist, discuss:
    - Reporting guidelines, procedures, formats, and timeframes for DART cables, situation reports, and final disaster reports.
    - Points of contact for reporting information to the USAID/Embassy, OFDA/W, UN, and affected country.
    - Obtain a list of the UN/PVO/NGO/IOs and donor countries, with names and numbers if possible, that are working on disaster relief in the affected country.

- Discuss with the OFDA/W information specialist responsible for the disaster, the guidelines, procedures, formats, and timeframes for preparing information.

- Identify, prepare, and arrange for shipping of special supplies for the planning function.

- Obtain adequate maps of the affected area and mapping supplies.

In-Country:

Immediate Actions:

- Perform an immediate initial evaluation of the information unit's needs. Coordinate with the administrative function.

- Assist in the preparation of the initial operational plan.

- Set up and maintain a tracking system for DART members.

- Work with the Logistics Officer to set up and maintain a tracking system for USG commodities. Use this information for the situation report.

- Establish local contacts and liaisons with USAID/Embassy.

- Prepare an initial map of the affected area.

- Establish a clearance process for situation reports and cables with the Team Leader.

- Develop a distribution list for situation reports and operational plans.

Ongoing Actions:

- Prepare and get clearance for situation reports according to identified procedures.

- Debrief Field Officer(s), Program Officer(s), and Technical/Scientific Specialist(s).

- Prepare and distribute DART operational plans as needed (see the *Planning Coordinator* section for elements of the plan).

- Coordinate information gathering and sharing with other UN/PVO/NGO/IOs, other donor countries, and the affected country. This includes attending coordination meetings.

- Take field trips and assist with assessments as necessary to collect onsite field information.

- Continually collect, verify, analyze, and update information on the general disaster status, progress of relief activities, areas of concern, maps, displays, and personnel and resource status locations from DART members and other sources.

- Document, distribute, and file the planning function information, including situation reports, maps, cables, field reports, operational plans, logs, and meeting notes.

- Make recommendations on future DART actions.

- Provide the press with access to displays and information at prearranged times.

- As requested, provide copies of documents for meetings and briefings.

- Individually record significant actions and events in the unit log each day and file.

- Collect and file unit logs from all DART personnel for use in the disaster chronology.

Demobilization:

- Assist with the preparation of the final disaster report by collecting all reports, evaluations, field reports, unit logs, and personnel time records from DART personnel and submit to Planning Coordinator.

- Ensure that the requested documentation is distributed to local USAID/Embassy prior to departure.

- Prepare planning function materials, supplies, and files for return shipment to the United States Account for missing items.

B. Field Officer

The Field Officer conducts field assessments of damage and the needs in the affected areas; monitors the effectiveness of relief activities conducted by the affected country, UN/PVO/NGO/IOs, and other donor countries; makes recommendations on areas of focus for USG relief efforts; and provides written assessment reports to the Information Officer. The Field Officer reports directly to the Planning Coordinator. Specific responsibilities of the Field Officer are as follows:

Predeparture:

- Contact the Planning Coordinator and receive a general briefing. In addition to the general checklist, discuss:
  - Guidelines, procedures, formats, and timeframes for field assessment reports.
  - Types and frequency of assessments required by the objectives.

- Obtain a list of the UN/PVO/NGO/IOs and donor countries, with names and numbers if possible, that are working on disaster relief in the affected country.

- Obtain maps of the affected area.

In-Country:

Immediate Actions:

- Obtain information on the locations of relief activities being conducted by the groups mentioned above.

- Transpose the above information to a map.

- Share the above information with the Information Officer.

- Begin an initial field assessment based on priorities in the initial operational plan.

Ongoing Actions:

- Continue field assessments as required.

- Continue to provide the Information Officer with assessment information.

- Provide inputs to the operational plan.

- Attend briefings and debriefings as required.

Demobilization:

See the general checklist at the beginning of this chapter.

C. Program Officer

The Program Officer assesses the effectiveness of USG-funded relief projects conducted by UN/PVO/NGO/IOs and coordinates with these groups and the planning staff to identify potential areas of focus for USG relief projects; performs initial reviews of grant/contract proposals submitted to the DART and/or OFDA/W by PVO/NGO/IOs; and makes recommendations on improvements to the proposals and on whether or not to fund projects. The Program Officer reports directly to the Planning Coordinator. Specific responsibilities of the Program Officer are as follows:

Predeparture:

- Contact the Planning Coordinator and receive a general briefing. In addition to the general checklist, discuss:
  - Types and frequency of monitoring/assessment of grant activities required.
  - Level of review expected for new proposals for relief projects.

- Obtain a copy of USG-funded relief activity grants and/or contracts in place in the affected country.

- Obtain a list of the relief projects being funded by UN/PVO/NGO/IOs and donor countries in the affected country. Try to get contact names and phone numbers if possible.

- Meet or contact the OFDA/W PVO coordinator to discuss UN/PVO/NGO/IO activities (occurring or expected) in the affected country.

- Meet or contact the OFDA/W staff members dealing with UN/PVO/NGO/IO grant/contract proposals to receive a briefing on the OFDA grant/contract review process.

- Obtain a copy of OFDA's guidelines for grant proposals.

- Obtain maps of the affected area.

In-Country:

Immediate Actions:

- Establish liaisons with UN/PVO/NGO/IOs presently performing USG-funded relief projects.

- Locate USG-funded relief grants/contracts projects.

- Transpose the above information to a map.

- Share the above information with the Information Officer.

Ongoing Actions:

- Conduct field assessments of USG-funded projects as required.

- Continue to provide the Information Officer with relief activity assessment information.

- Continue to coordinate with the USG-funded groups.

- Recommend relief activity areas that need to be addressed.

- Solicit new project proposals for these areas.

- Review and recommend changes to, and/or action on, new proposals.

- Provide inputs to the operational plan.

- Attend briefings and debriefings as required.

Demobilization:

See the general checklist at the beginning of this chapter.

D. Technical/Scientific Specialists

Technical/Scientific Specialists provide DART with technical and scientific expertise pertaining to specific areas of need caused by the disaster. These specialists assess the disaster situation; identify disaster relief/rehabilitation needs; review in-place USG-funded projects; and, with other DART members, make recommendations on the design of appropriate USG-funded interventions and programs.

Specialists assigned to a DART may be from several different technical/scientific fields, including shelter/housing, water, sanitation, food, health, infrastructure (transportation and utilities), volcanology, geology, hydrology, and fire suppression. Examples of these specialists include: Centers for Disease Control (CDC) doctors, Public Health service officers, Food for Peace officers, RHUDO officers, electrical engineers, transportation experts, disaster consultants, and Forest Service fire-suppression officers. These specialists should not be confused with Technical/Scientific Specialists assigned to the DART operations function who provide onsite technical/scientific support to DART operations and the affected country (see DART operations). Technical/Scientific Specialists report directly to the Planning Coordinator. Specific responsibilities of Technical/Scientific Specialists are as follows:

Predeparture:

- Contact the Planning Coordinator and receive a general briefing. In addition to the general checklist, discuss:
    - In-country support needs.
    - Current technical/scientific resources and relief commodities requested of USG by the affected country. Obtain a list.
    - Affected country's technical/scientific capabilities to use resources and commodities.
    - Availability of in-country support services.
    - Contact list for technical/scientific government officials and organizations in the affected country.
    - What other UN/PVO/NGO/IOs and other donor countries are doing and their capabilities.

- Coordinate the acquisition and shipping of equipment.

In-Country:

Immediate Actions:

- Establish contacts with technical/scientific experts at USAID/Embassy, UN/PVO/NGO/IOs, the affected country, and other donor governments to assess the status of relief activities to date and projected.

- Conduct assessments in areas not covered by the above groups.

- Prepare a report on the general situation by area of expertise, based on information from the above groups and a personal assessment. Include recommendations for follow-on actions and an assessment of the ability of the affected country and the groups mentioned above to make use of the technical/scientific resources and commodities proposed or provided by the USG.

Ongoing Actions:

- Monitor the actions of the above groups for the effectiveness of their response.

- Conduct further assessments and make further recommendations as necessary.

- Work closely with the Field Officer and Program Officer to ensure their inputs into DART recommendations.

Demobilization:

See the general checklist at the beginning of this chapter.

Note: The above position description is generalized for any Technical/Scientific Specialist assigned to a DART planning function. This Field Operations Guide does not contain position descriptions for every type of specialist that could be assigned to a DART. However, brief descriptions, and responsibilities, for some specialists that have been assigned to DART's in the past are listed below.

Types of Technical/Scientific Specialists:

The following specialist position description summaries represent types of Technical/Scientific Specialists that might be assigned to a DART.

1. Water and Sanitation Specialists

In-Country:

- Perform an immediate initial evaluation of the water and sanitation situation; discuss needs with local health and public works officials, USAID/Embassy, other response teams, and relief organizations dealing in water and sanitation; and assess the ability of the affected country's public works department to rehabilitate its systems.

- Conduct a thorough survey of the public water supply and waste management systems. Determine the needs for immediate repairs, and identify such areas on a map.

- Survey the water distribution and sanitation system in temporary shelter areas.

- Identify the areas in greatest need of corrective actions.

- Make recommendations on the best method of USG response to address the situation. Include ways to coordinate USG efforts with the local government, UN/PVO/NGO/IOs, and other donor government operations.

2. Health Specialists

In-Country:

- Perform an immediate initial evaluation of the health situation. Discuss needs with the affected country's health officials, USAID/Embassy, UN/PVO/NGO/IOs, and other donor countries.

- Coordinate or establish a disease and nutritional surveillance system and collect data as necessary. Determine the cause or source.

- Advise local health officials on findings and suggest control measures, including vector, food, and sanitation control, and their effect on food and water sources.

- Evaluate ongoing sanitary or public health programs.

- Investigate unconfirmed reports of disease outbreaks and malnutrition.

- Coordinate continuously with the above groups.

- Make recommendations on the best method of USG response to the situation.

3. Food Specialists

In-Country:

- Perform an immediate initial evaluation of the food security situation. Discuss with the affected country's officials, USAID/Embassy (Food for Peace Officer if present), UN/PVO/NGO/IOs, and other donor countries. Collect information on:
  - Affected country's normal food production rates.
  - Food production rates as a result of the disaster.
  - Food requirements (compare the affected government's estimates with other nongovernment estimates).
  - Amount of locally available food.
  - Amount of shortfall.
  - Amount of food in the pipeline from all sources.
  - Food for Peace commodities potentially available, from where, and how long delivery will take.
  - Normal food basket of the affected population, with acceptable alternatives.
  - Condition (from ports to victims) of the food distribution system, including the ability of food distribution organizations.
  - Availability of transport to move food within the affected country or from a third country into the affected country

- Review the food-sector portions of proposals for their appropriateness to the disaster situation.

- Monitor food distribution, quantify losses if possible, and make recommendations for improvements.

- Coordinate with the Food for Peace Officer (FFP) in-country and/or FFP/W and provide recommendations on commodity transfers and administrative funding requirements.

Administrative Officer

The Administrative Officer manages the DART's fiscal and administrative activities; hires and manages local personnel; and procures supplies, services, and facilities for the DART. The Administrative Officer reports directly to the Team Leader. Specific responsibilities of the Administrative Officer are as follows:

Predeparture:

- Contact the Team Leader and receive a general briefing. In addition to the general checklist, discuss the following:
  - Fiscal authorities and levels delegated to the Team Leader by OFDA/W and authorities that will be redelegated to the Contracts Officer, such as authority to sign relief grants and contracts and purchase orders.
  - Fiscal reporting requirements and timeframes for DART cables, situation reports, and final disaster reports.
  - Reporting relationships and points of contact with USAID/Embassy and OFDA/W.
  - Awareness of the USAID Financial Management Office of the deployment of the DART and its possible workload consequences.
  - Types (if any) of USG-funded relief grants and/or contracts in place in affected country at present.
  - Fiscal monitoring requirements for administrative function.
  - Types and levels of administrative support to be provided by administrative function to DART.
  - Funding cable for team support—amount, status, etc.
  - Warrant level for Contracts Officer.
  - Disaster funding by other USG agencies such as DOD, and DOS and how it is being administered.
  - DART member fiscal responsibilities and allowances such as per diem versus purchase order for lodging, local travel, phone call policy, and limits on petty cash reimbursements.
  - Ramifications for administrative function of the "Notwithstanding" clause of the FAA.
  - Emergency information on all DART members.

- Contact USAID/Embassy to discuss administrative support issues. Obtain names and telephone numbers of EXO and controller or person responsible for receiving DART allocations.

- Obtain copies of the pertinent USAID directives dealing with travel and administrative operations, disaster assistance, accountability, and contracts.

- Ensure the acquisition and proper shipment of computer equipment (hardware and software) and office supplies for the administrative function. If assigned by the Team Leader, obtain team support list items.

In-Country:

Immediate Actions:

- Establish contacts with USAID/Embassy. Determine reporting relationships; ability to support the DART with personnel, office equipment, space, transportation, and procurement; and the availability of local storage and work space, local hires, equipment, supplies, relief commodities, and transportation. Specifically discuss the following issues:
    - Setting up a petty cash account. Establish necessary recordkeeping, replenishment timeframes and levels, and local currency availability.
    - Methods of communication with USAID/Embassy (phone, fax, radios). What communications equipment/ services will the DART have to supply/pay for and how?
    - Motor pool procedures.
    - Procurement procedures.
    - Check-cashing policy for team members.
    - Travel office procedures.
    - Local hire procedures.
    - Potential FAAS or SEP budget issues.
    - Methods the DART can use to reduce its effect on the USAID/Embassy.

- Select a worksite, set up equipment, and begin operations.

- Develop staff work schedule by function.

- Hire local personnel as needed.

- Establish procedures for time and attendance and payroll.

Ongoing Actions:

- Establish a precise accounting and tracking system to ensure that all fiscal and administrative support actions are monitored, accurately documented, and filed in a safe place.

- Provide the Team Leader with regular reports on the amount of money spent and obligated by the DART.

- If appropriate and agreed to by USAID/Embassy, establish contacts at MFA to explain the DART's mission and needs, such as assistance with customs expediting and waivers.

- Contribute regularly to the team planning process.

- Advise other functions on cost estimates for proposed actions.

- Prepare DART support budgets as required. Provide for contingencies.

- Inform and oversee proper timekeeping procedures for all DART personnel.

- Ensure a complete transfer of knowledge of the operation of the administration function if replaced. Plan enough time for the transition.

Demobilization:

- Ensure that all rented facilities and equipment are inspected prior to turning over; and that the inspection is documented. Conduct the inspection with owners if possible.

- Ensure that all purchase orders (personnel, equipment, and facilities) and payments are closed and prepare documents for final billing.

- Ensure that requested documentation is distributed to the local USAID/Embassy prior to departure.

- Ensure that arrangements are made for the disposition of any remaining facilities, equipment, and supplies with USAID/Embassy.

- Ensure that the DART documentation package is prepared.

- Ensure that equipment, files, and records are accounted for and prepared for return shipment to the United States.

A. Procurement Specialist

The Procurement Specialist procures facilities, services, and supplies for the DART and establishes and administers DART vendor contracts. The Procurement Specialist reports directly to the Administrative Officer. Specific responsibilities of the Procurement Specialist are as follows:

Predeparture:

- Contact the Administrative Officer and receive a general briefing. In addition to the general checklist, discuss:
    - Fiscal authorities delegated to Administrative Officer and redelegated to Procurement Officer, such as the authority to sign service contracts, set up purchase orders, and administer petty cash.
    - Fiscal signing authorities of the DART.
    - Fiscal reporting requirements and timeframes for DART cables, situation reports, OFDA MIS, and final disaster reports.
    - Reporting relationships and points of contact with USAID/Embassy and OFDA/W.
    - DART member fiscal responsibilities and allowances such as per diem versus purchase order for lodging, local travel, phone call policy, and limits on petty cash reimbursements.
    - Types and levels of administrative support to be provided by administrative function to the DART.
    - Funding cable for team support—amount, status, etc.

- With the Administrative Officer, contact USAID/Embassy to discuss administrative and support issues. Get names and numbers of EXO and controller or whomever will receive DART allocations.

- Assist the Administrative Officer in obtaining pertinent copies of USAID directives dealing with travel and administrative operations, disaster assistance, accountability, and contracts.

- Ensure the acquisition and proper shipment of computer equipment (hardware and software) and office supplies for the administrative function. If assigned by the Team Leader, obtain team support list items.

In-Country:

Immediate Actions:

- With the Administrative Officer, establish contacts with USAID/Embassy. Determine reporting relationships and the availability of personnel support, including administrative, equipment rental, storage and work space, local hire, procurement of supplies and commodities, and transportation. Specifically discuss the following issues:

- Setting up a petty cash account. Establish necessary recordkeeping, replenishment timeframes and levels, and local currency availability.
- Methods of communication with USAID/Embassy. Phone, fax, radios; who supplies what; and who pays and how.
- Motor pool procedures.
- Check-cashing policy for team members.
- Contract travel office procedures.
- Local hire procedures.
- USAID/Embassy local banking procedures.

• Select a worksite, set up equipment, and begin operations.

• If necessary, arrange for the rental of buildings and equipment. Hire personnel as needed. Set up purchase orders with hotels. Prior to leasing or purchasing any facilities, vehicles, or equipment, inspect them with the owner and document the conditions.

Ongoing Actions:

• Ensure that all procurement actions are accurately documented and that information is filed in a safe, weatherproof area.

• Regularly provide the Administrative Officer with reports on the amount of money spent and obligated for DART support.

• Monitor vendor contracts.

• Ensure that proper safety and security practices and standards are observed.

• Establish a fiscal tracking system for all DART support expenditures.

• Set up a recordkeeping and filing system.

• Coordinate the acquisition and distribution of office supplies.

• Establish a facility, vehicle, and equipment maintenance system.

• Establish and monitor procedures for the contract/procurement and tracking of services provided to the DART.

- Contact American businesses and solicit assistance with labor, storage space, transportation, and interpreters.

- Points to consider when leasing or purchasing vehicles:
  - Country laws on liability, insurance, licensing, and leasing.
  - Cost analysis between leasing with a package (driver, insurance, license) versus purchasing plus cost of driver, insurance, and license.
  - Field use versus city use.
  - Accidents (budget for them).
  - Fleet size and capability mix.
  - Personal use policy.
  - Availability of taxis (the factor here is the ability to communicate with the drivers).
  - Maintenance.
  - Disposal at the end of DART assignment.

- Points to consider when hiring locals for DART support:
  - Country laws on hiring. May include very high taxes on wages or add-on charges.
  - Embassy procedures: hiring, firing, evaluation criteria and system, benefits, currency payment, citizenship, tribe, grade structure, seniority, and workmen's compensation.
  - Legality of using a purchase order to hire a local employee.
  - Forms of payment: Treasury check, dollars, or local currency (local hires almost always want cash).
  - Hiring PSCs has other issues such as scopes of work, job descriptions, liability, and efficiency reports.
  - Advertising for employment.
  - Testing potential employees.

- Points to consider when deciding on housing for DART members:
  - OE-funded versus program-funded employees.
  - Hotel costs per day are high, but provide convenience of maid service and possibly less logistical coordination for transportation of team members.
  - Hotels costs may be reduced with a purchase order for a block of rooms.
  - Consider morale factor of long-term hotel living.
  - Renting apartments or houses is cheaper by the month but may require additional logistical support, such as maid service for short-term TDYers or even for DART

members working long hours; extended travel time for pickups and dropoffs; and availability of restaurants or stores (markets) to purchase food.
- Apartments or houses may also require housecleaning contracts and maintenance contracts, and will have to be furnished.

- Points to consider when deciding to lease or purchase equipment:
  - Voltage and the need for generators, transformers, surge protectors, and/or power stabilizers.
  - Locally availability of parts and service.
  - Expected duration of the DART deployment.

Demobilization:

- Conduct a postinspection of rented facilities and equipment and document it. Conduct the inspection with the owner if possible.

- Conclude all contracts, purchase orders (personnel, equipment and facilities), and payments and prepare documents for final billing.

- Prepare requested documentation and distribute to local USAID/Embassy prior to departure.

- Make arrangements for disposition of remaining facilities, equipment, and supplies with USAID/Embassy.

- Assist with the preparation of the DART documentation package.

- Account for equipment, files, and records, and prepare them for return shipment to the United States.

B. Administrative Support Specialist

The Administrative Support Specialist provides administrative support to all DART functions. This position is usually filled by a local hire through USAID/Embassy network or directly from the affected community. The Administrative Support Specialist reports directly to the Administrative Officer for employment issues, but may take daily direction from any function that he/she is assigned to. Specific responsibilities of the Administrative Support Specialist are as follows:

In-Country:

Immediate Actions (upon being hired):

- Perform an immediate initial evaluation of administrative support needs. Consider the need for phones, radios, fax machines, typewriters, computers, electricity, work/storage space, and the ability to expand, if necessary. Identify needs to supervisor.

- Establish and monitor procedures for use of office equipment.

Ongoing Actions (performed for various functions):

- Assist with the development of an efficient recordkeeping system tailored to the DART's structure and space.

- Drive vehicles.

- Assume day-to-day responsibilities for processing purchase orders, petty cash transactions, payments for leases, payroll, time and attendance, and other financial responsibilities.

- Provide unofficial interpretive and translation services.

- As requested, type, file, fax, and copy.

- Answer phones and radios and keep communications logs.

- Act as a receptionist.

- Take and write up meeting notes.

- Assist in briefings.

- Provide expediting services as required.

- Assist in preparing maps.

- Assist in maintaining tracking systems by gathering information and filling out forms.

- Give general advice on local issues such as laws, customs, government and private sector, and locations of supplies, equipment, and commodities.

Demobilization:

- Assist with preparation of DART documentation package.

- Complete paperwork on time and attendance.

- Receive an evaluation.

- Ensure that equipment, files, and records are accounted for and prepared for return shipment to the United States.

Contracts Officer

The Contracts Officer is responsible for reviewing, negotiating, processing, approving, and signing grant proposals and contracts submitted by UN/PVO/NGO/IOs and contractors in the field. Contracts Officers are unique in that they bring with them to the field a USAID warrant authority. The Director of OFDA, through the Team Leader, delegates to the DART an authority to sign grants up to a certain amount per grant and a certain cumulative amount. The Team Leader does not have the warrant authority and therefore works with the Contracts Officer to ensure that the delegation of authority received from OFDA/W is followed. Because of the unique authorities and responsibilities inherent in the Contracts Officer's warrant authority, the Contracts Officer reports to the Team Leader for all DART activities except those inherent to the warrant. Specific responsibilities of the Contracts Officer are as follows:

Predeparture:

- Contact the Team Leader and receive a general briefing. In addition to the general checklist, discuss:
    - Fiscal authorities and levels delegated to Team Leader by OFDA/W and authorities that will be redelegated to the Contracts Officer, such as authority to sign relief grants and contracts and purchase orders.
    - The level of review desired for contracts and grants.
    - Fiscal reporting requirements and timeframes for DART cables, situation reports, and final disaster reports.
    - Reporting relationships and points of contact with USAID/Embassy and OFDA/W.
    - Awareness by USAID Financial Management Office of the deployment of the DART and its possible workload consequences.
    - Types (if any) of USG-funded relief grants or contracts currently in place or submitted for the affected country.
    - Fiscal monitoring requirements for grants and contracts.

- Relationships with other DART members regarding grants and contracts, such as Program Officer or Field Officer.
- Types and levels of contract support to be provided to DART by OFDA's grants or contracting review function and USAID's Contracts Office.
- Funding cable for team support—amount, status.
- Disaster funding and by other USG agencies such as DOS and DOD and administration of funds.
- Ramifications for contracts function of the "Notwithstanding" clause of the FAA.

- Contact USAID/Embassy to discuss contracting and support issues. Obtain names and telephone numbers of EXO and controller or person responsible for receiving DART allocations.

- Obtain copies of pertinent USAID Directives dealing with disaster assistance, Food for Peace, grants, and contracts.

- Obtain copies of the latest OFDA Grant Proposal Guidelines.

- Ensure the acquisition and proper shipment of computer equipment (hardware and software) and office supplies for the contracting function.

In-Country:

Immediate Actions:

- Establish contacts with USAID/Embassy. Determine reporting relationships and ability to support the DART with personnel, office equipment, space, transportation, and procurement. Determine availability of work space, local hires, equipment, supplies, and transportation. Specifically discuss the following issues:
  - Methods of communication with USAID/Embassy (phone, fax, radios).
  - Methods DART can use to reduce its impact on the USAID/Embassy.

- Select a work site, set up equipment, and begin operation.

- Develop staff work schedule (if any) for function.

- If necessary, prepare and execute contracts for the rental of buildings, vehicles, and equipment. Hire local personnel as needed.

Ongoing Actions:

- Establish an accounting and tracking system to ensure that all fiscal actions are monitored, accurately documented, and filed in a safe place.

- Provide Team Leader with regular reports on the amount of funds obligated by the contracts function.

- Contribute regularly to team planning process.

- Work closely with Program Officer in reviewing grant proposals for appropriateness to DART strategy, budget, implementation/completion timeframes, and ability of grantee to carry out proposal. Advise other functions on these actions.

- Ensure a complete transfer of knowledge of the operation of the contracting function if replaced prior to the demobilization of the team. Plan enough time for the transition.

Demobilization:

- If Contracts Officer demobilizes and is not replaced prior to team demobilization, coordinate closely with Team Leader and Program Officer to ensure transfer of knowledge as to the location and status of all appropriate files and paperwork.

- Ensure all contracts are closed and prepare documents for final billing.

- Ensure that requested documentation is distributed to local USAID/Embassy prior to departure.

- Ensure that arrangements are made for the disposition of any remaining facilities, equipment, and supplies with USAID/Embassy.

- Ensure the preparation of the DART documentation package.

- Ensure that equipment, files, and records are accounted for and prepared for return shipment to the United States.

- See also *DART Setup and Closeout Guidelines* in Chapter I, "General Responsibilities and Information."

Chapter V

Forms and Instructions

FORMS AND INSTRUCTIONS

This chapter contains samples of forms and instructions for use during disaster assessments and response. The forms can be used to document assessments, communications, individual activities, and team progress; request, manifest, and track resources and commodities; and account for commodities issued. These sample forms are offered as optional methods to perform required documentation, tracking, and accounting. Their use is not required in that Disaster Resistance Response Team (DART) members may already have in place other forms and methods to perform the same functions.

Transportation Tracking Form

The **Transportation Tracking Form** is used to track the movement by aircraft, vehicle, or boat of resources to, from, and within a disaster. This form will help the DART or responsible individuals know the status of inroute resources assigned and act as a safety check for personnel who are traveling, by tracking departures and arrivals against schedules.

Instructions

Block 1   **Disaster Name**—Enter the name given to the disaster by the Office of Foreign Disaster Assistance (OFDA) (for example, Hurricane Hugo, Armenia Earthquake).

Block 2   **Vehicle/Aircraft Type**—Enter the type of transport (for example, 2½-ton truck, C–130, boat).

Block 3   **Vehicle/Aircraft ID**—Enter the identification number or letters for the vehicle or aircraft (for example, United Airlines Flight #123, DOD N3456, with mission number if known).

Block 4   **Passengers/Cargo**—Enter the total number of passengers (pax) and the weight of the cargo for each portion of movement (for example, 5 pax/ 1,000#). For the names of the passengers and description of the cargo, see the Transportation Manifest Form.

Block 5   **Date**—Enter the date of travel (for example, 1/2/90).

Block 6   **From**—Enter the place of departure.

Block 7 **To**—Enter the destination point.

Block 8 **Transit Time**—Enter the estimated time of departure (ETD), the actual time of departure (ATD), the estimated time of arrival (ETA), and the actual time of arrival (ATA). Put all times in local times.

Block 9 **Remarks**—Enter any remarks that you feel are pertinent.

Note: For a specific listing of cargo/passengers, see request numbers on the Transportation Manifest and Resource Request Forms.

Transportation Tracking

Disaster Name		Vehicle/Aircraft Type		Vehicle/Aircraft ID			
1		2					3

Passengers/Cargo 4	Date 5	From 6	To 7	Transit Time 8			
				Depart		Arrive	
				ETD	ATD	ETD	ATD

Remarks 9

Transportation Manifest Form

The **Transportation Manifest Form** is used to document what resources (personnel, equipment, commodities, and supplies) are transported to, from, or within a disaster. This form should be filled out by the sending unit or the chief of party at the point of departure. It is a three-part form. Part 1 is to be left at the point of departure. Part 2 is for the receiving organization or responsible individual at the destination point. Part 3 is for the chief of party's records. If possible, once the form has been filled out, make copies of it, as the form contains useful lists for those who need to know the names of traveling individuals at intermediate stops and at the various check-in locations at the destination point.

Instructions

Block 1   **Disaster Name**—Enter the name given to the disaster by OFDA (for example, Hurricane Hugo, Armenia Earthquake).

Block 2   **Page __ of __** —Enter the page number and the total number of pages used in manifesting the resources.

Block 3   **Vehicle/Aircraft ID**—Enter the identification number or letters for the vehicle or aircraft (for example, United Airlines Flight #123, DOD C–130 N3456, with mission number if known).

Block 4   **Chief of Party**—Enter the name (if personnel are traveling) of the individual who is the point of contact for those traveling as a group.

Block 5   **Report To**—Enter the name of the person who is the point of contact or consignee at the destination. Be sure to include the phone number or radio frequency (for example, Paul Bell 234-4567 or 127.45 VHF).

Block 6   **If Delayed, Contact**—Enter the name of the person who is the point of contact if transportation is delayed or rerouted. Be sure to include the phone number or radio frequency.

Block 7   **Place of Departure**—Enter the name of the location from which the transportation is originating. Include the estimated time of departure (ETD) and the actual time of departure (ATD). All times should be listed in local times.

Block 8   **Intermediate Stops**—List any intermediate stops, with points of contact and estimated times of arrival and departure at those stops. Use the Remarks area if you need more room (for example, ETA 1/3/90 0345 Honolulu, HI, ETD 1/3/90 0600, Jim Smith 818-234-6789).

Block 9   **Destination**—Enter the final destination; the estimated time of arrival; and, upon arrival, the actual time of arrival. All times should be local (for example, ETA 1/4/90 1200 Tonga Int'l ATA 1/4/90 1345).

Block 10   **Request No.**—If known, enter the request number from the Resource Request Form for the item or person that is being transported. This will help reference back to the Resource Request Number that originated the request for the resources (for example, 6/29-1).

Block 11   **Resource Description and/or Pax Name**—Enter the resource description or name of the passenger (pax). Put the dressed weight of the passenger after his/her name (for example, blankets, water purification unit; Pete Bradford—195). You may also want to put in an abbreviation of the pax's home organization.

Block 12   **Cargo/Bag. Wt.**—Enter the weight of the cargo or passenger's bag(s). This is very important when manifesting for small aircraft.

Block 13   **Cubic/Dim.**—Enter the total cubic feet of each item and the dimensions of the largest piece of cargo being transported. This includes the bags and equipment of each person manifested. This will help when setting up transportation to meet specific requirements such as large cargo doors or an appropriately sized truck to pick up resources.

Block 14   **Remarks**—Enter any remarks as needed, such as intermediate stops not listed in item 8 or possible changes in carriers.

Block 15   **Print Name, Sign, and Date**—The person preparing the manifest should print his or her name and sign and date the form.

Transportation Manifest

Disaster Name	1	Page ____ of ____	2

Vehicle/Aircraft Identification No.	3

Chief of Party	4	Report To	5	If Delayed, Contact Phone No.	6
		Phone			

Place of Departure	7	Intermediate Stops	8	Destination	9
ETD (Local)				ETA (Local)	
ATD (Local)				ATA (Local)	

10 Req. No.	Resource Description and/or Pax Name 11	12 Cargo/Bag Weight	13 Cubic/Dim.

Remarks	14

Print Name, Sign, and Date	15

Resource Request Form

The **Resource Request Form** is used by the logistics function of a DART to track and document resources requested by the DART to support a disaster. It may also be used to keep an inventory of resources on hand as the resources are issued. These resources can include supplies, commodities, personnel, aircraft, and services.

Instructions

Block 1   **Disaster Name**—Enter the name given to the disaster by OFDA (for example, Hurricane Hugo, Armenia Earthquake).

Block 2   **Page __ of __** —Sequentially number the pages used.

Block 3   **Date/Request No.**—Enter a date/request number for each item requested. Start each day with the number 01 and continue consecutively (for example, 6/29–01, 6/29–02, 6/30–01, 6/30–02). This number will be a specific number that identifies the resources that are requested/received.

Block 4   **From**—Enter the initials and an abbreviation for the location of the person who is requesting the resources.

Block 5   **To**—Enter the initials and an abbreviation for the location of the person who is receiving the request for the resources.

Block 6   **Resource Description**—Enter a description of the items requested. Use standard OFDA descriptions whenever possible (for example, blankets, wool; water containers, 5-gallon). Be as descriptive as is required to make sure the request is clear (for example, Radio tech., with expertise in HF radios).

Block 7   **Quantity Requested**—Enter the quantity requested.

Block 8   **Unit of Issue**—Enter the unit of issue (for example, ea. = each, bx. = box, bbl. = barrel, cs. = case).

Block 9 **Quantity Received**—Use this block to identify how many of the requested resources have been received. Do this as the resources arrive. Use a pencil, as this quantity will change if the requested amounts come on several deliveries. Be sure to cable OFDA upon receipt of the requested items.

Block 10 **Quantity Issued**—Use this block to identify how many of the requested resources have been issued. Use a pencil, as this quantity will change as resources are issued. Maintaining an accurate number of quantities received and issued will provide an inventory of quantities on hand.

Block 11 **Remarks**—Use as needed to clarify information.

Resource Request

Disaster Name

3 Date/ Request No.	4 From	5 To	Resource Description	6	7 Qty. Req.	8 Unit Issue	9 Qty. Rec'd.	10 Qty. Issued	11 Remarks

Commodity Issue Form

The **Commodity Issue Form** is used when commodities are issued by the DART or by USAID or the U.S. Embassy in the affected country, or to private voluntary organizations (PVOs), nongovernmental organizations (NGOs), or international organiztions (IOs) for distribution. For complete tracking of commodities, the host country should also fill out this form or similar documentation when it reissues these commodities to the next level in the commodities distribution system. It is the responsibility of USAID, the Embassy, or the DART to retrieve a signed copy of this form from the host country or PVO/NGO/IOs upon completion of the distribution of the commodities. This form is required to document the movement of commodities and to balance the inventory of those commodities. This form should be filed with the final disaster documentation package. This form can also be used to hand-receipt returnable items, such as radios, to individuals.

The Commodity Issue Form has three parts. The first part remains with the issuing point. The second and third parts are taken by the transporter, along with the commodities. Upon receiving the commodities, the recipient or consignee signs the form and retains part 2. The recipient or consignee of the commodities sends part 3 back to the issuer to complete the accounting cycle. The bottom of the form will indicate who should retain which part.

Instructions

Block 1   **Disaster Name**—Enter the name given to the disaster by OFDA (for example, Hurricane Hugo, Armenia Earthquake).

Block 2   **Page __ of __**—Enter the page number and the total pages used of this form each time commodities are issued.

Block 3   **Date**—Enter the day and month of the transaction, excluding the year (for example, 4/21).

Block 4   **Method of Transportation**—Enter how the items were transferred from issue point to delivery point (for example, Truck #123, DOD C–130, Aircraft N3456).

Block 5 **From**—Enter the agency and location from which the commodities are being sent (for example, OFDA, USA).

Block 6 **To**—Enter the agency and location to which the items are being issued (for example, UNDHA, Yerevan, Armenia).

Block 7 **No.**—Sequentially number the commodities you are issuing.

Block 8 **Commodity Description**—Enter a description of the commodity that is being issued (for example, blankets, wool; water containers, 5-gallon; water; wheat; rice). If the form is being used as a hand receipt, be sure to include serial numbers or other identifiers (for example, chainsaw S/N 23456, radio MX–360 P/N 35678).

Block 9 **Quantity Issued**—Enter the amount of each commodity being issued.

Block 10 **Unit of Issue**—Enter the unit of issue (for example, box, bundle, carton, case) or unit of measure (for example, liters, gallons, pounds, kilos, metric tons).

Block 11 **Issued By**—Enter the printed name, signature, and title of the issuing party and date.

Block 12 **Transported By**—Enter the printed name, signature, and title of the transporting party and date. By signing, the transporter acknowledges that the items listed above have been received for transportation.

Block 13 **Received By**—Enter the printed name, signature, and title of the receiving party and date. By signing, the recipient acknowledges that the items listed above, unless otherwise noted, have been received.

Block 14 **Remarks**—Identify items listed above that have not been received or have been received in a damaged condition. Indicate in this box whether the recipient in Block 13 is a country, a PVO/NGO/IO, an individual, or an institution such as a hospital or a school and if the recipient is delivering relief supplies directly to victims. If the recipient is delivering directly to victims, estimate the number of victims who will receive assistance.

Commodity Issue

Disaster Name	1	Page ____ of ____	2

Date	3	Method of Transportation	4

From 5	To 6
Agency	Agency
Location	Location

7 No.	Commodity Description 8	Qty. 9 Issued	Unit 10 of Issue

Issued By (Print Name)	11
Signature	
Title	
Date	

Transported By (Print Name)	12
Signature	
Title	
Date	

Received By (Print Name)	13
Signature	
Title	
Date	

Remarks	14

T-Card

T-Cards have a variety of uses. They can be used to track or to maintain the status of people, equipment, and/or commodities. Using the different-colored T-Cards and the T-Card holder, T-Cards can visually organize information in a variety of ways and can be quickly referenced. T-Cards are easily transportable with the T-Card holder. How and if you use T-Cards will depend on your needs and other tracking and status equipment you have, but T-Cards provide a simple system for organizing information at a disaster.

Sample 1:
Header: Smith, Peter - Metro Dade

Assignment(s): Operations Coordinator
Date of Arrival: 6/18
Date of Departure: 6/30

Sample 2:
Header: Plastic Sheeting

Date(s) and Amounts Ordered:	3/24	500 rolls	
	3/30	250 rolls	
Date(s) Arrived:	3/26	225	via C-141 from Italy
	3/27	225	via C-141 from Italy
	3/29	50	via C-141 from Italy
	4/02	250	via C-5 from Italy

Date(s) Distributed and Consignee:

	3/26	175 rolls to Red Cross, Smith
	3/26	50 rolls to school superintendent, Brady
	3/28	125 rolls to St. Johns Mayor, Byrd

Sample 3:
Header: King Radio (S/N 384258)
Date Arrived: 6/21
Assigned To:
John Carroll—DART, 6/21
Sam Smith—Jamaica RC, 6/23
John Carroll—DART, 6/29
Released To:
OFDA, by John Carroll, 7/12

Smith, Peter — Metro Dade Fire

Position — Operations Coordinator

Deployed — 6/29 to Kingston

Deployed — 6/30 to Paradise

Departed — 7/15

KING RADIO - S/N 384258

Arrived — 6/21

Assigned To: John Carroll 6/21

Sam Smith — Jamaica RC 6/23

Chief Warden — Kingston FD 6/27

John Carroll (DART) 6/29

Released To OFDA by John Carroll — 7/1

Field Situation Reporting Format (SITREP)

This sample identifies the basic information needed by the DART planning function for planning and documentation purposes, and information needed by OFDA for use in assisting and supporting the DART and for assembling the OFDA Situation Report. Each disaster will dictate other information to be included in the field sitrep. Items to include are as follows:

1. DART field location, including city and country.
   Sitrep No.:
   Date:

2. Disaster Data:
   - Number affected.
   - Number of dead.
   - Number of injured.
   - Death rate.
   - Number of moderately and severely malnourished.
   - Availability of food and water.
   - Epidemics.
   - Number vaccinated.
   - Number of homeless/displaced.
   - Location of displaced camps.
   - Extent of damage (buildings damaged and destroyed, area of flooding, amount of damage to roads and bridges, area of drought, areas of civil strife, etc.).
   - Status of transportation systems for emergency response.
   - Short narrative on the overall situation.

3. Issues (political and others) arising or needing resolution and DART recommendations.

4. DART activities since last report (sample information to report):
   - Number of DART members and their locations.
   - Assessment of activities by function.
   - Accomplishments by function (persons assisted, meetings attended, commodities received from OFDA stockpile, or other shipments of USG donations, commodities distributed).
   - Estimated cost-to-date expended directly by the DART.
   - Coordination with other USG responders (USAID Mission, Embassy, DOD).

5. Activities of others:
   - Affected country.
   - Other donor countries.
   - UN.
   - PVO/NGO/IOs.

6. Actions requested of Washington:
   - Requests for personnel, equipment, supplies for DART.
   - Requests for relief commodities.
   - Status of previous requests (reference Sitrep No.).
   - Requests for information.
   - Answers to or status of issues raised previously (reference Sitrep No.).

Unit Log

A **Unit Log** should be used by all DART members to document important activities that occur during their assignment, such as work progress, meetings attended, people and organizations contacted, and personal movements. This Unit Log form is offered as an example of a form to document such activities. The important point is to make sure that you do have written documentation of your activities. Check with your DART supervisor to see how often you should turn in written documentation to the planning function. You may want to make a copy of your documentation for trip reports and also for travel voucher documentation purposes.

Instructions

The Unit Log is self-explanatory.

Unit Log

Name		Disaster
Date	Time	Major Events

Initials and Date

Communications Log

The **Communications Log** can be used to document information transmitted over phones, radios, or person to person, or as a DART Unit Log.

Instructions

Block 1   **Disaster Name**—Enter the name given to the disaster by OFDA (for example, Hurricane Hugo, Armenia Earthquake).

Block 2   **Pg___of____**—Number the pages of the log in sequential order.

Block 3   **Date/Time**—Chronologically enter information for better referencing at a later time.

Block 4   **Station (From/To)**—Identifies who is calling whom. Clarifies the context of the information sent or received.

Block 5   **Remarks**—Refers to main information sent or received during information exchange.

Block 6   **Initials**—Identifies who received or sent the information in the remarks column. It provides a method of contacting the person writing in the remarks column if more information or clarification is needed.

Communications Log

Disaster Name		Station				
3		4			5	6
Date / Time		From / To	Remarks			Initials
/						
/						
/						
/						
/						
/						
/						
/						
/						
/						
/						
/						
/						
/						
/						

Chapter VI

Reference Information

REFERENCE INFORMATION

This chapter contains reference information on Disaster Assistance Response Team (DART) communications systems; maps and mapping; aircraft use and capabilities; Office of Foreign Disaster Assistance (OFDA) stockpile commodities and DART support equipment and supplies, including detailed information on the use of plastic sheeting; and information on working with military organizations during field operations.

DART Communications

A. Requirements

The DART has the responsibility to communicate with the following:

- US Embassy/USAID Mission (USAID/Embassy).

- OFDA/Washington (OFDA/W).

- Affected country officials as required.

- Relevant parties within the DART organization and potentially at dispersed sites in the affected country.

- Private voluntary organizations (PVOs), nongovernmental organizations (NGOs), international organizations (IOs), and United Nations (UN) relief organizations.

B. Systems

1. General

There are three main types of communications systems used by a DART:

- Public switched telephone networks (PSTN), also called the "local phone system."

- Satellite (INMARSAT and VSAT) systems.

- Radio (HF/VHF/UHF) networks and systems.

Communications systems are chosen based on DART requirements. These include:

- Need for high-volume use.

- Portability.
- Ability to support various modes of communication, including among others:
  - Standard voice.
  - Computer data (networked or stand-alone e-mail connections).
  - Fax.
  - Text-only messaging and video conferencing.

2. The Local Phone System (PSTN)

Services—Services, quality, and availability vary with disaster locations. Following a disaster, if phone service is available, voice-grade lines will be available first (digital- and computer-grade lines may not be immediately available). Available phone circuits may be overloaded, and there may be difficulty accessing outside lines. Standard phone services are capable of providing ordinary voice and fax modes. Computer modes (e-mail/network) and extremely high-grade video conferencing modes require specially conditioned phone lines that are not always available.

Operating Range—Nearly all metropolitan areas worldwide offer some degree of telephone services, but they are not always available in rural areas.

Terrain Effects—Overhead telephone lines suspended on poles are often among the first casualties of natural or manmade disasters.

Weather Effects—Wet conditions may cause degradation or disconnection of telephone signals. Severe weather may knock down telephone poles, completely disrupting services.

Setup Time—It may take up to 10 minutes to learn and understand different dialing procedures. Because of overloaded circuits and the poor quality of telephone connections, patience may be required when attempting to make connections.

3. Satellite Terminal Systems

Services—Common telephone and data services are available from land-based terminals using the portable International Maritime Satellite (INMARSAT) or semifixed Very Small Aperture Terminal (VSAT) satellite network. These services include voice, fax, and e-mail communications. Any device that works with a common telephone device works with satellite systems. In addition to the above-mentioned services, some satellite terminals offer transfer of digital photographs or live video conferencing. Satellite signals may be digitally processed, giving your voice a computer-sounding characteristic. Table VI–1 contains additional information about satellite terminal systems.

Operating Range—Satellite terminal systems operate at any location between latitudes of 70° N. and 70° S., worldwide.

Terrain Effects—The satellite antenna or dish must have a clear, unobstructed view of the sky in the direction of the satellite.

Weather Effects—Heavy rains may impair the signal and high winds may disorient the antenna or dish placement.

Frequency Selection—The operating frequency is set and is not under user control.

Setup Time—
  – For portable INMARSAT terminals, setup can take 10 to 15 minutes.
  – For VSAT terminals, setup can take 30 minutes to 3 hours or more (depending on system complexity).

Voltage Requirements—These systems require 90 to 250 VAC 50/60 Hz, 10 to 30 VDC and generally will operate on any electricity available, including from most automobiles.

Shipping Requirements—Depends on system.

4. HF/VHF/UHF Radio Networks and Systems

Services—Transmission of voice and digital data may be accomplished with two stations that are similarly equipped for the desired modes of communications. Table VI–1 contains additional information about HF/VHF/UHF systems.

Operating Range—HF radio is most useful for long-distance communications. VHF/UHF are considered line-of-sight dependent, typically 3 to 10 miles. This range may be extended up to 30 to 40 miles with a high-mounted repeater and antenna. Range of special aircraft radios depends upon the altitude of the aircraft.

Terrain Effects—Trees, buildings, mountains, etc., may limit range of all radio systems. UHF radio waves are best to penetrate confined spaces such as collapsed buildings. VHF radio is a better choice for dense foliage such as jungles. *All* radio

Table VI–1. Characteristics of Radio and Satellite Communications

Type and Range	Equipment and Remarks
VHF/UHF, 3–25 miles, line-of-sight	Hand-held or mobile units. Antenna size and terrain have effect on range. Use for onsite coordination, personal security, and individual communications.
VHF/UHF with repeater, wider range	Same as above, but with a repeater station placed in the highest possible location.
HF (shortwave/voice), regional to worldwide	Mobile stations (car-radio size) and base stations. Range depends on antenna used. Use for regional communications, 50–1,000 miles.
HF (shortwave/data), regional to worldwide	Base station includes modem, laptop computer, power supply, and antenna. Needs qualified operator. Data links with similar stations worldwide.
Standard A, worldwide satellite terminal	Terminal in a suitcase, with parabolic antenna. Accessories in a separate box of 60 pounds. Use for phone, fax, and e-mail.
Standard B, worldwide satellite terminal	Digital version of Standard A; smaller antenna. Use for phone, fax, and e-mail. Some models offer high-speed data links and multiple phone/fax lines (with field public exchange).
Standard C, worldwide satellite terminal	Terminal in a suitcase, includes laptop computer, printer, and omnidirectional antenna. Built-in battery (4-hours standby). Use to send and receive e-mail and send fax; *no phone.*
Standard M, worldwide satellite terminal	Attaché case with flat antenna in lid. Use for phone, fax, or e-mail. Requires separate laptop computer or fax machine.

Note: Satellite terminals listed here are INMARSAT.

antennas (especially HF) must be mounted in a high location in a clearing for best results.

Weather Effects—With the exception of the most severe rains and wind, weather has only a minor effect on HF or VHF. Some degradation on UHF during heavy rains may be noticed. Quality of HF communications depends upon severity of solar activity (which changes throughout the day) in combination with the selected frequency. For this reason, multiple frequencies must be used throughout the day to effectively communicate with HF radio.

Frequency Selection—The Communications Officer determines specific operating frequencies. Use of existing USAID/ Embassy frequencies may be authorized and are preferred. Frequency allocation from foreign governments takes time and is not automatic. Organizations such as UN/PVO/NGO/IOs, MARS (Military Affiliate Radio Systems), amateur radio networks, etc., may have prior frequency arrangements of which the DART, if authorized, may take advantage.

Setup Times—Initial base stations or repeaters require 30 minutes to 2 hours to set up. Installation (if required) of taller antennas, additional data modes, or more complex network systems may take several hours. Programming of radio frequencies may require up to 10 minutes per unit.

Voltage Requirements—These systems require 90 to 250 VAC 50/60 Hz, 10 to 30 VDC and generally will operate on any electricity available, including from most automobiles.

Shipping and Handling—Radios are considered by many governments to be controlled items. Special considerations (licenses, declarations, or authorizations) may be required before importation into the host country.

C. Policy on the Use of Frequencies

In all cases, the host government has both the authority and the responsibility to control the use of communications equipment within its borders. A reasonable attempt must be made by the DART to obtain authorization from the host government for the use of radio communications equipment. The DART Communications Officer will request authorization through USAID/Embassy. Written authorization is preferred, but may not be possible to obtain in time of disasters. Frequency selection by the DART is the responsibility of the Communications Officer.

D. Radio Identification and Communications Procedures

1. Radio Identification

Radio identifications or call signs will be assigned by the Communications Officer in accordance with international agreements, host government laws, or USAID/Embassy policies. As a security precaution, coordinate with the embassy in the selection of a call sign that does not indicate you are a ranking official or authority figure.

2. Communications Procedures

The following radio communications procedures should be used:

- Speak clearly, using plain language and no codes.

- Begin the transmission with the call sign of the station you are calling, followed with your call sign.

- If a reply is expected, end your transmission with "over."

- If no reply is anticipated, end your transmission with "out."

- Use standard phonetics as illustrated below for call signs, station identifications, and spelling of words and names that may not be easily understood.

3. Phonetic Alphabet

A	alpha	J	juliet	S	sierra
B	bravo	K	kilo	T	tango
C	charlie	L	lima	U	uniform
D	delta	M	mike	V	victor
E	echo	N	november	W	whiskey
F	foxtrot	O	oscar	X	x-ray
G	golf	P	papa	Y	yankee
H	hotel	Q	quebec	Z	zulu
I	india	R	romeo		

Maps and Mapping

Assessment Teams and DARTs can both use and make maps of factors affecting disaster relief operations. Assessment Teams and DARTs will be referred to as "Field Teams" because the information here on maps and mapping is used by both. Typical map applications include general orientation and reference, operational and strategic planning, results monitoring, and communication of information. Although any Field Team member may wish to obtain and use maps or contribute to creating them, the Team Leader should consider the operational and planning potential of maps, determine an appropriate level of effort, and delegate responsibilities accordingly.

A. Predeparture

Predeparture preparations include obtaining maps for field use, and, if warranted, making predeparture arrangements for additional data collection and map production during field operations.

1. Obtaining Maps for Field Use

OFDA has access to both general and thematic maps from government and commercial sources. General orientation maps showing major populated places, roads, topography, national and subnational administrative boundaries, etc., are available from the National Imagery and Mapping Agency (NIMA), U.S. Department of State Library, Library of Congress, and local map stores. Thematic maps expressing specific details such as agricultural zones, ethnic groups, rainfall, etc., are also available from a wide variety of sources. When requesting maps, the following map specifications should be considered:

- **Size**—How big should the map be? Sizes range from page-size to multiple sheets covering an entire wall.

- **Geographic coverage**—What is the geographic window that the maps should cover? Regional, national, or subnational coverage may be desirable.

- **Features**—What features (that is, roads, rivers, airports, administrative boundaries) need to be shown on the map for it to serve its purpose? Is the map general or thematic?

Size and geographic coverage determine a map's scale, typically expressed as a ratio of units on the map to units on the ground. A scale of 1:10,000 is considered large-scale, appropriate for showing a detailed street plan of a city. Another common large scale is 1:50,000, which shows subnational detail. Several 1:250,000 medium-scale sheets will cover a small country. Small-scale maps are available at 1:1,000,000 and 1:2,000,000. Three large 1:4,000,000 sheets are sufficient to cover the entire continent of Africa.

Map products that have proven useful in the past include the NIMA's 1:250,000 Joint Operations Graphics; the State Department's page-size, general country maps; and tourist or road maps of selected countries. **NIMA maps in larger than 1:250,000 scales are marked "Official U.S. Government Use Only" and may not be distributed otherwise without permission from NIMA.** Such permission may be obtained in disaster situations, however.

2. Predeparture Arrangements for Field Data Collection and Map Production

Procedures for collecting and mapping field data are described below. Such efforts will be facilitated with planning prior to departure. Any Field Team member designated by the Team Leader as responsible for field mapping should review the following sections and make appropriate predeparture arrangements.

B. Mapping in the Field

The Planning Coordinator, Information Officer, Field Officer, and Administrative Support staff (specifically on a DART) all potentially have responsibilities for map data collection and map production. Training can be provided to equip these individuals for specific related tasks, as the Team Leader designates. In general, map data collection is a subset of the normal data collection undertaken by personnel in these positions. It can be done in the normal course of Field Team operations with little additional effort. Digital cartography for producing maps in the field, however, is time-consuming and requires special skills. If field production of anything other than simple maps is anticipated, either a specialist should be recruited or extra training provided. This section defines key terms and concepts and outlines procedures, required materials, and production options for generating up-to-date maps of key features of a disaster situation.

1. Field Applications

A common map application in the field is orientation (that is, knowing where things are). Off-the-shelf maps are the preferred option for this purpose. As OFDA often works in regions that are not well mapped, however, it is conceivable that a Field Team might need to specially commission maps for orientation after ascertaining that no serviceable maps already exist.

Specifications and procurement in such instances should be done in consultation with OFDA/W.

Field Teams may also wish to transfer situation-specific information—such as assessment data, relief organization locations, security incidents, relief assets, or locations and numbers of affected people—to a map for planning or communication purposes. These thematic maps may involve data collected firsthand by a Field Team or data from secondary sources. Procedures for collecting data and producing situation-specific thematic maps are described below.

Vulnerability maps are a commonly encountered type of thematic map. These are useful for guiding assessments to geographic areas that are likely to be hardest hit during a disaster. Vulnerability mapping is a task for specialists, requiring significant expertise in indicator selection and substantial resources for data collection. It is possible, however, that Field Teams may be involved in such efforts or even perform vulnerability assessments using rapid survey techniques.

2. Terms and Concepts

Feature—A point, line, or area object in the real world—a well, a road, or an administrative district, for example.

Attribute—Information about a feature—for example, a well can be operational or dry.

Theme—A geographic distribution of some phenomenon such as rainfall, population density, agricultural productivity, etc.

Symbol—A representation of something in the real world on a map. Like features, symbols are classified as point, line, or area, and also include text.

Scale—Relationship between map distances and ground distances. Commonly expressed as a ratio (for example, 1:10,000) or as a line labeled with the ground distances it represents.

Legend—A description of the symbols used on the map.

Reference Information—Includes the date, title, data sources, and an orientation symbol.

Various standard types of maps have been developed for conveying certain types of information. Graduated symbol maps use symbols of varying sizes to represent quantities. Choropleth maps use shaded or hatched unit areas to convey quantitative information. Dot density maps are well suited for communicating continuous distributions. Reference maps may simply consist of text or pictorial symbols to communicate locations of features of interest.

Map data manipulation and production is often accomplished using a computer, even when the output is a paper product.

3. Options for Thematic Map Production

This section outlines three options for generating and distributing maps from the field.

Adding features to existing paper maps—When the map will be used primarily in the field, data can be drawn onto an acetate overlay of a wall map or indicated with stickies or colored push-pins. For wider distribution, black-and-white page-sized paper base maps can be annotated and photocopied. Page-size maps are limited, however, in the amount of information that can be added to them without crowding. Wall maps cannot be easily distributed but can convey more information than a page-size map because of their larger size. Such base maps should be obtained prior to departure if possible.

Adding features to digital maps in the field using a computer—This option has greater technical requirements than working with paper maps. These include a computer that has been equipped with appropriate software, a printer, base map data, a reliable electricity source, a protected environment, and a cartographic specialist or someone who has received special training.

In-the-field–Washington coproduction of digital maps—Under this option, data is collected in the field but the maps are produced in Washington. Distribution back to the field is accomplished via electronic file transfer, pouch, or fax. Both Washington and the Field Team view the same map, which enhances communication. The Field Team is relieved of the cartography burden, and a professional cartographer executes the map. This option requires the greatest amount of preparation, however, and start-up coordination may be difficult. Additionally, the Field Team must be equipped with the proper hardware if files are to be electronically transferred or map graphic files are to be printed in the field. Special training may be required.

4. Procedures

The following procedures apply to most Field Team mapping applications, although they can be followed less formally in simple cases. Map production proceeds in the following steps:

- **Define the purposes**—Purposes include briefings, situation reports, activity tracking, results monitoring, and strategic and operational planning.

- **Design the map**—Determine the map's size, geographic coverage, base data, and thematic data requirements.

- **Data collection and georeferencing**—All data to be mapped must be georeferenced. A georeference indicates where each data item is located. Features for which precise location is unimportant can be mapped by eye. Place names can serve as georeferences. The most useful level of geo-referencing for page-size maps is often at the level of the first subnational administrative unit (for example, the province). Very precise locational data (within 100 meters) can be obtained using a Global Positioning System (GPS), available from OFDA. GPSs are useful for giving geographic coordinates of features that are not already associated with existing named locations, such as refugee camps, or features for which the exact location is important, such as boreholes. GPS georeferencing requires physically going to the location to obtain its position.

- **Select the appropriate production option**—Refer to *Options for Thematic Map Production,* above. Transfer the georeferenced data to a base map, using appropriate symbolization and cartographic design principles, and generate the final product.

- **Distribution**—Determine quantities and distribution format (that is, digital or hardcopy) in advance.

Aircraft Information

A. General

OFDA frequently uses aircraft to support disaster response activities. It may use either commercial aircraft or DOD aircraft.

OFDA must first check the availability of commercial air carriers to meet disaster response needs. If commercial aircraft are available, they are chartered by OFDA logistics, through USAID's Office of Transportation. Often, commercial air carriers do not have the aircraft available to meet the short timeframes required by OFDA. Only if commercial aircraft are not available may OFDA request assistance from DOD. If DOD approves the request, OFDA will work directly with the Joint Chiefs of Staff's (J–4) Logistics Readiness Center to work out the details on needs, availability, timeframes, and accountability. Be advised that anytime DOD aircraft are used, OFDA must follow all DOD regulations on weights, cubes, manifesting, hazardous cargo, and takeoff and landings. If more information is needed on DOD regulations or restrictions, contact OFDA's Logistics Officer.

When loading and offloading any type of aircraft, the pilot or the crew chief are in charge. They will make the final determination on a "go/no-go" for the flight, based on the load, weather conditions, runway conditions, and any conditions specific to the flight.

Always think SAFETY around aircraft!! Follow the instructions of the pilot or crew chief.

B. Points to Consider when Dealing with Aircraft

Whenever possible, all materials to be airlifted should be stored in containers (for example, suitcases, backpacks, metal and cardboard boxes) for rapid handling and for stacking onto pallets.

All individual containers must be small enough to fit through passenger doors of commercial aircraft in case cargo space is not available.

Personal gear should be well-packaged (for example, in a pack or suitcase), with the owner's name clearly marked, to allow for rapid customs processing.

Packages containing hazardous materials or chemicals must be well-marked and kept separate from all other cargo so they can be left behind if they are refused by the carrier.

Individual pieces of cargo should not weigh more than 200 pounds to allow for movement by two people. Each DART member is responsible for his or her personal luggage.

The length of the flight will determine fuel requirements and, thus, the cargo capacity of the aircraft. The more fuel required, the less weight for cargo.

Crew duty day times are very important and must be followed. Aircraft at your disposal do not represent an unlimited resource. Find out the flight crew's duty times for your planning purposes, considering the following:

- Crew duty day refers to the maximum time that a flight crew can be engaged in standing by for a flight or actually flying in an aircraft (normally this is 15 hours combined).

- Crew flight time refers to the maximum time a flight crew can spend physically flying or maintaining an aircraft. Sometimes certain preflight and postflight aircraft activities are included in crew flight time duty. This should be verified with the flight crew in advance.

C. Aircraft Loading and Offloading Methods

Aircraft may be loaded in four ways:

- **Bulk Loaded**—Cargo is loaded on the floor and held in place by nets, straps, or ropes.

- **Palletized**—Cargo is preloaded onto pallets; held in place by nets, straps, or ropes; and then loaded onto the aircraft.

- **Containerized**—Cargo is preloaded into closed containers and then loaded onto the aircraft.

- **External (helicopters only)**—Cargo is placed in a net or suspended from a line and picked up and moved by the helicopter using a belly hook.

Bulk loading may increase the usable cargo space on an aircraft; however, securing cargo in place may be more difficult. Bulk loading also slows loading and offloading, sorting, distribution, and customs processing.

Palletizing cargo is the method most often used to move OFDA commodities. OFDA usually uses DOD (U.S. Air Force) aircraft for short-timeframe disaster support, and the DOD's preferred method of cargo packaging is using pallets and netting. Commercial aircraft can also use pallets.

Military pallets, officially called dual rail 463L pallets (nicknamed "cookie sheets"), measure 88 × 108 inches, are made of aluminum, and weigh 356 pounds. The loaded pallets can range in weight from 2,000 to 6,000 pounds. **These pallets are reusable and must be returned. Do not leave them!** They are used on the C–5s, C–17s, C–141s, C–130s, and some commercial aircraft. For logistical planning purposes, when building pallets, limit the height of a stack to 96 inches for these aircraft unless authorized to stack higher by the crew chief.

The size of commercial pallets varies, but is most often 88 × 108 inches or 88 × 125 inches . They are used on DC–8s, B–727s, DC–10s, and B–747s and weigh over 300 pounds. These pallets are also reusable. Commercial Hercules also use a pallet that is 88 × 118 inches.

It is possible to build up pallets on the aircraft, but it is more difficult and very time-consuming. Remember, flight crew duty time is ticking!

Containerizing cargo is a method used to load large commercial aircraft such as 747s and DC–10s. Cargo containers come in a great variety of shapes and sizes, and their maximum loaded weights can range from less that 1,000 pounds to 25,000 pounds. Each type is designed to be loaded and offloaded with cargo in place using a mechanized loading system or a forklift. Containerizing is very difficult and time-consuming, and sometimes it is impossible to hand-load or unload containers once they are on the aircraft.

If a forklift will be used to load or offload containers or pallets, make sure that the forklift can carry the largest pallet, has tines long enough to counterbalance the weight, and that the highest point of the forklift is lower than that portion of the aircraft (wing, tail, or door in open position) where it must move to retrieve the container or pallet.

External loading of cargo is done with helicopters. Helicopters normally can lift and move more cargo externally (slinging) than internally. The external cargo is loaded into specially made nets that are connected to a cargo hook on the belly of the helicopter. Cargo may also be suspended on cables (leadlines). Make sure leadlines and nets are approved for slinging cargo.

Remember: Pallets, containers, nets, and leadlines are reusable. They may also need to be returned quickly to their point of origin so they can be used for loading more cargo. Always think in terms of "backhauling" cargo equipment for reuse or when it is no longer needed.

D. Points to Consider when Planning To Receive Aircraft Cargo

- Ramp space for parking the aircraft. If there is no ramp space and you will have to unload on the active runway, consider offloading time and the schedules of other aircraft arrivals.

- The weight of the loaded aircraft and the ability of the ramp to support parked aircraft.

- Availability of trucks and laborers if the aircraft will be manually offloaded. Remember, planes may arrive at all hours.

- Availability of a correctly sized forklift, if the aircraft will be offloaded using a forklift. Think again about arrival times. If no forklift is available, OFDA logistics may be able to get approval from DOD for the Air Force to bring one along on the arriving aircraft. This, however, may reduce the amount of relief commodities that will fit on the aircraft.

- Storage space near the ramp if the commodities will be stored close to the offloading point. Consider whether the location of the storage area will cause security problems.

Tables VI–2 and VI–3 list some types of fixed-winged and rotary-winged aircraft that have been or might be used by OFDA during disaster operations. They include specifications for the different categories of aircraft. The purpose of these tables is to assist in planning for the movement of people and commodities. Note however that **these figures represent *approximate* aircraft specifications.** Figures for each aircraft will vary based on individual aircraft configurations and ratings, operating range, runway conditions, temperature, altitude, wind speed, and direction. Always check with local aviation authorities as to what type of aircraft can operate in and out of local airports. This chart does not include specifications for aircraft capable of spraying insecticides. These specifications are available through the OFDA Logistics Officer.

Note: The cargo capacities and cruise speeds listed below are averages for that type of aircraft. Actual capacities will vary based on the altitude, ambient air temperature, and fuel actually on board. Table VI–4 lists some overland transport capabilities.

Table VI–2. Types of Aircraft That May Be Used by OFDA During Disaster Operations

Aircraft Type	Fuel Type	Cruising Speed (knots)	Runway Length (ft.)	Cargo Weight (lbs.)	Cargo Volume (cu. ft.)	Door Size (H x W in inches)	Pallet Size (H x W in inches)	Pallet Qty.	Container Types
C-5	Jet	423	7,700	130,000	13,000	150 x 228	88 x 108	36	open pallet
C-17	Jet	410	4,500	90,000	20,900	126 x 216	88 x 108	18	open pallet
C-141B	Jet	410	6,300	40,000	4,500	106 x 123	88 x 108	13	open pallet
C-130	Jet	280	3,000	25,000	2,000	108 x 123	88 x 108	6	open pallet
Antonov 124	Jet	450	10,000	300,000	30,000	173 x 238	all	n/a	all
Beach 18	AvGas	135	1,800	2,500	285	n/a	n/a	n/a	n/a
Beach 99	Jet	225	1,750	5,000	n/a	n/a	n/a	n/a	n/a
B-377/C97	AvGas	220	5,000	32,000	n/a	173 x 162	n/a	n/a	n/a
B-707-320C	Jet	450	8,000	80,000	6,000	89 x 134	88x108/125	13	all
B-727-100	Jet	495	7,000	35,000	8,100	89 x 134	88 x 125	9	A, A-2
B-727-200	Jet	495	8,300	55,000	8,100	120 x 134	88 x 125	30	A, A-2
B-747-100	Jet	490	9,400	223,000	20,750	n/a	88 x 125	29	A, A-2
B-747-200	Jet	490	10,700	229,000	22,175	n/a	88 x 125	37	A, A-2
Casa C-212	Jet	195	2,500	4,000	n/a	n/a	n/a	n/a	n/a
Cessna 340 A (Propjet)	Jet	195	2,500	n/a	n/a	n/a	n/a	n/a	n/a
Cessna 414	Jet	200	2,400	n/a	n/a	n/a	n/a	n/a	n/a

Table VI–2. Types of Aircraft That May Be Used by OFDA During Disaster Operations (contd.)

Aircraft Type	Fuel Type	Cruising Speed (knots)	Runway Length (ft.)	Cargo Weight (lbs.)	Cargo Volume (cu. ft.)	Door Size (H x W in inches)	Pallet Size (H x W in inches)	Pallet Qty.	Container Types
Cessna 421–C (Propjet)	Jet	185	2,400	n/a	n/a	n/a	n/a	n/a	n/a
C–46	AvGas	150	3,000	12,000	3,300	n/a	n/a	n/a	n/a
DHC–6 Otter (Propjet)	Jet	160	1,900	3,500	506	50 x 56	n/a	n/a	n/a
F–28 (Propjet)	Jet	380	5,200	15,000	3,400	n/a	n/a	n/a	n/a
F–27 (Propjet)	Jet	240	6,000	7,500	1,980	n/a	n/a	n/a	n/a
Transall C–160	Jet	n/a	3,300	37,000	4,900	n/a	n/a	n/a	n/a
L–188 Electra (Propjet)	Jet	310	6,000	32,000	3,700	78 x 140	88 x 108	8	all
L–55 Learjet	Jet	460	4,500	n/a	n/a	n/a	n/a	n/a	n/a
L–100-10 Hercules	Jet	275	4,300	25,000	4,500	108 x 120	88x108/118	6	open pallet
L–100-20 Hercules	Jet	275	4,500	37,000	5,300	108 x 120	88x108/118	7	open pallet
L–100-30 Hercules	Jet	280	4,300	40,000	6,057	108 x 120	88x108/118	8	open pallet
Skyvan	Jet	130	1,500	3,500	780	72 x 72	n/a	n/a	n/a
Westwind I 124	Jet	450	4,900	1,190	n/a	n/a	n/a	n/a	n/a
Cessna 185	AvGas	130	1,400	900	n/a	n/a	n/a	n/a	n/a
Cessna 206	AvGas	130	1,500	1,100	n/a	n/a	n/a	n/a	n/a

Table VI–2. Types of Aircraft That May Be Used by OFDA During Disaster Operations (contd.)

Aircraft Type	Fuel Type	Cruising Speed (knots)	Runway Length (ft.)	Cargo Weight (lbs.)	Cargo Volume (cu. ft.)	Door Size (H x W in inches)	Pallet Size (H x W in inches)	Pallet Qty.	Container Types
Cessna 207	AvGas	130	1,900	2,500	340	n/a	n/a	n/a	n/a
Caravan	Jet	170	1,900	2,500	340	n/a	n/a	n/a	n/a
Turbo Porter	Jet	142	620	1,400	100	n/a	n/a	n/a	n/a
Helio Courier	AvGas	130	610	1,200	140	n/a	n/a	n/a	n/a
Dash 7	Jet	225	2,200	11,300	2,100	n/a	n/a	n/a	n/a
Dash 8	Jet	250	2,700	8,500	1,400	n/a	n/a	n/a	n/a
Ilyushin 76	Jet	430	2,800	75,000	8,300	n/a	n/a	n/a	n/a
DC–8 51F	Jet	480	8,000	61,000	n/a	n/a	n/a	n/a	n/a
DC–8 54F	Jet	480	8,000	95,800	n/a	n/a	n/a	n/a	n/a
DC–8 55F	Jet	480	8,000	97,000	n/a	n/a	n/a	n/a	n/a
DC–8 73F	Jet	480	8,000	102,000	n/a	n/a	n/a	n/a	n/a
DC–8 61F	Jet	480	8,000	83,000	n/a	n/a	n/a	n/a	n/a
DC–8 63F	Jet	480	8,000	94,000	n/a	n/a	n/a	n/a	n/a
DC–8 70F	Jet	480	8,000	85,000	n/a	n/a	n/a	n/a	n/a
DC–9	Jet	450	7,000	35,000	4,500	n/a	n/a	n/a	n/a

Table VI-3. Types of Helicopters That Might Be Used by OFDA During Disaster Operations

Helicopter Type	Fuel Type	Cruising Speed (knots)	Internal Cargo Weight (lbs.)	External Cargo Weight (lbs.)	No. of Passengers
B-204	Jet	100	2,600	3,100	10
B-205	Jet	100	2,600	3,100	14
B-206B	Jet	110	760	910	4
B-206L	Jet	110	970	970	6
B-212	Jet	100	2,600	3,100	14
B-214	Jet	100	3,000	7,000	12
A-STAR	Jet	125	1,100	1,400	5
Allouette II SA 318C	Jet	95	900	1,300	4
Hughes 500C	Jet	125	700	900	4
Hughes 500D	Jet	125	700	900	4
Allouette III	Jet	110	1,400	1,600	6
Lama SA 315B	Jet	100	1,400	1,400	4
BV-107	Jet	125	7,000	9,000	cargo only
BV-234	Jet	130	22,500	22,500	44
Hiller FH 1100	Jet	105	700	900	4
Bell G-47	AvGas	75	800	1,000	2

Table VI–4. Overland Transport Capacities

Surface Carrier	Payload
Standard railway car	30 MT (52 m^3)
Standard sea/land container	
–20 ft. (6.1 m)	18 MT (30 m^3)
–40 ft. (12.2 m)	26 MT (65 m^3)
Large lorry and trailer	20–30 MT
Large articulated lorry	30–40 MT
Medium lorry	5–8 MT
Long-wheelbase Land Rover/	
Land Cruiser or pickup	1 MT
Typical water tanker	8 MT (8 m^3)
Hand-drawn cart	300 kg
Camel	250 kg (more for short distances)
Donkey	100 kg
Bicycle	100 kg

Note: MT = metric tons.

OFDA Stockpile Commodities and DART Support Equipment

OFDA maintains stockpiles of standard relief commodities at four locations around the world. The purpose of these stockpiles is to position relief commodities closer to potential disaster sites to make relief commodities more immediately available to disaster victims. The prepositioning of these commodities also reduces the delivery costs.

Stockpiles are located in Maryland, Panama (closing in 1998), Italy, and Guam. The Panama, Guam, and Italy stockpiles are located on U.S. military installations, and the military by agreement assists with the handling and storage of these commodities. In Maryland, the stockpile is maintained through a contract with a private organization.

To access commodities in the stockpiles, the OFDA Logistics Officer notifies the stockpile managers of the type and amount of items needed for a disaster and coordinates the pickup and delivery of the commodities to the affected country. The types and amounts of commodities withdrawn from the stockpiles are based on the acceptance of needs assessments conveyed to OFDA from the affected country.

There is a chance that the initial stockpile commodities released to a disaster may precede the arrival of a DART. Upon arrival at a disaster site, DART members should be prepared to assist or take on the responsibility of locating or receiving, offloading, inventorying, issuing, tracking, and accounting for these commodities. If at any time during a disaster the DART needs further stockpile commodities, a request with a description of the need must be processed through OFDA. A DART cannot access the stockpiles directly.

Stockpile commodities may be released to UN/PVO/NGO/IOs that are qualified to distribute and instruct in the use of the commodities.

OFDA Logistics is constantly reviewing the usefulness, quality, and feasibility of both stockpile commodities and DART support equipment. OFDA Logistics also looks for new items for relief commodities and team support. Therefore OFDA may have commodities or support equipment available that are not listed below. For example, OFDA now owns a variety of vehicles for DART use. These vehicles have a range of capabilities including gas or diesel, left- or right-hand drive, armored or unarmored. If you have a need or an idea, convey that to OFDA Logistics and they may be able to assist you.

Information critical to the planning of all aspects of the ordering, movement, tracking, and accounting of OFDA stockpile commodities and DART support equipment is provided below. This section also contains detailed information about obtaining and using plastic sheeting to construct temporary shelters.

A. OFDA Office Supply Kit

The OFDA office supply kit is designed to provide the DART with office supplies. It will assist with the administration and secretarial needs of the DART. **Each kit weighs 117 pounds, displaces 6.6 cubic feet, and is packaged in two boxes. One box has general supplies. The other box contains an easel with easel pads.** Table VI–5 lists the items contained in the OFDA office supply kit.

Table VI–5. Contents of OFDA Office Supply Kit

Item	Quantity	Unit
Bands, rubber, assorted	1	Box
Binders, 3-ring	10	Each
Box, interfile	1	Each
Calculator	1	Each
Calendar	1	Each
Carbon paper	1	Package
Carton, 23 × 19 × 10 in.	1	Each
Chalk, white	1	Box
Clips, binder, med.	1	Box
Clips, paper	1	Box
Clipboards	2	Each
Diskettes	1	Package
Dispenser, tape	1	Each
Easel, w/folding legs	1	Each
Easel board, dry eraser	1	Set
Envelopes, mailing	10	Each
Envelopes, unfranked	50	Each
Eraser, chalk	1	Each
Erasers, rubber gum	6	Each
Folders, file	12	Each
Highlighters, 4-color	2	Set
Jackets, filing	10	Each
Markers, felt tip, 3-color	2	Set
Pads, easel, 27 × 34 in.	2	Pad
Pads, post-it note (12 pads/package)	10	Package
Pads, ruled, tablet	4	Pad
Pads, writing, DI–5A	25	Each
Paper, copier	1	Ream
Pens, ballpoint	24	Each
Pens, marking, dry-eraser	1	Set
Pens, nylon tip, black	3	Each
Pens, nylon tip, blue	3	Each
Pens, nylon tip, red	3	Each
Pencils, #2	12	Each

Table VI–5. Contents of OFDA Office Supply Kit (contd.)

Item	Quantity	Unit
Pencils, wax, black	2	Each
Pencils, wax, blue	2	Each
Pencils, wax, green	2	Each
Pencils, wax, red	2	Each
Pins, push, assorted	1	Box
Portfolios, DBL pocket	4	Each
Punch, paper, 3-hole	1	Each
Punch, paper, single	1	Each
Rags	1	Pound
Reinforcements, gummed	1	Package
Remover, staple	1	Each
Ruler, 12 in.	1	Each
Sharpener, pencil	1	Each
Shears, office	1	Each
Sheeting, plastic (5 sheets, 40 × 48 in.)	5	Each
Staplers, desk	2	Each
Stapler, heavy-duty	1	Each
Staplers, plier-type	2	Each
Staples	1	Box
Staples, heavy-duty	1	Box
Stenographer pads	10	Pad
Tacks, thumb	1	Box
Tape, cellulose	4	Roll
Tape, filament, 1 in. × 60 yds.	5	Roll
Tape, masking	1	Roll

B. OFDA Individual Support Kit

The purpose of the OFDA individual support kit (or "OFDA backpack") is to provide the necessary items to allow OFDA personnel sent to the field to be able to support themselves for 48 to 72 hours, under adverse field conditions if necessary. Many items are useful to an individual during a relief operation. Remember: It is a support kit, not a survival kit, and is not intended to complement personal items that DART members bring on a deployment. **Each kit measures 18 × 18 by 12 inches, displaces 3 cubic feet, and weighs 23 pounds.** Table VI–6 lists all the items contained in the individual support kit. All the items listed are packed into a backpack.

C. Tents

OFDA stockpile tents are lightweight summer tents, designed for a family of six to eight people. Each tent is 10 by 14 feet, and has with an external supporting tubular frame and a floor. Tent flies will be sent as a separate item upon request. The tent material is flame-retardant. **Each tent is boxed, displaces 8 cubic feet, and weighs 85 pounds with dimensions of 20 × 8¼ × 47½ inches. There are 10 tents per pallet (shrink-wrapped). Approximate numbers per USAF aircraft are: 350 per C–130, 500 per C–141, and 1,500 per C–5.**

D. Blankets

1. Wool Blankets

Wool blankets are used by disaster victims in cool climates. **Blankets are packaged in bundles of 25 each. A bundle weighs 85 pounds, measures 32 × 22 × 20 inches, and displaces 9 cubic feet. Each blanket weighs 3.3 pounds and displaces 0.6 cubic foot.**

2. Polyester Blankets

Polyester blankets are used by disaster victims in warm climates. **Blankets are packaged in bundles of 25 each. The bundle weighs 85 pounds and displaces 9 cubic feet. Each blanket weighs 3.3 pounds and displaces 0.6 cubic foot.**

Table VI–6. OFDA Individual Support Kit

Description	Quantity	Unit
Bags, plastic, zipper-lock, 12 × 12	10	Each
Bags, trash, plastic, 10 gal.	5	Each
Bandana, cotton	1	Each
Bowl, plastic w/cover, 6 in.	1	Each
Candles, emergency, dripless, 7.5 hr	12	Each
Candle lantern, 6 in. × 2 in.	1	Each
Canteen, plastic w/cover, 1 qt.	1	Each
Compass, azimuth w/mirror	1	Each
Cord, parachute, 550 lb. test, 100 ft.	1	Hank
Dust mask	5	Each
Ear plugs with case, 1 med. pair, 1 lg. pair	2	Pair
Emergency blanket	2	Each
Eye wash	1	Bottle
First-aid kit	1	Kit
Flagging, 50 yd., day-glo pink	1	Roll
Flashlight, Mini-Mag	1	Each
Flashlight bulbs (2/package)	1	Package
Flashlight headband	1	Each
Gloves, latex	5	Pair
Handwipes, germicidal	50	Each
Insect-bite swabs, sting-kill, 10/box	1	Box
Insect repellent, lotion	2	Bottle
Knife, pliers head survival, w/sheath	1	Each
Matches, waterproof, 25/box	4	Box
Meal, MRE	8	Package
Mirror, heavy-duty	1	Each
Mug, plastic, w/cover	1	Each
Poncho, clear color	1	Each
Sunscreen, SPF-30	2	Bottle
Tape, fiberglass	1	Roll
Towel, cotton	1	Each
USAID patch	1	Each
Utensil kit, 3-pc., metal	1	Kit
Water purification tablets	1	Bottle

E. Chainsaw Kits

Chainsaws are used to cut blown-down tree and brush debris, usually debris resulting from a hurricane. The kits include safety chaps, goggles, gloves, an extra chain, a chain sharpener, oil, rags, and a saw tool. **Chainsaws can be deadly tools and should only be issued to individuals who can prove that they have previous experience operating and maintaining chainsaws.** Chainsaws should not be used to cut up debris that has been submerged during a flood, because dirt and silt embedded in the debris will quickly dull the chain and make the saw useless. **The kits weigh 54 pounds, measure 36 × 18 × 18 inches, and displace 5.2 cubic feet.**

F. Water Container, 5-Gallon Collapsible

These water containers are for use by disaster victims and relief workers for moving and storing potable water. **There are 50 per box, with dimensions of 47 × 20 × 10 inches. The boxes displace 7 cubic feet and weigh 38 pounds.**

G. Water Tank, 3,000-Gallon (10,000-Liter) Collapsible—UNICEF Type

These water tanks are made from polyester coated with PVC and are suitable for drinking water storage. The tank is totally sealed, unlike the U.S. military type (see below). This tank comes in a box with 12 outlet taps, tools for setup and repair, and 30 feet of semirigid waterpipe. **The box measures 39½ × 31½ × 20 inches, weighs 352 pounds, and displaces 14.1 cubic feet.**

H. Water Tank, 3,000-Gallon Collapsible—U.S. Military Type

These water tanks have an open top with a cover. Once the tank is assembled, water tank access must be managed to prevent the polluting of the water in the tank. **Each 3,000-gallon tank has a collapsed size of 30 × 25 × 44½ inches. The tank weighs 125 pounds and displaces 18 cubic feet.**

I. Plastic Sheeting

1. General

OFDA has developed and maintains a limited stock of plastic sheeting at four worldwide locations (New Windsor, Maryland;

Guam; Panama (closing in 1998); and Italy). This sheeting is specially designed for shelter, and it can be used to replace damaged or destroyed roofing or to construct temporary shelter for those in need. Because of its high cost and unique qualities, the sheeting should be utilized only to meet temporary human shelter requirements. This plastic sheeting should last over 1 year under normal field conditions, and it functions extremely well in hot climates.

This plastic sheeting (24 feet by 100 feet) is boxed at one roll per box weighing 136 pounds. Each box is 42 × 24 × 16 inches. One roll is 2,400 square feet and has heat-sealed seams 6 feet apart along the length of the roll. These seams allow for quick separation because they will easily "zipper" apart. Figure VI–1 shows an example of the dimensions of the plastic sheeting. A 40-foot container holds 216 rolls, while a 20-foot container holds about 96 rolls. The USAF C–130 airplane holds 180 to 200 rolls, a C–141 airplane holds 300 rolls, and a C–5 airplane holds 1,200 to 1,300 rolls. One box is 9.3 cubic feet, and there are 10 boxes banded to a standard wood (42-inch × 48-inch) pallet. The weight of a 10-box pallet is about 1,400 pounds. One pallet is 99.2 cubic feet. The cost of the sheeting is about $350 per roll plus transportation costs to the disaster.

The plastic is coated on both sides with a black scrim net that makes it strong (it cannot be torn) and nontransparent. The white side is ultraviolet-deflective and treated to reduce the heat

---

Figure VI–1. Plastic Sheeting

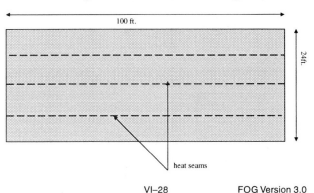

heat seams

from the sun in hot climates. The other side is a light beige color and should be faced outward in colder climates. An 8-inch USAID emblem is printed on the plastic at 3-foot intervals. It has tick marks down both sides at 5-foot intervals for measuring purposes. Also enclosed are six rolls of adhesive tape constructed from the same material as the plastic. Each roll of tape is 30 feet long and 1¾ inches wide.

Although the material is fire-retardant, open fires should not be allowed in or near the shelter for safety reasons.

One reported flaw of this sheeting is that, like most tents, moisture will condense (sweat) inside when the plastic is made into enclosed tent-like shelters and is used in high altitudes or cold climates (the sheeting is nonporous and does not breathe). To remedy this, use a second layer of plastic over the structure, keeping it from touching the frame of the building.

2. Distribution

The OFDA plastic sheeting was designed for distribution directly to disaster victims and for use on community buildings such as schools and hospitals, and not for use on government or business buildings or churches (unless they are utilized as temporary mass shelter facilities).

Before unpacking and unrolling the sheeting, move the distribution operation to a large area, such as a school gym, football field, or airport hanger, that preferably is protected from the weather. For distribution purposes, the sheets can easily be separated at the heat seams by peeling the seams apart. Normally a single sheet is split at the center seam, which allows strips of 12 feet by 100 feet. These are then cut to the appropriate lengths for distribution. With measurement tick marks at every 5 feet, cutting lines can be quickly established. **The most common size for a small family is a 12-foot × 20-foot piece. This may be enlarged according to family size, weather conditions, and other considerations, such as the need for roofing patches or replacements.**

3. How to Use Plastic Sheeting

If wood shelter frames are constructed to be covered with the plastic, the walls should be slightly less than 6 feet high. This allows the plastic to be split quickly and easily by hand at the 6-foot seams. Walls slightly less than 6 feet high will allow all four sides of a structure to be wrapped with a single strip.

To wrap a structure, staple or nail one end of a 6-foot-wide piece of sheeting to the corner upright, pull or wrap it around the structure to the same beginning corner, and staple or nail it to the same upright. Then go back and staple or nail the sheeting to the other uprights and crosspieces. A door can be cut as a slit until the final door is established or designed. Nails should be hammered through thin wood or metal disks or strips, such as soft drink cans and lids, to prevent the nail head from pulling through. Staples, if available, work best because they cross over the scrim netting. Use the enclosed adhesive tape to seal seams, patch rips and cuts, and seal nail and staple holes in the roof. The roof should be a single piece of plastic when possible to prevent leaks in the center.

a. Hot-Weather Conditions

- Turn the white side of the sheeting toward the outside to reflect as much of the Sun's heat as possible.
- Make the roof of any new building as high as possible. 10 feet at the highest point is good.
- Vent the roof to let super-hot air escape and to reduce the temperature inside the building. Ventilation through doors and windows helps but is not enough.

b. Cold-Weather Conditions

- Turn the long side of the building towards the warmth of the Sun.
- Turn the dark (beige) side of the sheeting toward the outside to absorb the heat of the Sun.
- Make the roof of any new building as low as possible. 7 feet at the highest point is good.
- Shovel dirt or even snow against the outside of the building walls to help hold the heat inside.
- Special care must be taken when heating the shelter, because plastic sheeting will burn.
- Tack a second layer of OFDA plastic or any other material on the inside to create a double layer for insulation.

c. Useful Construction Techniques

Plastic sheeting can be stretched over a building and then anchored to the ground with ropes and stakes like a tent in several ways.

- Wrap the ends of the plastic that will be staked down around a stick. Poke holes in the plastic along the stick and tie ropes around the stick. Then stake the ropes.

- Place a small rock under the sheeting. Twist the sheeting around the rock. Tie a rope around the twisted sheeting. Then stake the rope.

- Use as many stakes or anchors as needed to keep the plastic as tight as possible.

Plastic sheeting can be stretched over a building and nailed to the frame of the building.

- Stretch the sheeting over the roof. Pull the plastic sheeting as tight as possible before connecting it to the roof frame.

- To get the sheeting tight, pull it firmly in all four directions.

- It is very important to stretch the plastic tight and to attach it securely to the roof frame or to anchor it to the ground.

- Hammer the nails through some type of washer such as a piece of tire, rubber, or a flattened bottle cap. Or, hammer the nail through a batten.

Precautions:

- During windy weather, loose sheeting will flap violently and cause (more) damage to the structure.

- During rainy weather, loose sheeting will collect rainwater which can cause (more) damage to the structure.

After a strong wind or rain storm, look at the building for signs of wear and tear. Tighten all ropes and use additional nails if needed to tighten the sheeting.

Use two 6 × 26 foot pieces to cover an 8-foot, square roof. Place seams along the supports and secure the ends tightly.

Doors should be slit in after connecting to offer a tight opening against sand and dust. Leftover, narrow, 1- and 2-foot pieces can serve as curtains over slits and windows.

J. Other Supplies

1. Hard Hats

Orange safety hard hats are provided for victims and relief workers helping to remove rubble from collapsed structures after an earthquake. **There are 20 per box, with dimensions of 18 × 18 × 24 inches. The boxes displace 4.2 cubic feet and weigh 17 pounds.**

2. Face Masks

Respiratory dust face masks are provided for victims and relief workers helping to remove rubble from collapsed structures after an earthquake. The face masks are not fine enough to filter out volcanic dust or toxic fumes. **There are 500 per box, with dimensions of 15 × 11 × 16 inches. The boxes displace 1.4 cubic feet and weigh 9 pounds.**

3. Gloves

Leather-palm work gloves are used by disaster survivors and relief workers assisting with relief efforts. **There are 72 pairs per box, with dimensions of 12 × 17 × 26 inches. The boxes displace 3.9 cubic feet and weigh 50 pounds.**

Working with the Military in the Field

The following information is intended to inform Assessment Teams and DARTs about working with military organizations during field operations. This information will focus mainly on those response activities where OFDA works with the U.S. military, but the information may be applicable to working with coalition and multinational military forces such as NATO. The information includes how the military organizes and conducts field operations and how, when, and where Assessment Teams and DARTs can coordinate OFDA's disaster response operations with military operations.

A. Military Operations Involving Coordination With OFDA Disaster Response Activities

1. Point-to-Point Logistical Support

When OFDA's response option to a disaster is to provide relief commodities from OFDA stockpiles, and commercial aircraft are unable to meet the time or operational requirements for delivery of those commodities, OFDA will request the use of Department of Defense (DOD) aircraft. These U.S. military aircraft may be used to provide airlift of OFDA relief commodities to a point close to the disaster site or to shuttle relief commodities within the area of the disaster. To arrange for this military airlift support, OFDA's Logistics Officer prepares documentation that specifically details when, where, and what type of support is needed and how that support will be reimbursed. Once the requirements have been identified and accepted by DOD, OFDA Logistics will continue to coordinate with the appropriate military staffs to expedite the delivery of the commodities. OFDA Logistics may request assistance from an Assessment Team or DART with customs, off loading, consignment, and accounting for the relief commodities.

OFDA/W also works very closely with the State Department's Office of Political/Military Affairs (PM). PM serves as a facilitator between DOD and OFDA. For example, when DOD receives a request for support to an NGO that requires validation or (in the case of DOD-initiated disaster response activities) when no military presence is available in an affected country, OFDA will work with PM to assist in validating and targeting the response activities.

2. Peace Operations

Peace operations are military operations conducted in support of diplomatic efforts to establish and maintain peace. These operations may also have a humanitarian relief component. Peace operations are usually one of the two following types:

- **Peace Keeping**—Military operations undertaken with the consent of all major parties to a dispute, designed to monitor and facilitate implementation of an agreement (cease-fire, truce, etc.), and support diplomatic efforts such as negotiations, mediation, arbitration, and judicial means to reach a long-term political settlement. If the military force is deploying under a UN mandate, this type of operation is usually referred to as a **"Chapter VI operation,"** referring to Chapter VI of the UN Charter, which is titled "Pacific Settlement of Disputes."

- **Peace Enforcement**—Application of military force or threat of its use to compel compliance with resolutions or sanctions designed to maintain or restore peace and order. If the deployment in this case is under a UN mandate, this type of operation is usually referred to as a **"Chapter VII operation,"** referring to Chapter VII of the UN Charter, which is titled "Action with Respect to Threats to the Peace, Breaches of the Peace, and Acts of Aggression."

3. Disaster Relief

When the military is involved in disaster relief activities (which may be referred to by the military as foreign humanitarian assistance [FHA] or humanitarian assistance operations [HAO]), military assets are provided *primarily* to supplement or complement the relief efforts of the affected country's civil authorities or of the humanitarian relief community. This support may include providing logistics, transportation, airfield management, communications, medical support, distribution of relief commodities, or security. In such cases, OFDA will assign personnel to work at different levels of the military organization (see *Military Structure During Operations*), including the field or tactical levels, as liaisons between the military and the relief community to ensure that the efforts of both are mutually supportive and not duplicative. The military has recognized OFDA liaisons and representatives as valuable members of their staff and has looked to them to foster a unity of effort in humanitarian assistance.

When the military's mission is in support of humanitarian assistance, the DART will have a much more significant involvement and input into the military's operational planning and activities. If, however, the military mission is to carry out a Chapter VI, Chapter VII, or another more traditional military mission, the DART's involvement will be mainly with that portion of the military operation dealing with issues affecting relief efforts, but not controlled by the military. In these cases, humanitarian relief issues will be of secondary importance to the military.

B. Characteristics of Military Culture

1. Organizational Culture

Most organizations have a distinct organizational culture, an often unwritten set of rules, regulations, viewpoints, perspectives, and operating procedures. This culture is based on the unique history, mission, structure, and leadership of the organization. The military's distinct organizational culture is reflected in the characteristics listed below. These characteristics, which make the military very effective in combat, may frustrate relief organization personnel, who may find the military inflexible. DART members who are more aware of the military environment and culture will be more prepared to deal with the frustrations of relief community members who have not dealt with the military. Here are some of the main characteristics:

- Highly structured, hierarchical, chain-of-command.
- Authoritarian, "Who's in charge?"
- Goal oriented, "What's the mission?" (both explicit and implied).
- Rules and regulations run the organization.
- Process and scheduling are adhered to, "daily battle rhythm."
- Work ethic, "work hard, play hard."
- Highly competitive.
- Respect for tradition.
- Respect for physical and mental toughness.
- Respect for age.
- Training priority is on combat readiness.
- Emphasis on battle skills.
- Emphasis on physical fitness.
- Emphasis on equipment maintenance.
- Trained to be insensitive for battlefield survival.
- Trained to be secretive for operational security.

- Leaders are taught to be assertive, decisive, tenacious, and confident. "Make a decision and make it now!"
- Concepts such as cooperation, collaboration, and non-conformity are avoided.

The following section describes how the military's cultural norms may be displayed to the relief community during an operation.

2. Meetings

Military personnel expect meetings to be highly structured and efficiently managed. A leader is expected to listen to succinct presentations, usually consisting of overheads or slides of the issues, and to make clear decisions without hesitation. They will come to meetings expecting everyone to leave with their "marching orders." Meetings attended by autonomous agencies expecting a consensus approach to issue resolution may be viewed by the military as lacking a leader. Some military personnel will judge such meetings as weak in leadership and inefficient and may attempt to assert leadership intending to help. Others may become very frustrated, lose interest, and not participate.

3. Coordination

Concern for operational security will likely result in a reluctance to share information about planned activities, although the military can be expected to want indepth information about civilian activities. The military will respond well to clearly stated missions, efficient processes, organization, responsibility, and competence. It will judge harshly any operation weak in these areas and may show insensitivity when expressing that judgment.

4. Operational View of the Mission

Some military leaders may be concerned that humanitarian operations degrade combat readiness. Sensitivity to suffering may not be viewed as a virtue on the battlefield. This may result in a desire to minimize participation in some operations. Although humanitarian operations may be viewed with mixed feelings organizationally, the military is excellent at dutifully executing national direction. If that direction is clearly to support humanitarian operations, the response can be delivered effectively with a single-minded purpose.

5. Deployment

The military deploys with a comparatively high standard of support, and the number of personnel, support packages, and "baggage" may seem excessive. This support is designed to make the military as self-sustaining and self-reliant as possible.

The military support systems can be used to assist displaced civilians. However, the military standard of support is based on DOD policy determinations and may differ from humanitarian relief agency standards.

What the military will be constantly trying to avoid is **mission creep,** which occurs when armed forces take on broader or additional missions than those for which they initially planned.

Overriding all other priorities will be internal **force protection.** Force protection is the security program designed to emphasize the protection of soldiers, civilian employees, facilities, and equipment that are part of the military organization. How force protection is implemented may have an effect on how, where, and when the military will become involved in relief activities.

Each military operation will have **rules of engagement** (ROE), which delineate the circumstances and limitations under which the military will initiate or continue combat engagement. The ROE in turn, will have significant impacts on disaster relief operations, affecting freedom of movement, security, logistics, and the perception of neutrality of the relief community in the eyes of competing factions.

C. Military Structure During Operations

1. Chain of Command

The Department of Defense receives direction from the **National Command Authority (NCA),** which consists of the President of the United States and the Secretary of Defense, or their duly authorized alternates or successors. The NCA has the constitutional authority to direct the Armed Forces of the United States. NCA direction is passed to the chairman of the Joint Chiefs of Staff. The **Joint Chiefs of Staff** (JCS) consists of the chairman and the chiefs of staff of the various services (Army, Navy, Marines, and Air Force). The chairman then directs commanders of various **areas of responsibility** (AOR) to carry out operational activities. The military divides the world into five geographic areas. A geographic-area combatant commander at the admiral or general officer level heads U.S. military operations in each AOR. They are referred to as the **commanders in chief (CINC)** for that particular AOR. The AORs are as follows:

- **US Atlantic Command (USACOM)**—the Atlantic Ocean and the islands within it. Headquarters is in Norfolk, Virginia.

- **European Command (EUCOM)**—Europe, all countries of Africa (except those bordering the Red Sea), the Mediterranean Sea and bordering countries. Headquarters is in Stuttgart, Germany.

- **Pacific Command (PACOM)**—Pacific Ocean, part of the Indian Ocean including Madagascar, and East and Southeast Asia. Headquarters is in Honolulu, Hawaii.

- **Central Command (CENTCOM)**—Countries bordering the Red Sea (Horn of Africa) and the Persian Gulf. Headquarters is in Tampa, Florida.

- **Southern Command (SOUTHCOM)**—Latin America land area and the Caribbean Sea. Headquarters is in Miami, Florida.

Note: The land areas of Mexico, Canada, and the former Soviet Union are not assigned to any CINC. Humanitarian responses to these locations will be assigned to a command on a case-by-case basis as the need arises.

In addition to geographical commands, OFDA works with two other **functional commands** on a regular basis. They are:

- **Special Operations Command (SOCOM)**—In command of special operations units that include Special Forces, Civil Affairs, and Psychological Operations. Headquarters is in Tampa, Florida

- **Transportation Command (TRANSCOM)**—Unified command for providing management of all surface/air/sea lift. Headquarters is at Scott Air Force Base in Illinois.

2. CINC Authorities During Critical Humanitarian Relief Situations

Each area CINC is responsible for all U.S. military operations within his or her AOR. CINCs almost always seek NCA guidance, though they have the legal authority to take unilateral action on what they consider a critical humanitarian relief situation within their AOR. These usually involve life and death, fast onset disasters that may or may not have been a "declared disaster" by the U.S. embassy in the affected country. OFDA may work with the CINC to share costs on certain relief activities.

3. Humanitarian Assistance Survey Team

Some CINCs have developed what they call a **Humanitarian Assistance Survey Team** (HAST) to assess existing conditions after a disaster and the need for military forces. HASTs usually focus on the requirements for military support to the relief effort and the ability of the affected country to handle the deployment of follow-on forces (for example, airport or seaport capabilities). Assessment Teams or DARTs may encounter HASTs in the field. There may be confusion between the HAST mission and the OFDA mission if the HAST is assessing humanitarian or emergency victim needs as well as the support capabilities and requirements of the affected country to handle follow-on military forces. If Assessment Teams or DARTs encounter HASTs, they should first ascertain the objectives of the mission of the HAST. If the HAST mission involves identifying victim needs, it is important to determine what the HAST has identified as priority requirements and its recommendations. Separate and different needs analysis and recommendations may lead to confusion at the decision-maker levels within the AOR and at the OFDA/W level. If there are differences between what the Assessment Team or DART and the HAST have recommended, both sides should attempt to reach a consensus on the differences. If this cannot be accomplished, the Assessment Team or DART should notify OFDA/W through normal reporting channels, which should include the U.S. embassy in the affected country, of the differing needs assessments and the reasons for the differences.

4. Joint Task Force

The CINC will normally set up a **Joint Task Force** (JTF) for the field management of large military activities. A JTF is established when a mission involves two or more military services on a significant scale and requires close integration of effort to meet specific military objectives. The CINC designates a **commander for the JTF** (CJTF) who is responsible to the CINC.

The JTF is broken into six main command staff designations. They are:

J–1 Administration (deals with internal personnel issues).

J–2 Intelligence (gathers, analyzes, and reports on information, including classified information).

J–3 Operations (mainly focuses on current operations).

J–4 Logistics (provides internal support for the JTF and may include support to disaster victims).

J–5 Plans and Policies (normal location of CMOC [see below]).

J–6 Communications (provides all telecommunications needs for JTF).

5. Civil Military Operations Center

The DART will work most often with the JTF through the **Civil Military Operations Center** (CMOC), which usually functions under the J–5 designation but may also function under the J–3 or may report directly to the CJTF through his or her chief of staff. NATO uses the term **CIMIC Center (the Civil-Military Cooperation Center)** for its CMOC operation. Wherever it is placed, the purpose of a CMOC is to coordinate and facilitate the U.S. and any multinational force's humanitarian operations with those of international and local relief agencies and with affected country authorities. A CMOC is not restricted to the JTF level; a field commander at other geographic locations may establish a CMOC based on the need to coordinate with civilian agencies.

The following tasks may fall under CMOC auspices:

- Screen, validate, and prioritize UN/PVO/NGO/IO military support requests.

- Act as intermediary, facilitator, and coordinator between JTF elements and UN/NGO/PVO/IOs.

- Explain JTF (military) policies to UN/PVO/NGO/IOs and conversely explain UN/PVO/NGO/IO policies to the JTF.

- Screen and validate UN/PVO/NGO/IO requests for available passenger airlift space.

- Administer and issue identification cards (for access into military-controlled areas).

- Convene ad hoc mission planning groups when complex military support or numerous military units and PVO/NGO/IOs are involved.

- Provide JTF operations and general security information to UN/PVO/NGO/IOs as required.

- Facilitate or coordinate activities such as airlift and sealift to avoid duplication and inefficiency of efforts and to increase safety.

- Assist in the creation and organization of food logistics systems, when requested.

- Provide liaison between JTF and other humanitarian coordination groups or centers.

- Exchange information.

The CMOC will look to the DART representatives to provide advice to the CMOC staff and assist in screening and validating requests for military support from the relief community. DART representatives can also provide a valuable service to the CMOC by informing the CMOC staff of the capabilities, areas of expertise, and operational methods of the relief organizations. Similarly, the DART representative can also advise and educate the relief organizations about the military. This liaison/facilitator role is the priority role that a DART representative can play during these military humanitarian relief operations.

In some military operations, CMOCs play a larger role than just coordinating the military's involvement in humanitarian relief efforts. The CMOC may be involved in repairing infrastructure and supporting the reinstitution of civil administration such as a police force and a judicial system. Restoring government capabilities are actually more traditional CMOC activities. During Operation Uphold Democracy in Haiti, the military set up a **Humanitarian Assistance Coordination Center** (HACC) to focus specifically on humanitarian assistance coordination issues that involved the military while the CMOC took on the expanded role of coordinating civilian-military interface issues. In this setting, the HACC was a subunit of the CMOC and DART representatives worked with the HACC and the CMOC. However, HACCs can also be established at higher echelons of the military structure to provide links between the military and other governmental and nongovernmental agencies that may participate in the relief operation at the theater-strategic level (CINC level). No matter how they are labeled at the various levels within the military structures, the CMOCs and the HACCs are the centers of gravity for cooperation and coordination between the military and civilian organizations in disaster relief operations.

6. Civil Affairs

CMOCs and HACCs are usually staffed by personnel from Army **Civil Affairs** (CA) units from both active duty and reserve component forces whose function is to provide the interface between the military and the civilian populace, organizations, and government. CA personnel are a part of the Special Operations Command and are trained in skills such as governmental functions, economics, and public infrastructure management, which makes them an optimal choice to form the core of the CMOC staff, into which other functional military specialists integrate. CA personnel are capable of supporting humanitarian assistance operations in a variety of functional areas. CA units may serve as the CJTF's primary advisor on the impact of military activities on the civilian sector. They also provide a primary military liaison with local civil authorities in the affected country.

7. Psychological Operations

Another Special Operations Command group that DART representatives may encounter in a JTF setting is **Psychological Operations** (PSYOPS). PSYOPS units convey messages and themes intended to have an impact on selected target audiences. Their objective is to influence behavior and attitudes and constrain undesired actions. PSYOPS personnel can provide the JTF commander with analysis of perceptions and attitudes of the civilian population and the effectiveness of ongoing information campaigns and humanitarian assistance operations. They also provide language capability and equipment such as radio broadcasting, print, loudspeakers, and audiovisuals to disseminate necessary information to the affected population. It is important that DART representatives track PSYOPS actions closely to ensure that the goals and operational activities of OFDA's field staff and those of the JTF, through PSYOPS, are tracking consistently, so as to avoid a conflict in the message and actions of the USG toward the victims and the relief community.

D. Your Deployment with the Military

1. Before Departing

Both OFDA and the military appreciate the value of having you, a DART representative, present with the JTF. But not all military commanders have worked with or are even familiar with the mission and field operational methods of other USG agencies, including OFDA. Therefore it is important that OFDA/W coordinate with the appropriate CINC staff to define your scope of work (SOW). Some military offices may refer to a SOW as a terms of reference (TOR). OFDA/W should then request through the CINC staff a point of contact for you, to facilitate your entry into the military organization and also to request that your SOW/TOR be forwarded to the JTF. OFDA/W should also cable your security clearance level in a message cable to the geographical CINC and the CJTF if possible. Without that information, the JTF may be reluctant to include you in planning meetings and briefings. If at all possible, have the CINC's staff send a welcome/concurrence letter on military letterhead back to OFDA/W, prior to your departure, that concurs with the purpose of your mission with the JTF.

2. Arrival

Upon arriving at a JTF, you may be engulfed in a "sea of green uniforms" that look the same. (Table VI–7 lists the titles, ranks, and insignias of U.S. military commissioned officers.) You should request that the JTF point of contact meet you to help you gain entry into the JTF and to assist with any in-processing procedures. If you do not have a point of contact, you may even be stopped at the door/gate/wire and told by a 19-year-old with a rifle that DART doesn't mean anything to him or her. Show the letters you may have (SOW/TOR and a military welcome letter). You could also show your USG ID or your travel authorization. Tell the guard you want to see someone from the CMOC. Ask to see someone from the J–5 if the guard says there is no CMOC.

3. Getting Visibility

Once you have made the proper contacts within the CMOC, as early as possible make an appointment with the CJTF and other senior staff. The "gatekeeper" for the CJTF is often the CJTF's chief of staff, whom you may need to educate on your liaison role with the military operation. The CJTF's availability to you and your importance to him or her will again depend on the operational mission of the JTF. If the operation's focus is not

Table VI-7. Title, Insignia, and Rank of U.S. Military Commissioned Officers

Army, Air Force, and Marines Title	Insignia	Rank	Equivalent Navy Title
Second lieutenant	1 gold bar	O-1	Ensign
First lieutenant	1 silver bar	O-2	Lieutenant (junior grade)
Captain	2 silver bars	O-3	Lieutenant
Major	gold oak leaf	O-4	Lieutenant commander
Lieutenant colonel	silver oak leaf	O-5	Commander
Colonel	silver eagle	O-6	Captain
Brigadier general	1 star	O-7	Rear admiral (lower half)
Major general	2 stars	O-8	Rear admiral (upper half)
Lieutenant general	3 stars	O-9	Vice-Admiral
General	4 stars	O-10	Admiral

humanitarian relief, your access to the CJTF will be limited. If it is humanitarian relief you may find yourself dealing directly with the CJTF on a continual basis. The point here is *visibility* and to stress to the CJTF the value of having a DART member assigned to work with the JTF.

4. Your Mission

You will work most closely with the CMOC and with whomever is the commanding officer or director of that staff. The CMOC will usually have coordination meetings with the relief community to share information and to map out the requirements, capabilities, and mutual concerns. Your job is to observe and advise, not facilitate or run CMOC meetings. That is the job of the CMOC staff. CMOC meetings will be held as required, probably daily. It is important that both the military and the humanitarian relief community understand that your mission is to advise and assist both sides to work toward a coordinated effort. This will mean that at times you may be caught between competing or conflicting desires and objectives. It is important to not compromise your status, because if either side sees or perceives you as favoring the other, your credibility and effectiveness in the job will be diminished. Your main task is to encourage the military's operation to be as cooperative and supportive to the humanitarian relief effort as possible. But it is important also to realize that the military may have to temper that support within the context of its mission objectives.

5. Meetings and Briefings in the JTF

Within the time constraints that always exist in these types of operations, attend as many of the JTF planning meetings and briefings as possible, based upon their relative value to the humanitarian relief effort. These will keep you informed about what the military is doing and about the problems and constraints that they are encountering. Depending on the mission and how the JTF is organized, CMOC staff may be a part of the commander's briefings. If they are, encourage the CMOC briefer to spend a minute or two educating the various JTF staffs on what the humanitarian relief community is doing and how they are doing it. For example, to a soldier, food is food, but to a hungry child a high-energy protein biscuit or a cup of blended foods may be much more important than a cup of wheat. When this type of issue is explained, it can reduce the frustrations of soldiers who think that loading one type of food instead of another makes no sense. "Show and tell" can also be effective in briefings, where relief commodities are not only explained but also shown, such as vegetable oil bottles, plastic sheeting, or high-energy biscuits.

6. Contact and Visibility with the Affected Country, UN/PVO/NGO/IOs, and Donor Governments

The other aspect of this DART assignment is maintaining contact and visibility with the relief community to better understand how their activities are faring and what issues are arising. Make every effort to attend coordination meetings. Affected country relief officials, relief organizations, or donor governments may arrange these meetings. The mechanism for coordination among these organizations will depend on the ability of the affected country or other lead coordinating agency to organize them. If there is no affected country capability or other coordinating agencies are unable to perform their role, other coordinating groups will arise.

The UN (UNHCR, UNOCHA [formerly DHA], UNICEF, WFP) may take on a coordination role by setting up coordination centers where PVO/NGO/IOs and UN relief agencies can discuss operational activities. These coordination centers may have various names such as **Humanitarian Operations Centers** (HOCs, the military term for this type of center), or **On Site Operations Coordination Centers** (OSOCC, run by OCHA), or sectoral coordinating committees for such issues as health, nutrition, water, or sanitation. The PVO/NGO/IOs may also set up coordination groups in addition to or instead of other efforts. The CMOC director or staff will want to participate in these meetings, at least as interested observers, as another way to gather information and to inform the relief community of the mission, capabilities, and limitations of the JTF to support relief operations.

7. Staffing

DART staffing for the JTF assignment is another important issue. You may be the only DART representative to a JTF or it may require several staff members to assist in the effort. How large and how spread out the military operation is will determine the number of DART members needed. If the military has broken the JTF into geographical subunits with CMOCs, there may be a need to staff each CMOC. Another factor determining staff size is the amount and timing of the reporting requirements. It will be difficult to remain visible and involved with the military, work with the affected country and the relief community and other donor governments, travel to relief sites, and still maintain a regular reporting schedule. For example, you may need to have support from an Information Officer who can focus on the reporting aspects of the assignment.

8. Reporting

Before you leave OFDA in Washington, the reporting require- ments must be decided: to whom, how often, and in what form. If the JTF is spread out and there are several DART members with the JTF staff, what will be the reporting chain? When you are preparing your reports there are several important issues to keep in mind. The JTF will prepare at least one situation report a day. It may all be unclassified, partly classified (the usual case), or totally classified. Be aware that the information they have collected may have come from your situation report, the relief organizations, or CMOC staff directly. If the information they have collected is useful to the DART, make sure what you report through your reporting chain does not duplicate information you and other members of the DART in other locations have already reported. Clarify any differences in reporting data, such as tonnage carried or gallons of water purified. And don't forget that the U.S. military figures will not be in the metric system while most of the relief community information will be. Also make sure the military information you report is not from the classified portion of their information. Be aware not only of classification but also of the sensitivity of military reports and information. You may be privy to their reporting, which may take several forms such as situation reports, commander's reports to the CINC, lessons-learned reports, and others. You must realize that what is submitted by the JTF may not be the total information or the same analysis or the same decision that comes out in Washing- ton through the Joint Chiefs of Staff. If you report what you read or overheard at the JTF as the military position, you may find that in reality the military position is much different in Washing- ton than at the JTF level. And if the word gets back that you have been reporting incomplete information that has caused confu- sion up the chains of command of OFDA and the military, your credibility and effectiveness will certainly be compromised.

9. Support

When planning for your assignment, define with the Team Leader or OFDA/W how you and other DART members as- signed to the military will be supported, especially if the JTF is not colocated with the DART headquarters. Will your support come from the USAID Mission, from the U.S. Embassy, the DART Administration Officer, through an allotment to the mission or embassy to pay for your support, or will you have to fend for yourself using a beefed-up travel authorization and increased cash advance? Identify in advance how you will be housed, fed, transported to and from the JTF, and what type of telecommunications equipment you will have access to or should bring with you. What about simple issues like office supplies? It is best to be as self-sufficient and independent of the JTF as possible because the JTF will be burdened enough with its own logistical and administrative issues. Your need for support may reduce your flexibility to respond to humanitarian relief issues and it will affect your credibility with the JTF. You may be viewed as another support requirement instead of as an asset to the operation.

10. When Are You Done?

When is your job complete? Because you are closest to the military and humanitarian relief issues, you will be relied on by the DART Leader to define when your DART assignment is no longer necessary. Every effort should be made to ensure that the JTF's needs have been met. Be advised, if you have been useful and quite independent of JTF support, there is often a tendency to want to keep you around for as long as possible, even when the value of your support has greatly diminished. You have to think in terms of the DART's needs as well as the JTF's.

11. Closeout

The closeout of a DART from a JTF is similar to any DART closeout. You must make sure that those groups that have been supporting you (Mission, Embassy, DART Administration Officer) are aware of the closeout assistance required. Enough lead time is always important. Complete any reporting requirements with the military, including exchanging any pertinent documents. Make sure that the relief community is aware of your departure, if the military will or will not remain, and how they can access DART or OFDA if they have questions or concerns.

12. Other Assignments

On occasion, OFDA has assigned individuals to work with military organizations that are of a multinational nature, such as North Atlantic Treaty Organization (NATO) military forces. Under these circumstances, the individuals assigned will be working more independently of a DART. They are referred to as **Humanitarian Advisors** (HUMADS). The HUMAD takes on the role of representing the interests of the entire relief community, not just the USG. If you are assigned to serve as a HUMAD, it is critical that you have a well-defined scope of work and that all parties that you will be working with, both civilian and military, understand the scope and limitations of your role.

As a final point, it is important to remember that a military operation with the magnitude of a JTF is very complex and there will be many times when issues arise that are internal to the military and the JTF. Out of courtesy to the military, if you are present when internal issues arise where there is no need for your presence, you may want to excuse yourself until these discussions are completed. This will be appreciated by the military and may prevent you from observing situations that may prove embarrassing to certain members of the JTF staff, especially when their actions (or lack thereof) are being discussed.

E. More Information

There are several military publications available through the Operations Support Division dealing with military doctrine for humanitarian relief activities if you wish to review these issues in more detail. Chapter VII, " Commonly Used Acronyms and Terminology," has additional DOD terms.

Chapter VII

Commonly Used Acronyms
and Terminology

COMMONLY USED ACRONYMS AND TERMINOLOGY

This chapter has two parts. The first section lists acronyms and terms used by the Office of Foreign Disaster Assistance (OFDA) and the humanitarian relief community. The second section is a list of acronyms and terms used by the Department of Defense (DOD) that the team member may read or hear if she or he is coordinating assessment or relief activities with the military. (For more information on DOD, also refer to *Working with the Military in the Field*, in Chapter VI, "Reference Information.")

OFDA Acronyms and Terms

Affected Country—Term used to define a country stricken by a disaster.

Affected Population—People requiring immediate emergency assistance from outside sources as a result of a disaster situation or event.

AID—See USAID.

ARC (American Red Cross)—U.S. PVO. Channels financial aid, material, and technical personnel to victims of natural disasters worldwide, multilaterally through the IFRC and directly through sister national societies. Assists ICRC in providing relief to victims of armed conflict. Contributes to disaster preparedness of other national societies.

ARI (Acute Respiratory Infections)—ARIs are serious, potentially fatal infections in a displaced and malnourished population.

Assessments:

> **Damage assessment**—The process of evaluating the damages and losses caused by a disaster.

> **Situation assessment**—The process of evaluating the situation caused by a disaster, such as the number killed, injured, and affected.

> **Needs assessment**—The process of evaluating the needs of the affected population as a result of the disaster.

Assisting Country—Term that more specifically defines a country providing aid to a disaster-stricken country (affected country). Assisting countries may or may not be a donor country.

ATA—Actual time of arrival.

ATD—Actual time of departure.

At-Risk Populations—A group that may suffer the effects of drought, conflict, food insecurity, or other phenomena resulting in humanitarian hardship. Includes but is not limited to vulnerable groups (see definition).

Bailey Bridge—Transportable (in pieces) temporary bridge.

Blended Foods—Foods such as Wheat-Soya blend, Corn-Soya blend, and Soy-Fortified Bulgur are fortified/processed commodities used for targeted vulnerables in an at-risk population.

Bureau of Populations, Refugees, and Migrations (PRM)—Bureau in the U.S. Department of State that has primary responsibility for formulating U.S. policies on populations, refugees, and migration, and for administering U.S. refugee assistance, admissions funds, and programs.

Cable—Secured (classified) and unsecured (unclassified) hard copy telecommunications system used by USAID and U.S. Department of State to pass information back and forth worldwide.

Cargo Abbreviations and Terms:

Air Way Bill (AWB)—A document serving as a guide to a carrier's staff in handling, dispatching, and delivering the consignment. It is a nonnegotiable document.

Bill of Lading—A receipt for goods, contract for their carriage, and documentary evidence of title to goods. As such it is a Bill of Exchange, a negotiable document of title. Usually issued in sets of three originals and several copies.

C and F—Cost and Freight. The shipper pays for freight to the named port of destination.

CIF—Cost, insurance, and freight.

COD—Cash on delivery.

Dead Weight (DWT)—A vessel's dead weight in the number of tons (2,240 pounds) required to sink the vessel in the water to its load line. DWT includes cargo, bunkers, and stores. DWT cargo capacity is the weight available for cargo after all other allowances have been made.

FAS—Free Alongside Ship. Price of goods dockside at port of discharge.

FOB—Free on Board. The price of goods covers transportation to the port of shipment, loading, and stowage, not transportation costs to final destination.

Long Ton—A measure of weight equivalent to 20 hundredweight (cwt.) of 112 lb. each = 2,240 lb. = 1016 kilos.

MT—Metric Ton. MT = 1,000 kilos = 2,205 lb.

Short Ton—2,000 lb. = 907.2 kilos

CDC (Centers for Disease Control and Prevention)—A part of the U.S. Public Health Service, located in Atlanta, Georgia. CDC specialists often support OFDA assessments in the areas of nutrition, health, and epidemiology.

CHE—Complex humanitarian emergency.

CIDA (Canadian International Development Agency)—Canadian government's foreign assistance and development agency.

CM (Chief of Mission)—Refers to the highest-ranking official in a country's embassy.

Cold Chain—The refrigerated transportation system for vaccines from the manufacturer to the individual.

Country Team—The senior, in-country U.S. coordinating and supervising body, headed by the Chief of the U.S. diplomatic mission, and composed of the senior member of each represented United States department or agency, as desired by the Chief of the U.S. diplomatic mission (Joint Pub 1-02).

CSB (Corn-Soya Blend)—A fortified cereal blend used for targeted vulnerables in an at-risk population.

Cyclone—Name given to severe tropical storms in the Indian Ocean and South Pacific Ocean with wind speeds in excess of 120 km/hr.

DART (Disaster Assistance Response Team)—Name for OFDA's field operational response capability.

DCM (Deputy Chief of Mission)—The second-ranking person in an embassy.

Death Rate—See Mortality Rate.

Denton Amendment—Law allowing the U.S. military to airlift or sealift donated humanitarian relief commodities for NGOs, on a space-available basis, to countries affected by disasters.

DHA—See OCHA, an agency listed under the heading "UN."

DFID (Department for International Development)—British government foreign assistance and development agency.

Displaced Person—An individual temporarily uprooted from his or her home who is expected to eventually return. Internally displaced persons have relocated within their country, while externally displaced persons have crossed an international border. Depending upon the reason for flight, externally displaced persons may be entitled to recognition as UNHCR-mandated refugees.

DOD—Department of Defense.

Donor Country—Country that provides aid to a developing country.

DRD (Disaster Response Division)—An OFDA division that is responsible for developing and implementing OFDA's disaster response strategy.

DSM—Dry skim milk.

DTP (Diphtheria-Tetanus-Pertussis)—Immunization for small children against these diseases.

DWM—Dry whole milk.

Earthquakes—Movements of the Earth's crust generates intense deformations in the Earth's interior, accumulating energy that is suddenly released in the form of waves that move the land surface, resulting in earthquakes. The point of the wave's origin within the Earth is called the **focal point**. The point on the Earth's surface located above the focal point is called the **epicenter**. The **Richter scale** measures the magnitude of the quake. The scale of **magnitude** goes from 0 to 8.9

and measures the energy dissipated in the quake. The modified **Mercalli scale** measures the intensity of the quake. The scale of **intensity** goes from 1 to 12 and measures the destructive effects at the site where it is measured. Instruments can barely detect 1 and 12 represents almost total destruction.

EC (European Community)—Twelve European nations pledged to unite by 1999 into a federation with a single currency, central bank, and a common defense and foreign policy. Headquarters are in Brussels, Belgium.

ECHO (European Community Humanitarian Office)—ECHO's mandate from the Community covers the following specific areas:
- General humanitarian aid, for those fleeing long-running civil wars.
- Emergency humanitarian aid, financing crisis management, and food aid for victims of natural catastrophes or civil wars.
- Aid for refugees or displaced people who need it, both in the country or region that hosts them or in their own country when they return.
- Financing for disaster preparedness in the areas of early warning systems and disaster prevention in high-risk countries.

EDP—Extended delivery point.

EPI—Expanded program for immunization.

Epicenter—See Earthquakes.

ETA—Estimated time of arrival.

ETD—Estimated time of departure.

ETE—Estimated time en route.

Ex-pat (Expatriate)—Individual residing in a country other than their own.

FAA—Foreign Assistance Act of 1961, as amended.

Fairfax—Fairfax County (Virginia) Fire and Rescue Department. Specially trained members of the department are deployable on OFDA DARTs in the SAR component.

FAS (U.S. Department of Agriculture, Foreign Agricultural Service)—Office within USDA responsible for procurement and shipping of food commodities under P.L. 480.

Fast Onset Disasters—Also known as sudden or quick onset disasters. Disasters such as earthquakes, hurricanes, volcanic eruptions, floods, and tsunamis.

FEMA (Federal Emergency Management Agency)—U.S. agency responsible for coordinating federally declared disasters in the United States and its territories.

FEWS (Famine Early Warning System Project)—Information system designed and financed by USAID. Mandate is to identify problems that could lead to famine conditions in 11 African countries so that such conditions can be preempted, helping to ensure food security in these countries.

Fly—Term used to describe weather covers for a tent or shelter cover set up to keep individuals sheltered from the elements.

Food Basket—The particular selection of food commodities that are handled by the assistance operation and included in the rations distributed to the target beneficiaries.

Food Categories or Types—Food distributed in disaster relief usually falls into four categories or types:

    Cereals—Corn, wheat, rice, sorghum.

    Pulses—Beans, peas, and lentils.

    Oils—Vegetable oil, butter oil.

    Blended foods—Wheat-soya blend, corn-soya blend, and soy-fortified bulgur.

Food for Peace (FFP)—Refers to the overseas food aid donation program authorized by Title II of P.L. 480. The Office of Food for Peace within USAID's Bureau for Humanitarian Response administers P.L. 480 Title II food aid grants to cooperating sponsors for use in development and emergency assistance programs overseas. These cooperating sponsors include PVO/NGO/IOs and UN relief organizations.

Food for Work—Disaster relief intervention designed to use capabilities of the affected population to improve infrastructure and support systems within the community by paying workers with food.

Food Pipeline—Term used to describe the various location points and the amount of food going to an affected population. Locations include the port of origin, the ship on the high seas, the port of entry, and the distribution system in the affected country.

Forest Service—OFDA has a RSSA with the Forest Service to provide disaster management training and technical specialists for DARTs.

GMT (Greenwich Mean Time)—Time synchronized worldwide to the time at the zero meridian. Also called Zulu Time and Coordinated Universal Time.

GO_—Three letter abbreviation for Government of _____, such as GOK (Government of Kenya) or GOJ (Government of Japan).

GPS—Global positioning system.

Grant (as defined by OFDA)—The transfer, by the United States, of money to various PVO/NGO/IOs and UN relief agencies to perform predefined relief activities.

GTZ (German Technical Assistance Agency)—The German government's foreign assistance and development agency.

Hazard—An external risk factor, represented by the potential for a natural or human-caused event to occur in a specific location, with a given intensity and duration.

HDR (Humanitarian Daily Ration)—DOD ration introduced in October 1993 for use by DOD in humanitarian relief efforts. Designed to be acceptable by all ethnic and religious groups. The purpose of HDR is to provide extra energy and high protein in a daily ration to maintain a moderately malnourished person's health at a stable level for a short period of time (approximately 30 days or until special arrangements can be made for targeted foods to be provided through traditional relief efforts). The HDR is used as a stopgap feeding asset until other foods chosen to meet specific or multiple nutritional deficiencies can arrive. Each HDR has approximately 2,000 calories and costs about $4.00.

HF Radios (High Frequency Radios)—Radio communication system that does not rely on line of sight.

Host Country—Country in which USAID has a development or disaster assistance program.

HQ—Headquarters.

Hurricane—Name given to severe tropical storms in the eastern Pacific and western Atlantic with wind speeds in excess of 120 km/hr.

IBRD (International Bank for Reconstruction and Development)—The World Bank.

ICRC (International Committee of the Red Cross)—Private, international relief organization with headquarters in Geneva. It works principally in cases of civil conflict, ensuring legal protection for victims and acting as a neutral, independent humanitarian organization in complex emergency situations. At times it may get involved in humanitarian operations. The Red Cross is neutral with regard to politics, religion, and ideology. Its international character derives from its mission, which is enshrined in the Geneva Conventions.

ICVA (International Council of Voluntary Agencies)—Independent, international association for nongovernmental and nonprofit organizations active in humanitarian assistance and sustainable development. ICVA provides a means for voluntary agency consultation and cooperation and undertakes advocacy work on issues of common concern to its members. It is not a funding agency and does not implement field projects. Its headquarters are in Geneva, Switzerland.

IDP—Internally displaced person. (See also Displaced Person.)

IFRC (International Federation of Red Cross and Red Crescent Societies)—Formerly known as the League of Red Cross and Red Crescent Societies. Located in Geneva, Switzerland. This is the umbrella organization for all Red Cross and Red Crescent Societies.

InterAction (American Council for Voluntary International Action)—A membership association of over 150 U.S. PVOs engaged in international humanitarian efforts, including relief, development, refugee assistance, public policy, and global education.

IO (International Organization)—Acronym for organizations such as ICRC, IFRC, and IOM that are international in their scope.

IOM (International Office for Migration)—Geneva-based international organization that provides arrangements for the transport of refugees and migrants and provides other resettlement services worldwide to meet the specific needs of the receiving countries.

ITSH (Inland/Internal Transport, Storage, and Handling)—Costs associated with the internal transport, storage, and handling of relief commodities from the seaport of entry to the distribution point.

JICA (Japan International Cooperation Agency)—Japanese government's foreign assistance and development agency.

Life Lines—Public services that provide water, sanitation, power, communications, and transportation. They are linear systems, which are vulnerable to different events and in different magnitudes.

Maize—Another name for corn.

MCH (Mother-Child Health)—Refers to programs that are targeted at improving the health of mothers and children.

MDRO (Mission Disaster Relief Officer)—This is the individual in a USAID Mission who has the responsibility for developing and implementing a Mission Disaster Relief Plan. Normally the point of contact for OFDA Washington and a DART during fast onset disasters.

Metro Dade—Metro Dade County (Florida) Fire and Rescue Department. Specially trained members of the department are deployable on OFDA DARTs in the search and rescue component.

Mitigation—See PMPP.

Monetization—Relief assistance programs where local merchants sell relief commodities (usually the most sought-after types) to affected populations using local currencies. Merchants are able to purchase the commodities at subsidized rates from participating donor countries. Donor countries use profits from the sales to fund community improvement projects that are carried out by the local affected population. Monetization attempts to increase the purchasing power of the affected population, who can then begin the process of reestablishing economic cycles within the community.

Morbidity Rate—Measure of the frequency of illness (morbidity) within specific populations. Time and place are always specified. Commonly used morbidity rates include point and period of prevalence, incidence, and attack.

Mortality Rate—Also known as death rate. A ratio of deaths/10,000 persons/day, based on the number of deaths times 10,000, divided by the number of days, times the population.

MOU (Memorandum of Understanding)—A common form of agreement, usually with USG agencies, that is less formal than a contract.

MUAC (Mid-upper-arm circumference)—Method of rapidly assessing the nutritional status of young children by measuring the mid-upper-arm circumference.

NGO (Nongovernmental Organization)—Refers to transnational organizations of private citizens that maintain a consultative status with the Economic and Social Council of the United Nations. NGOs may be professional associations, foundations, multinational businesses, or simply groups with a common interest in humanitarian assistance activities (development and relief). NGO is a term normally used by non-U.S. organizations as the equivalent of the term PVO (see PVO) as used in the United States.

OAS (Organization of American States)—Intergovernmental organization of all North, Central, and South American and Caribbean countries except Cuba and Canada.

OAU (Organization of African Unity)—An organization of independent African states established to promote unity, coordinate policies, and protect the independence of the continent. The OAU headquarters is in Addis Ababa, Ethiopia.

OE (Operating Expenses)—Money given to OFDA to fund travel, per diem, salary, and office expenses of USAID direct-hire employees.

OFDA (Office of U.S. Foreign Disaster Assistance)—Part of USAID's Bureau for Humanitarian Response. Office responsible for the coordination of all USG assistance to foreign countries after a natural or manmade disaster.

ORT (Oral Rehydration Therapy)—Treatment used for dehydrated patients, usually children, to prevent death from dehydration, which is often the result of diarrheal diseases.

ORS (Oral Rehydration Salts)—Electrolyte replenishing salts that often come in premixed packages. Used in ORT.

OS (Operations Support)—OFDA division responsible for conducting the operational implementation of OFDA's disaster response strategy.

OSOCC (On-Site Operations Coordination Center)—UN/OCHA term for a coordinating group set up near a disaster and composed of staff from affected country, local officials, personnel from assisting country, and UNOCHA and which meets to coordinate the use of assisting country capabilities. An OSOCC reports to and receives direction and priorities from local officials and is set up at the request of the affected country. An OSOCC may be co-located with the affected country's operations center. It may also be referred to as the "Center."

OTI (Office of Transition Initiatives)—Part of USAID's Bureau for Humanitarian Response. OTI manages USAID's assistance to nations in the wake of social, political, and economic trauma resulting from disasters. Its assistance supports efforts to make the transition from crisis to fundamental sociopolitical stability, which may serve as the foundation for longer-term, sustainable development programs.

PAHO (Pan-American Health Organization)—UN agency responsible for monitoring health training, health systems, and disaster-related health issues in the Americas. PAHO is a part of the World Health Organization (WHO).

PEM (Protein-Energy Malnutrition)—Major cause of death among infants and young children, usually caused by low food intake and infection. There are three types of PEM: nutritional marasmus, kwashiorkor, and marasmic kwashiorkor.

P.L. 480 (Public Law 480)—The Agricultural Trade Development and Assistance Act of 1954, Public Law 480 has been the principal legislative authority for channeling U.S. food to needy countries. The parts of the law that OFDA and the Office of Food for Peace are associated with are as follows:

– Title I: Administered by USDA. Food aid sold to countries able to pay for food but experiencing foreign exchange difficulties. Local currency generated by sale of food on local markets is used by country governments for agriculture, trade promotion, and public infrastructure.

- Title II: Administered by USAID. Provides emergency and nonemergency food aid in support of development projects—in many cases the food is given directly to individuals—through programs such as supplementary feeding, Food for Work, and disaster assistance.

- Title III: Administered by USAID. Provides food to needy countries that are ranked according to need based on the food security index. Eligibility for Title III can be based on:
  1. Daily per capita consumption is less than 2,300 calories;
  2. Mortality rate of children under 5 years of age in the country is in excess of 100 per 1000 births; and
  3. Country is unable to meet its food security requirements through domestic production or imports because of a shortage of foreign exchange earnings.

Plastic Sheeting—OFDA contracts for the manufacture of a specially coated, scrim net, plastic sheeting that is both durable and long lasting. OFDA distributes the plastic sheeting in rolls (one roll/box) that are 24 feet wide and 100 feet long.

PMPP (Prevention, Mitigation, Preparedness, and Planning)—An OFDA division that is responsible for developing OFDA's long-term strategies in disaster prevention, mitigation, and preparedness.

- Prevention: Encompasses those activities taken to prevent a natural phenomenon or potential hazard from having harmful effects on either persons or economic assets. Includes channeling the direction of debris flow away from population centers, construction of dams or dikes to eliminate flooding, and safe destruction of outdated hazardous materials.

- Mitigation: Concentrates on reducing the harmful effects of a disaster. Accepts the occurrence of disasters, but attempts to limit their impact on human suffering and economic assets. Includes improving building standards, installing hurricane straps to reduce wind damage to roofs, and modifying crop patterns to reduce vulnerability.

- Preparedness: Aims to limit the impact of a disaster by structuring the response and providing quick, effective actions after the disaster. Addresses actions in both the predisaster and postdisaster phases. Also includes early warning systems.

PRM—U.S. Department of State's Bureau for Population, Refugees, and Migration.

Program Money—Money given to OFDA to fund its program activities, such as RSSAs, PSCs, and grants.

PS (Program Support)—OFDA division responsible for managing office budgets and finances, procuring technical services, performing contract administration, and overseeing the management information system and computer services.

PSC (Personnel Services Contractor)—Individuals contracted by OFDA to assist OFDA in Washington and the field.

Pulses—Beans, lentils, and peas.

PVO (Private Voluntary Organization)—Private nonprofit humanitarian assistance organizations, registered with USAID, that are involved in development and relief activities. PVO is the equivalent term of NGO, which is normally used by non-U.S. organizations. (See also NGO.)

Rapid Onset Disaster—See fast onset disaster.

Ration—The particular amount of food provided by an assistance program for beneficiaries in a specified target group to meet defined nutritional objectives. The "daily ration" is the amount provided per person per day. The "distribution ration" is the quantity provided to each individual or household at each distribution.

Reconstruction—Medium- and long-term repair of physical, social, and economic damage to a condition or level of development equal to or better than before the disaster.

REDSO (Regional Economic Development Support Office)—USAID offices located in Abidjan, Cote d'Ivoire (closing in 1998 or 1999), and Nairobi, Kenya, that assist USAID Missions in Africa with economic and development programs.

Reftel (Reference Telegram)—In cable traffic "Reftel" means to reference information in a previous telegram (cable).

Refugee—A person who is outside of his or her country of origin and who, because of a well-founded fear of persecution, is unable to return to the country or to prevail upon that country for protection.

Rehabilitation—Short-term recovery of basic services and initiation of repair of physical, social, and economic damages.

Reproductive health (RH)—RH activities include safe motherhood; prevention and management of the consequences of sexual and gender-based violence; prevention and care of sexually transmitted diseases (STDs), including HIV/AIDS; family planning; management of other reproductive health concerns; meeting the special needs of adolescents; and reproductive health surveillance and monitoring.

Resrep—See UNDP, an agency listed under the heading "UN."

Response—Actions carried out in the face of an adverse event aimed at saving lives, alleviating suffering, and reducing economic losses.

Richter Scale—See Earthquakes.

Risk—Probability of exceeding a specific value of social, environmental, and economic damages, in a given place and during a specific exposure time.

RSSA (Resources Support Services Agreement)—An agreement between USAID and another U.S. agency or department that authorizes work.

SAR (Search and Rescue)—Component of the DART operations function, responsible for searching for and rescuing victims trapped in collapsed buildings, usually as a result of an earthquake. Also referred to as urban search and rescue.

SATCOM System (Satellite Communications System)—Refers to International Maritime Satellite (INMARSAT) communications system, which can provide almost worldwide communications for voice, data, and fax using a system of geostationary satellites.

Seeds and Tools—Distribution of seeds and tools is a relief intervention designed to give affected populations an opportunity to become more self-sufficient in food production.

Selective Feeding—A collective term used for all feeding and food distribution programs in which food is provided to specifically selected beneficiaries. It typically includes both supplementary and therapeutic feeding.

Septel (Separate Telegram)—In cable traffic, reference to a "septel" means that information will be contained in a separate telegram (cable) to follow.

SDCA (Swiss Development and Cooperation Agency)—The Swiss Government's agency responsible for international development and assistance.

SDR (Swiss Disaster Relief)—Office within SDCA that is responsible for coordinating the Swiss Government's international disaster relief activities.

SFP (Supplementary Feeding Program)—Feeding program offering extra calories for vulnerable populations of displaced persons.

Sitrep—A situation report on the current disaster situation and on the current U.S. response activities. Completed as required.

Slow Onset Disasters—Disasters that develop over a period of time. Examples are famine, civil strife, and insect infestations.

STDs—Sexually transmitted diseases.

Sudden Onset Disasters—See Fast Onset Disasters.

TA (Travel authorization)—USG form that authorizes someone to travel as stated on the TA.

TDY—Temporary Duty.

TFP (Therapeutic Feeding Program)—Intensive feeding program offering total calories for severely malnourished infants and small children in a health care setting (sometimes referred to as "nutritional rehabilitation").

Tropical Storms—Tropical cyclonic systems with wind speeds between 64 km/h and 119 km/h. If the wind speed is <64 km/h, the system is referred to as a **tropical depression**.

Tsunami—Progression of large sea waves that are capable of propagating for thousands of kilometers and that are caused by the sudden displacement of volumes of water. Tsunami are generated by earthquakes, volcanic eruptions, or underwater landslides.

Typhoon—Name given to severe tropical storms in the western Pacific with wind speeds in excess of 120 km/hr.

UAC (Unaccompanied Children)—Minors who are separated from both parents and are not being cared for by any adult who, by law or custom, is responsible to do so.

UHF Radios (Ultra High Frequency Radios)—Radio systems that are dependent on line of sight or repeaters.

UN (United Nations)—International organization formed to promote international peace, security, and cooperation under the terms of the UN Charter. The following are UN organizations with which OFDA works in the field:

FAO (Food and Agriculture Organization)—This UN agency serves as the organizing and coordinating agency that plans and executes development programs within the whole range of food and agriculture, including forestry and fisheries. Headquartered in Rome.

OCHA (Office for the Coordination of Humanitarian Affairs)—Focal point in the UN system for disaster relief coordination. The **Resident Representative (Resrep)** may take on the title of **UN Relief Coordinator** during a disaster response. OCHA was formerly UNDHA.

UNDAC Team (United Nations Disaster Assessment and Coordination Team)—An OCHA team designed for rapid assessment and onsite coordination missions following a fast onset disaster. Team members are specially trained and equipped for such missions. Members are OCHA Relief Coordination Officers and emergency managers from governments cooperating with the program. The UNDAC Team works for the UN Relief Coordinator and OCHA in Geneva.

UNDP (United Nations Development Program)—This is the central UN development agency in developing countries. In most of these countries, UNDP has a resident representative (Resrep). During a disaster the Resrep leads the UN incountry team in needs assessment and local relief coordination of aid from the UN system. Headquartered in New York.

UNHCR (The United Nations High Commissioner for Refugees)—This UN agency is responsible for protecting refugees, seeking permanent solutions to refugee problems by facilitating voluntary repatriation and resettlement, and providing supplementary aid and emergency relief to refugees as necessary. Headquartered in Geneva.

UNICEF (United Nations International Children's Emergency Fund)—This fund provides money for programs for health, education, and welfare for children and mothers in most developing countries. Headquartered in New York.

WFP (World Food Program)—UN organization responsible for procuring, accepting, and distributing food commodities to NGOs and needy countries. Headquartered in Rome.

WHO (World Health Organization)—UN organization responsible for coordinating international public health work. Headquartered in Geneva.

USAID (U.S. Agency for International Development)—The official USG agency responsible for international assistance and development.

USAID/Embassy—Refers to the USAID and State Department presence in a country.

USAID Mission—Name used to describe the office of the U.S. Agency for International Development in a foreign country.

USG—United States Government.

USGS (U.S. Geological Survey)—Provides earthquake information and technical specialists to OFDA as required.

USPHS (U.S. Public Health Service)—The lead USG agency for medical/health policy and operational activities. The CDC is under USPHS. USPHS officers are assigned to OFDA to assist with public health issues such as water and sanitation, drugs, and medical supplies.

USUN—United States Mission to the United Nations. There are two USUN missions, one in New York and one in Geneva.

VHF Radios (Very High Frequency Radios)—Radio system that is somewhat dependent on line of sight or repeaters.

VITA (Volunteers in Technical Assistance)—Provides OFDA with an information clearinghouse called the Disaster Information Center (DIC) located in Rosslyn, Virginia, which is designed to track private sector donations and offers of volunteer technical assistance for use by OFDA and PVOs responding to foreign disasters. The DIC also provides a computer bulletin board system, VITANet, which enables PVOs to easily access the offers of private sector disaster assistance that are collected by VITA.

Vulnerable Groups—Children, especially unaccompanied children, the unaccompanied elderly, persons who are handicapped or chronically ill, single women, and single heads of households.

Vulnerability—Internal risk factor of a subject, object, or system exposed to a hazard that corresponds to its intrinsic susceptibility to damage.

Weight-for-Height—Method of measurement to assess the nutritional status (malnutrition levels) of young children by comparing the weight and height of random samples of children (age 60 months or younger) in an area at regular intervals (see also Z-Score).

WHO Emergency Kit—Standard list of drugs and medical supplies WHO has identified and can make available as needed for an emergency. The kit is configured to be used by 10,000 people for 3 months.

WSB (Wheat-Soya Blend)—A fortified cereal blend used for targeted vulnerables in an at-risk population.

Zulu Time—Also known as Greenwich Mean Time (GMT) or Coordinated Universal Time. Method of synchronizing time worldwide to the time at the 0 meridian.

Z-Score—Standard measurement used during nutritional surveillance. "Z" represents the mean. A Z-Score represents the standard deviation above or below the mean. Children with Z-Scores of less than −2 are considered malnourished. Z-Scores of less than −3 are considered severely malnourished.

Department of Defense Acronyms and Terms

AC—Active component of the military.

Aircraft Types:

 C–5—(Galaxy) U.S. Air Force's largest cargo aircraft.

 C–12—U.S. military small passenger aircraft. Commercial version named King Air.

C–17—(Globemaster III) New generation military cargo aircraft.

C–130—(Hercules) U.S. military turbo-prop cargo aircraft.

C–141—(Starlifter) U.S. Air Force jet cargo aircraft.

CH–47—(Chinook) U.S. Army heavy-lift helicopter.

CH–53A—(Sea Stallion) U.S. Navy heavy-lift helicopter.

H–3—(Sea King) U.S. military medium-lift helicopter.

OH–58—(Kiowa) U.S. Army light helicopter.

UH–1H—(Huey) U.S. military medium helicopter.

UH–60—(Blackhawk) U.S. military medium helicopter.

AFFOR—Airforce Force.

ALCC—Airlift Control Center.

AMC—Air Mobility Command.

AO—Area of Operation.

AOR—Area of Responsibility. The U.S. military divides the world into five geographical areas of responsibility, which are each supervised by area commanders in chief (area CINCs). There are other commands with worldwide responsibilities (see SOCOM and TRANSCOM). The commands are:

SOUTHCOM (Southern Command)—Latin America land area and the Caribbean. Headquarters in Miami, Florida.

PACOM (Pacific Command)—Pacific Ocean, part of Indian Ocean, and East and Southeast Asia. Headquartered in Honolulu, Hawaii.

CENTCOM (Central Command)—Countries bordering the Red Sea and the Persian Gulf. Headquartered in Tampa, Florida.

EUCOM (European Command)—Europe, Africa not in CENTCOM, the Mediterranean Sea, and bordering countries. Headquartered in Stuttgart, Germany.

USACOM (Atlantic Command)—The Atlantic Ocean excluding the Caribbean. Headquartered in Norfolk, Virginia.

SOCOM (Special Operations Command)—Worldwide. Headquartered in Tampa, Florida.

TRANSCOM (Transportation Command)—Unified command providing management of all surface/air/sea lift. Headquartered at Scott Air Force Base in Illinois.

APC—Armored Personnel Carrier.

AR FOR—Army Force.

ARG—Amphibious Readiness Group.

BDE—Brigade, Army or Marine Corps, 2,000 to 3,000 personnel.

Billet—To quarter or house troops.

BN—Battalion, Army or Marine corps, 600 to 800 personnel.

CA (Civil Affairs Units)—Able to assist civil governments and their citizens in disasters. Part of SOF.

CAP—Crisis Action Planning.

CAT—Crisis Action Team.

CCO—Complex Contingency Operations.

CFST (Coalition Forces Support Team)—In a multinational operation, this team coordinates actions with coalition units.

CIMIC (Civilian Military Cooperation)—NATO term analogous to CMO in U.S. military terminology.

CIMIC Center—NATO term analogous to a CMOC in U.S. military terminology.

CINC—Commander in Chief of an AOR.

CJTF—Commander, Joint Task Force.

CMO—Civil Military Operations.

CMOC (Civil Military Operations Center)—A center established by the JTF commander to carry out decisions.

CMOT (Civil Military Operations Team)—A small, mobile group of personnel who travel in the affected area, liase with the PVO/NGO/IO community, and report to the CMOC.

CO—Commanding Officer.

Command Staff designations: S=Special, G=General, J=Joint

    S/G/J 1 = Administration
    S/G/J 2 = Intelligence
    S/G/J 3 = Operations
    S/G/J 4 = Logistics
    S/G 5   = Civil Affairs
    J 5   = Plans and Policies
    S/G/J 6 = Communications

CONOPS—Concept of Operations.

CONUS—Continental United States.

CP—Command Post.

CTF (Combined Task Force)—Military force made up of two or more allied nations. May also be called a Coalition Task Force.

DAO—Defense Attaché Office.

DATT—Defense Attaché.

DIV—Division, Army or Marine Corps, 8000 to 12,000 personnel.

DSN (Defense Switching Network)—DOD telephone system.

Echelon—A subdivision of a headquarters, that is, rear echelon or forward echelon.

FAO—Foreign Area Officer.

FHA (Foreign Humanitarian Assistance)—Programs or operations conducted to relieve or reduce the results of natural or manmade disasters or other endemic conditions that might present a serious threat to life or that can result in great damage to or loss of property.

FUNCplan—Functional Plan.

General Orders—Permanent instructions issued in "order form" that apply to all members of a command, usually concerning matters of policy or administration.

HA—Humanitarian Assistance.

HACC—Humanitarian Assistance Coordination Center.

HAST (Humanitarian Assistance Survey Team)—Deployed by CINC to assess existing conditions and need for followup forces.

HMMWV (hum vee)—The Highly Mobile Multipurpose Wheeled Vehicle, successor to the "Jeep."

HOC (Humanitarian Operations Center)—Established by a CJTF, it is a group of decision-makers from the JTF and PVO/NGO/IOs, USAID/OFDA, and host nation authorities.

HRO (Humanitarian Relief Operations)—Also referred to as HUMRO.

HUMINT (Human Intelligence)—A category of intelligence derived from information collected and provided by human sources.

JCMOTF—Joint Civil Military Operations Task Force.

JCS—Joint Chiefs of Staff.

JFC—Joint Force Commander.

JIB (Joint Information Bureau)—The focal point for the interface between the military and the media.

JMC (Joint Movement Center)—Coordinates the employment of all means of transportation supporting the CJTF's concept of the operation. May also be referred to as JMCC or Joint Movement Control Center.

JOA—Joint Operations Area.

JOPES—Joint Operations Planning and Execution System.

JPOTF—Joint Psychological Operations Task Force.

JSOTF—Joint Special Operations Task Force.

JTF (Joint Task Force)—DOD force made up of two or more military services and used in an operation.

LNO—Liaison Officer.

LOC—Line of Communication.

LOGCAP—Logistics Civilian Augmentation Program.

MARFOR (Marine Force)—A component of a joint force.

MEF—Marine Expeditionary Force.

MEU—Marine Expeditionary Unit.

METL—Mission Essential Task/Training List.

METT-T—Mission Enemy Terrain Troops-Time.

MNF—Multinational Force.

MOOTW—Military Operations Other Than War.

MPS—Marine Prepositioned Ship.

MPF—Marine Prepositioned Force.

MRE (Meal, Ready-to-Eat)—Complete individual combat meal in a pouch. Usually heated in boiling water.

NAVFOR—Navy Force.

NBC—Nuclear, Biological, Chemical.

NCA (National Command Authorities)—The President and the Secretary of Defense.

NEO—Noncombatant Evacuation Operations.

O-CONUS—Outside CONUS.

OOTW—Operations Other Than War.

OPCOM—Operational Command.

OPCON—Operational Control.

Operation _____—Name designator for each military operation, for example, Operations Provide Hope, Sea Angel, Provide Comfort, Restore Hope.

OPLAN—Operations Plan.

OPORD—Operations Order.

OPS—Operations.

OPSEC—Operations Security.

PDD25 (Presidential Decision Directive 25)—Presidential policy on reforming multinational peace operations.

PDD39 (Presidential Decision Directive 39)—Presidential policy on response to NBC terrorism acts.

POLAD (Political Advisor)—An expert in the politics of a particular country or region who advises a CINC.

PSYOPS (Psychological Operations)—Part of SOF.

RC—Reserve Component of the military.

ROE (Rules of Engagement)—Defines when and how force may be used.

ROROs (Roll-on-roll-off)—Refers to a type of transport ship that rolls equipment and supplies up into one end of the ship and rolls it off the other end at the port of delivery.

SECDEF—Secretary of Defense.

SF—Special Forces.

SJA (Staff Judge Advocate)—A legal advisor attached to a JTF staff.

SOFA—Status of Forces Agreement.

SOF—Special Operations Forces.

SSC—Small Scale Contingencies (see also OOTW).

TACOM—Tactical Command.

TACON—Tactical Control.

TALCE—Tanker Airlift Control Element.

TDY—Temporary Duty.

TPFDD—Time-Phased Force Deployment Data.

TF—Task Force.

Theater—Region of the world for which a CINC has responsibility for U.S. military operations.

WMD—Weapons of Mass Destruction.

WWMCCS—World Wide Military Command and Control System.

Zulu—See Zulu Time in nonmilitary portion of this chapter.

Notes

Notes

Notes

Notes

Miscellaneous Conversion Information

Centigrade to Fahrenheit

Centigrade × 1.8 + 32 = Fahrenheit

Fahrenheit to Centigrade

Fahrenheit − 32 × 0.555 = Centigrade

Weight of water by volume (at 16.7 °C or 62 °F)

1 liter	=	1 kilogram
1 U.K. gallon	=	10 pounds
1 U.K. gallon	=	1.2 U.S. gallons
1 U.K. gallon	=	4.54 liters
1 U.S. gallon	=	0.833 U.K. gallons
1 U.S. gallon	=	8.33 pounds
1 U.S. gallon	=	3.79 liters
1 liter	=	0.26 gallons
1 cubic foot of water	=	62.3 pounds (7.48 gallons)

Distance

1 nautical mile = 1.152 statute miles = 1.852 kilometers

How to Calculate Area and Volume

$$\text{Area} = \text{Width} \times \text{Length}$$

$$\text{Area of a circle} = \Pi r^2$$

where $\Pi = 3.14$

$r = $ (½ the diameter of circle)

$$\text{Volume} = \text{Width} \times \text{Length} \times \text{Height}$$

$$\text{Volume of a cylinder} = \Pi r^2 H \text{ or } \Pi r^2 L$$

where $L = $ length of a cylinder

$H = $ height of cylinder

Metric to English

To convert	into	multiply by
Lengths		
millimeters	inches	0.0394
centimeters	inches	0.3937
meters	inches	39.3700
meters	feet	3.2808
meters	yards	1.0936
kilometers	yards	1093.6133
kilometers	miles	0.6214
Surfaces		
square centimeters	square inches	0.1550
square meters	square feet	10.7639
square meters	square yards	1.1960
square kilometers	square miles	0.3861
hectares	acres	2.4710
Volumes		
cubic centimeters	cubic inches	0.06102
cubic centimeters	liquid ounces	0.03381
cubic meters	cubic feet	35.31467
cubic meters	cubic yards	1.30795
cubic meters	gallons (USA)	264.17205
liters	cubic inches	61.02374
liters	cubic feet	0.03531
liters	gallons (USA)	0.26417
milliliters	teaspoon	0.20289
milliliters	tablespoon	0.06763
milliliters	fluid ounces	0.03381
liters	cups	4.22675
liters	pints	2.11338
liters	quarts	1.05669
Weights		
grams	grains	15.4324
grams	ounces	0.0353
kilograms	ounces	35.2740
kilograms	pounds	2.2046
kilograms	tons (USA)	0.001102
kilograms	tons (long)	0.000984
tons (metric)	pounds	2204.6226
tons (metric)	tons (USA)	1.1023
tons (metric)	tons (long)	0.9842

For sale by the U.S. Government Printing Office
Superintendent of Documents, Mail Stop: SSOP, Washington, DC 20402-9328
ISBN 0-16-049721-3

ISBN 0-16-049721-3

90000